The North Carolina One-Day Trip Book

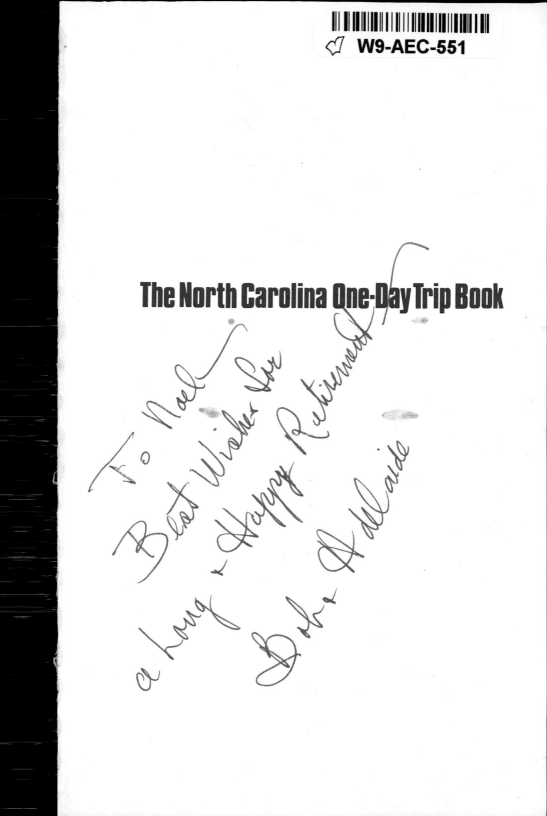

To Noel —

Best Wishes for
a long + Happy Retirement

Bob + Adelaide

For Jerry Bloch
. . . *first, last and always!*

Jane Ockershausen

The North Carolina One-Day Trip Book

150 excursions in the land of dramatic diversity

EPM Publications
McLean, Virginia 22101

Library of Congress Cataloging-in-Publication Data

Ockershausen, Jane.
  The North Carolina one-day trip book : land of dramatic
diversity / Jane Ockershausen.
      p.   cm.

    ISBN 0-939009-38-2
      1. North Carolina—Description and travel—1981—Tours.
I. Title.
F252.3.035   1990
917.5604'43—dc20   90-34997
                                                                   CIP

EPM Publications, Inc., 1003 Turkey Run Road,
  McLean, Virginia 22101

Printed in the United States of America

Cover and book design by Tom Huestis
Photographs courtesy of North Carolina Division
of Travel and Tourism, Department of Commerce

Contents

THE NORTH CAROLINA ONE-DAY TRIP BOOK

BREVARD/FRANKLIN/MURPHY AND VICINITY

GREAT SMOKY MOUNTAINS AND VICINITY

NANTAHALA NATIONAL FOREST AND VICINITY

=====NORTHERN FOOTHILLS=====

GREENSBORO, BURLINGTON AND REIDSVILLE VICINITY

WINSTON-SALEM

HIGH POINT

GOLDSBORO VICINITY

FAYETTEVILLE AND PINEHURST VICINITY

═══════════NORTHERN COAST═══════════

MAINLAND

ALONG RIVERS AND SOUNDS

OUTER BANKS AND ROANOKE ISLAND

NEW BERN AND VICINITY

BEAUFORT, MOREHEAD CITY AND VICINITY

WILMINGTON AND VICINITY

From the splendor of the Appalachian Mountains to the sand and surf of Cape Hatteras, North Carolina's diverse beauty beckons millions of appreciative day-trippers every year.

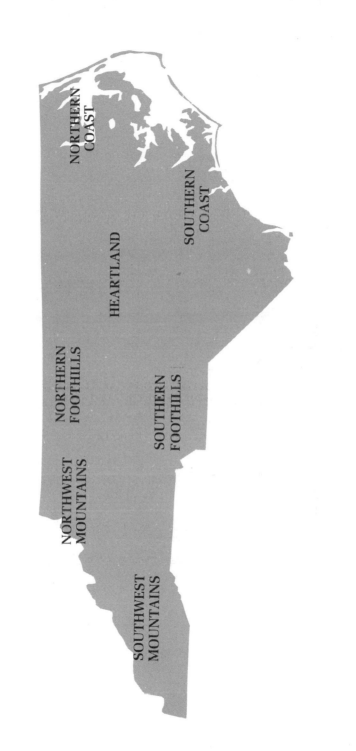

=Discover North Carolina=

The North Carolina One-Day Trip Book offers life-long residents, newcomers and visitors a wide diversity of unexpected discoveries and experiences, plus little-known facts and stories often omitted in guidebooks and overlooked on brief visits.

North Carolina is noted for an impressive series of firsts, all of which have sites that can be visited. In 1587 near present-day Manteo on the southern coast, Virginia Dare was born, the first English child born in the New World . At Reed Gold Mine the first gold nugget found in America was discovered by 12-year old Conrad Reed. For a time this 17-pound rock was used as a doorstop! At Kitty Hawk, Wilbur and Orville Wright made the world's first powered aircraft flight on December 17, 1903. The Wright brothers built their plane in six months at a cost of a about $1,000, but it took 50 craftsmen three years and a half million dollars to reproduce it. Cape Hatteras was the nation's first National Seashore. Morehead Planetarium was the first to be owned by a university, and the North Carolina Zoo was the first zoo in the world planned around a totally natural habitat.

There are trips for all interests, seasons and ages throughout this dramatic state. These selected sites trace the state's history from prehistoric rock formations and early human paintings to the days of the Cherokee Nation and pre-colonial explorers; from the battlefields of the American Revolution and the Civil War to the dynamic hustle-bustle of North Carolina's present industrial centers. The places recommended for their natural beauty range from the rugged coast of Cape Hatteras to the rolling hills and lakes of the Heartland and on to the waterfalls and majestic peaks of the Blue Ridge and Smoky Mountains.

Day trips take only a few hours, so you can pursue new challenges, revive old hobbies, or just concentrate on and expand your current interests. When you pick a destination or check out a spot you've already decided to visit, read about the other options in the area. It is often possible to combine several nearby attractions for a diverse day's fun. You can easily plan a weekend or week-long vacation in any of the seven regions of the state. The book follows the same geographical organization the state's Department of Tourism uses.

Where to go and what to see are important decisions, but you must also decide when to go. The Calendar of Events alerts you to fairs, festivals, birthday celebrations, blooming cycles, holiday festivities, sports events, concerts, competitions and much more. For some travelers these special activities are the main attraction. Other travelers prefer to visit at less crowded times. Read the entire section before you set out; you don't want to arrive to find the site closed. It is always advisable to call ahead to check fees and possible changes in hours.

When I wrote the first One-Day Trip Book in 1975 most families did their traveling during an annual two-week vacation. In the intervening years there has been a growing trend towards short mini-vacations. The seven One-Day Trip Books are written for these travelers. They realize that short excursions spaced weekly or monthly throughout the year can offer an escape from the winter doldrums, a jump on spring, or a whole series of summer holidays as well as a chance to enjoy an almost unbelievable range of autumn delights. It is true as the official North Carolina line puts it: "The Beauty Only Begins with the Scenery."

NORTHWEST MOUNTAINS

Boone, Blowing Rock and West Jefferson Vicinity
1. Blowing Rock and Bolick Family Pottery
2. Churches of the Frescoes
3. Grandfather Mountain
4. *Horn in the West*, Hickory Ridge Homestead, Daniel Boone Native Gardens
5. High Country Sports
6. Mast General Store and Valle Crucis
7. Tweetsie Railroad

North Wilkesboro Vicinity
8. Stone Mountain State Park and Old Wilkes Walking Tour

Spruce Pine and Vicinity
9. Linville Caverns and Linville Falls
10. Museum of North Carolina Minerals and Emerald Village
11. Penland School of Crafts and Artists' Studios

═Northwest Mountains═

A number of North Carolina's oldest travel attractions are found in the Northwest Mountains, or High Country as it is also called. Here you can visit Grandfather Mountain with its mile-high swinging bridge, Blowing Rock, a tourist mecca since the 1920s, and Linville Caverns whose fame had spread as early as 1849. The reason these attractions have remained part of the travel scene for so long is simple—they are nature's signature on the area.

But it isn't nature alone that inspires the traveler. The marvelous art adorning the Churches of the Frescoes—Holy Trinity and St. Mary's—is part of a moving story that touches hearts deeply.

This is also a region for fun. Sports options span the calendar with winter skiing, summer white-water rafting, and horseback riding, canoeing, trekking and hiking that begin in the spring and continue through autumn.

Consider this a hands-on region. Enjoy many different sports activities, enroll in a wide range of art classes at Penland School of Crafts or try your hand at panning for gems at places like Emerald Village. Ride an old steam train at Tweetsie Railroad theme park and attend the outdoor drama *Horn in the West*, the story of the Appalachian Mountain settlers during the American Revolution. Whatever you choose, you experience North Carolina firsthand in the Northwest Mountains.

BOONE, BLOWING ROCK AND WEST JEFFERSON VICINITY

Blowing Rock and Bolick Family Pottery

Blowing in the Wind

It is said that if you speak words of love on top of **Blowing Rock**, the wind carries them to your beloved. This romantic notion may stem from Indian legends. One tale concerns a Chicksaw chieftain's lovely daughter. Fearful of the white man's admiration of his child, the chief took her from the plains to the mountains of the High Country. Once they arrived the girl fell in love with a Cherokee brave she spied from her rocky perch. Time passed quickly after the lovers met, but when the sky reddened with warning fires, the brave felt he had to return to help his plains tribe in their time of trouble. The girl entreated him not to leave her. Torn by love and duty the brave leaped from the rock into the void. Grief-stricken the girl prayed daily to the Great Spirit. Her prayers were answered when a gust of wind blew her lover back into her arms. It is said that from that day on, winds have blown up from the valley below.

Other explanations of the upward draft are less romantic. Another tale speaks of a blacksmith with a nagging wife. One day he became so exasperated he hit her over the head and threw her off the rock. Having led a far from blameless life she landed in hell, where she so annoyed the devil that he tossed her back up through the roof of hell. Since then a wind has always blown up towards Blowing Rock.

Whichever explanation you prefer, the rebound phenomenon is striking. Robert Ripley in a "Believe it Or Not" column said the rock was the only place in the world where it snows upside down. The actual reason why small items thrown from the rock are blown back up is that the rocky walls of the gorge form a flume through which the northwest wind blows, thus explaining the upside down snow.

Blowing Rock is an immense cliff formed of metamorphic rock, geologists classify as gneiss, 4,000 feet above sea level. The rocky promontory juts dramatically out over the Johns River Gorge 3,000 feet below. This dramatic perch is North Carolina's oldest travel attraction. As early as the 1920s people were picnicking on it. In the 1930s it was offered for sale to the state as a public park, but that project was scuttled due to lack of funding. In 1935, the site opened privately as a tourist attraction with paid admission.

A 30-foot-high observation tower provides one of the most famous views in the entire Blue Ridge chain. Clearly visible is Grandfather Mountain, Hawksbill Mountain and Table Rock, flanking the Linville Gorge and Mount Mitchell, the highest peak east of the Rockies. There is also a small garden, a snack bar and a large gift shop. Blowing Rock is open daily April through October from 8:00 A.M. to 8:00 P.M. and during March and November weather permitting.

Down the road is another genuine North Carolina attraction, a family pottery business run by Glen Bolick with his wife, Lula Owens Bolick, and his son, Jeff. The Bolicks are fifth-generation potters; Lula Owens is from the Seagrove area (see selection), where her family has a long tradition of pottery making. As Glen

16

sings in a song he wrote and recorded on his folk album, his "daddy's daddy's daddy was a sawmill man." Singing is not Glen's only talent; he was the 1988 Champion at "hollerin" in the Spiveys Corner competition. Hollerin is a folk art, and each family had their own "tune," not a melodic line but a distinctive sound. Through this mountain tradition families pass messages from one farm to another. With a little coaxing, Glen, a master folk artist, will demonstrate how it's done and talk about his appearance on the "Pat Sajak Show." His prize-winning performance included the yells he gives while cutting timber, his grandmother's call to dinner (she would yell "let's eat" but it sounded like "SSE"), the hollerin done while rabbit hunting and an unbelievable rendition of "Rudolph the Red-Nosed Reindeer." Glen intersperses his hollerin with humorous recollections. In 1989, he won the Fox Horn Blowing Championship, and sometimes he can be persuaded to get out his hunting horn and demonstrate his prowess. You can purchase the family's distinctive pottery as well as Glen's mountain tapes at the Bolick Family Pottery, open 8:00 A.M. to 5:00 P.M. daily.

A wider variety of mountain crafts can be found at the nearby **Moses H. Cone Memorial Park** where one of the region's most outstanding craft galleries is located in the 20-room Cone Manor House (originally called Flat Top Manor) built by Moses H. Cone, the "Denim King," at the turn of the century. Craft items created by members of the Southern Highland Handicraft Guild are for sale in the manor's downstairs rooms.

Just a few yards from the manor is Craftsman's Trail, a short 20-minute loop walk that was a favorite with the Cones. Even this brief exposure reveals Moses Cone's deep interest in preserving and enriching the natural beauty of the North Carolinan highlands. He built and stocked three lakes, added an apple orchard and planted extensive white pine forests and hemlock hedges. The Blue Ridge Parkway passes through the Moses H. Cone Memorial Park for 2.5 miles, and adjacent to the park is the 4,200-acre **Julian Price Memorial Park** where you can hike, picnic and camp.

Directions: From I-85 take I-40 to Winston-Salem, then head north on Route 421 towards Boone. Before Boone take Route 105 south until it intersects Route 321/221. Continue south on Route 321 to Blowing Rock. Just three miles south of Blowing Rock, ½ mile off Route 321 on Blackberry Road, you will see the Bolick Family Pottery. For Moses H. Cone Memorial Park take the Blue Ridge Parkway exit off Route 321 (you will turn right on parkway) and drive south just a short distance.

Churches of the Frescoes

Faith of Our Fathers

The story of Father Hodge and his mountain churches demonstrates just what can be accomplished with a little muscle and a lot of faith. When Father Hodge was appointed the "rector for all Episcopal souls for Ashe and Alleghany counties" in 1972, **Holy Trinity Church** in Glendale Springs was abandoned and decayed, and **St. Mary's Church** in Beaver Creek barely clung to life. St. Mary's had a mere 13 communicants, and the last full-time priest had left Holy Trinity in 1934.

Father Hodge had no vestments, no altar candles, no processional cross, no prayer books, no hymnals and no money. The organist had been playing at St. Mary's for 29 years and knew only three hymns. But by returning to a simpler style of worship and by reaching out to his flock, Father Hodge enlarged his congregation to 140 full-time parishioners by the end of his first year.

If the mountain parish had continued to grow in this manner, its success would have been a matter for local congratulations, but its story would never have reached a larger audience. In 1973 Father Hodge attended a party in nearby Blowing Rock and met Ben Long. This young artist had been traveling around North Carolina seeking a chance to paint a fresco. Long had studied fresco painting in Florence, Italy under Pietro Annigoni, an acknowledged master of this vanishing art form.

Frescoes, often confused with murals, are paintings done on a plaster wall by mixing earth and mineral pigments with lime, sand and mortar. The fresco technique dates back to the ancient Egyptians, about 3,000 years ago. The most famous frescoes were done by Leonardo da Vinci and Michelangelo during the Renaissance.

Ben talked with Father Hodge about painting a fresco in St. Mary's Church honoring the Virgin Mary. Months passed before the project was realized, but without any financial assistance and with only a couple of student assistants, Ben eventually finished a stirring life-size painting of a pregnant Holy Mother, the only one like it in the world. When a Presbyterian minister told the young people in his congregation to stay away from the evil painting, they flocked to see it, and as a result attendance at Sunday services continued to grow.

The attention captured by the fresco *Mary, Great with Child* encouraged both artist and minister to continue their work together. Long painted two more frescoes, *John the Baptist* and the *Mystery of Earth,* and when he was awarded the prestigious Leonard da Vinci International Art Award, the story of the Blue Ridge church spread far beyond the Carolina mountains.

18

Having revived one of his mountain churches, Father Hodge turned his attention to Holy Trinity, which was "about two good stiff winds away from falling down" as one local described it. Hodge was seriously considering tearing down the derelict building, selling the land and using the money to continue expanding St. Mary's. But Ben Long was anxious to paint a large fresco of the Last Supper on the dilapidated chancel wall. In the summer of 1978, as Father Hodge was debating whether to repair the church or level it, a couple stopped to see Holy Trinity where the man's mother had worshiped decades earlier. On learning of the church's perilous condition, they donated money to finance the needed repairs.

By the end of the summer, 20 artists were in Glendale Springs helping Ben Long paint *The Last Supper*. The job of feeding and housing these American and foreign artists was formidable, but Father Hodge's congregation and those of nearby churches pitched in. Visitors who stopped to see the frescoes also made donations. By the end of the summer the collection totaled almost $30,000, which paid for the rest of the repairs to the church and mission house.

In the undercroft of Holy Trinity there is a fresco, *The Departure of Christ* by Jeffrey Mims, a student of Ben Long. There is also a large mosaic called *Christ the King* and a wood carving of *Christ's Agony in the Wilderness* done by a young Jewish artist. Christ's heart is a natural formation of the wood. In the adjacent mission house, work by regional artists is displayed. In St. Mary's visitors are fascinated by *The Laughing Christ* done by 19-year-old Bo Bartlatt. This Gothic-style church also has beautiful stained-glass work.

Each year more than 200,000 tourists stop to view these mountain church frescoes. The doors of the churches never close. An audio message welcomes all and gives the background on the frescoes and their significance. It isn't really necessary to have a guided tour, but if you would like to arrange one, call (919)982-3076.

If you are in Glendale Springs around lunch or supper time, be sure to stop at Glendale Springs Inn & Restaurant. The 1895 General Adams Inn, noted for its excellent French-inspired cuisine, offers a bounteous buffet on Sunday and antique-filled rooms for overnight guests. From the porch of this Queen Anne-style inn you'll be able to see the **Greenhouse Craft Shop**, which is across the street from Holy Trinity Mission House. The shop has a large selection of well-made regional craft items. If you're looking for eatable items then, when visiting St. Mary's outside West Jefferson, drop in at the **Ashe County Cheese Company**. The plant, between Main and Fourth Street, produces cheddar, mellow colby and Monterey Jack cheeses. Weekdays from 8:00 A.M.

to 5:00 P.M. you can watch cheesemaking through a special viewing window; call to be sure that they are making cheese on the day you plan to visit, (919)246-2501. Then visit the retail shop where you'll find an assortment of cheeses and cheese accessories. The factory sells about eight million pounds of cheese a year. A sign here informs visitors that, "A dinner without cheese is like a kiss without a squeeze."

Directions: From I-85 take I-40 to Winston-Salem, then head north on Route 421. At Wilkesboro take Route 16 north. Holy Trinity Church is off Route 16 in Glendale Springs. The best way to get to St. Mary's Church is to retrace your route south on Route 16 to Horse Gap and pick up Route 163 north. Just before West Jefferson turn right on Beaver Creek Road for the second Church of the Frescoes.

Grandfather Mountain

Rock Face

It doesn't take a lot of imagination to make out the profile of an old man gazing skyward on the north slope of **Grandfather Mountain**. The pioneers named it for the profile, but the Indians, who associated the mountain with the raptors that they believed guarded the sacred peaks, called the mountain Tanawha, meaning "a fabulous hawk" or "eagle."

The rock formations on Grandfather Mountain date back over 650 million years. Scientific studies indicate that the mountain itself was formed through three distinct metamorphisms, each pushing a massive granite peak into the sky. This repeated upward thrust has prevented the mountain from leveling off over the millenniums. Grandfather's age and unique rock formations provide geologists with a window into the past.

It isn't just the mountain's age that awes visitors, it is also the grandeur and majesty of its alpine-like summits. These are the highest peaks in the Blue Ridge chain, rising a mile or more above nearby valleys. In fact, Grandfather Mountain's foot bridge added by owner Hugh Morton in 1952 was dubbed the "Mile High Swinging Bridge," referring to its elevation above sea level. Despite the name, the suspension bridge is actually only 100 feet or so above a small crevice separating the visitor center area from Linville Peak. The panoramic views from the bridge and mountain peaks are breathtaking.

About one-fifth of the 5,000-acre natural preserve is accessible to visitors via a summit road leading to the Linville Peak visitor center. Along the way are a wildlife habitat area, a new nature museum and several picnic areas. However, the back country around Grandfather Mountain is a mecca for outdoor enthusiasts who hike the more than 30 miles of trails in the preserve.

Two of the nine trails, the Grandfather Trail and the Daniel Boone Scout Trail, are National Recreation Trails. The Boone Trail climbs a ridge that forms the Eastern Continental Divide. In 1907 (it was reissued in 1934) Shepperd Dugger wrote *The Balsam Groves on the Grandfather Mountain*, a classic tale about hiking on another of the mountain's trails, the Shanty Spring Trail. His work had far more than just regional appeal; it was the first book about the southern mountains to make *The New York Times* Bestseller List.

In 1987, the last link of the Blue Ridge Parkway was completed around Grandfather Mountain. This led to the creation of three new trails that offer easier hiking than the older routes. One, the Tanawha, is a National Park trail and does not require a hiking permit, as do all the other trails. Permits are easily available at local outlets.

The 12-mile Tanawha Trail, from Beacon Heights to Price Park Campground, connects with the Boone Trail and Grandfather Trail. All the trails are popular throughout the year, but they make for an especially glorious hike in October and from about May 20 through June when the red rhododendron, flame azalea and mountain laurel bloom.

Another of the new trails is the 2.6-mile Profile Trail, offering an excellent view of the rock face from which the mountain got its name. This trail joins Shanty Spring Trail. The steepest of the new trails, the one-mile Crag Way Trail, rewards those with the stamina to climb it with absolutely spectacular views.

Though sneakers are acceptable footwear, even some of the new and easier trails are best tackled in hiking boots. On the most rugged trails, boots are a must as are a small pack with food, rain gear, warm clothes, a flashlight and a trail map.

You don't have to depend on the vagaries of nature to spot wildlife on Grandfather Mountain. There are six environmental habitats designed by Hyatt Hammong, who is also responsible for the North Carolina Zoological Park (see selection). The star attraction is Mildred with her family of adult black bears and cubs. You'll also see habitats for cougars, white-tailed deer, bald eagles and golden eagles.

A **Nature Museum** is scheduled to open in the early spring of 1990. Geological and botanical exhibits will include a look at rare and endangered plants and animals found on Grandfather Mountain. Other displays will center on the Indians of this region as well as the explorer Daniel Boone, who lived and hunted here for about ten years in the forefront of the other pioneers.

Two events at Grandfather Mountain have become annual favorites. The first, a full day of gospel singing called "Singing on the Mountain" occurs on the fourth Sunday in June and is a free event. The Grandfather Mountain Highland Games and Gathering of Scottish Clans take place the second full weekend in July when 120 Scottish clans and societies gather for what *Better Homes & Gardens* calls "the best Highland Games in North America."

Calling Grandfather Mountain "Carolina's Top Scenic Attraction" is not advertising hyperbole. You can visit Grandfather Mountain daily; summer hours are 8:00 A.M. to dusk, winter hours 9:00 A.M. to 4:00 P.M. weather permitting.

On September 11, 1987, three decades after the parkway was begun, the last stretch, or missing link, of the Blue Ridge Parkway was dedicated—the 7,500-ton **Linn Cove Viaduct**. One of the "most complex bridges ever built," the S-shaped viaduct, seemingly suspended in mid-air, leaves Grandfather Mountain and some of the oldest rock formations in the world undisturbed. This engineering marvel is the first of its kind in the United States; the Rombas Viaduct in France provided the inspiration. Linn Cove Viaduct uses 153 precast concrete segments, only one of which is straight. The Linn Cove Viaduct visitors center opened in the fall of 1989. There are trails from the parkway parking lot to observation points beneath the viaduct.

Directions: From I-40 take US 421 west at Winston-Salem. At Boone go south on Route 105/221 to Linville where you will see the entrance to Grandfather Mountain. Grandfather Mountain is one mile off the Blue Ridge Parkway and two miles from Linn Cove Viaduct.

Horn in the West, Hickory Ridge Homestead and Daniel Boone Native Gardens

Horn of Plenty

Frontier life in the Blue Ridge Mountains is brought to life by diverse means on the grounds of the Daniel Boone Amphitheater where the outdoor drama *Horn in the West* is presented.

For nearly 40 years, the nation's third oldest outdoor historic drama (the other two are also in North Carolina: *The Lost Colony* and *Unto These Hills*, see selections) has told the story of the struggle of the Appalachian Mountain pioneers to obtain religious, political and economic freedom. The play is about the Regulators who settled in the western wilderness after the Battle of Alamance (see Alamance Battleground selection). When Major Ferguson demanded that the Regulators cease their rebellion

22

against the crown or he would "lay waste to their country with fire and sword," he badly misjudged their mood. Instead of obeying, the mountain men heeded the "horn of freedom," reputedly blown by Colonel Ben Cleveland (see Old Wilkes selection) and marched over the mountain to fight at Kings Mountain.

This exciting story is told on an outdoor stage in a star-lit setting that suggests the scenic splendor in which the pioneers lived. The amphitheater is located four miles off the Blue Ridge Parkway in Boone, about halfway between the Shenandoah National Park and the Great Smoky Mountains National Park, at opposite ends of the parkway. Unlike some of North Carolina's nine outdoor dramas, this play is miked. Nevertheless, it is still a good idea to get a seat near the stage so you can follow the dialogue, and to take along a bug repellent. There are three categories of seats: general admission, reserved seats and box seats. Your best bet is a reserved seat in the first ten rows. The drama runs nightly at 8:30 (except Mondays) from mid-June through mid-August. For reservations call (704)264-2120.

Don't wait until curtain time to arrive. You should allow enough time to visit the **Hickory Ridge Homestead**. The seven homestead buildings are the real-life set where pioneers, like those depicted in *Horn in the West*, actually lived. Visitors are encouraged to help with such frontier chores as weaving, candlemaking and open-hearth cooking. A small exhibit gallery is located in the 1875 log house of Tom Coffey where frontier tools, household articles and wearing apparel are displayed.

It is the authentically garbed staff at the Tatum Cabin who really bring the late 18th century to life. The Tatum Cabin, home to five generations, was moved to this location from Elk Crossroads (now Todd). William Tatum lived in the North Carolina mountains when the area was still one of the Lost Provinces, belonging to no colony. It wasn't until sometime between 1760 and 1765, however, that another member of the Tatum family, Captain James Tatum, a descendant of an English settler at Jamestown, put his family and belongings in a canoe and followed the river west to the Boone area. The Tatum family was in this log cabin as early as 1785, and perhaps even earlier. It's hard to imagine James and his wife living in this modest-sized log cabin with their ten children, but somehow they managed.

While visiting the cabin notice the gun slots—pieces of logs loosely set into the wall so that they could be easily removed if the Indians attacked. To save space, there was no ladder to the sleeping loft, just climbing pegs in the wall logs. Since the house came to the Southern Appalachian Historical Association in 1958 directly from the Tatum family, there are original furnishings and household articles like the foot warmer, grease lamp, long-handled waffle iron, English ironstone and cord beds. One interesting piece is a cradle with one rocker longer than the other so a mother could rock it by foot while doing chores.

The self-sufficiency of the mountain settlers is apparent throughout. You'll see a smokehouse, barn, weaving cottage and spring house as well as the kitchen garden where vegetables and herbs were raised to augment the diet. The homestead also has a museum shop where local arts and crafts are sold. The Hickory Ridge Homestead is open daily (closed Mondays) from 1:00 P.M. to 8:30 P.M. when the drama is playing, and from May to late June and mid-August through October it is open on Saturdays from 7:30 A.M. to 1:00 P.M. A nominal admission is charged.

Six acres of North Carolina trees, bushes and flowering plants are encompassed in the **Daniel Boone Native Gardens** adjacent to the amphitheater. Enter this informal garden through the iron gatehouse, made by Daniel Boone VI, a direct descendant of the great pioneer. The path winds through seven kinds of gardens including a sunken, a fern and a meditation garden. The colors are at their peak in the spring when the flame azaleas bloom and again in the fall when the leaves turn. Tucked away in the gardens is the Squire Boone Cabin, named for, but never inhabited by, the father of Daniel Boone. Although Daniel Boone never camped in this cabin, he did hunt and explore throughout this part of North Carolina. The Boone Gardens are open at a nominal fee daily May through September, and October weekends from 10:00 A.M. to 6:00 P.M. While the drama is in production the gardens stay open until 8:00 P.M.

Directions: From Winston-Salem take Route 421 west to Boone. From Charlotte take I-77 north to the I-40 intersection in Hickory. Go west on I-40 to the intersection with Route 321, then go north on Route 321 to Boone. From Route 321 turn right on Route 105 for the *Horn in the West* amphitheater.

High Country Sports

High Ranked

The mountainous northwestern part of North Carolina is ideal for a variety of adventure sports. Half of the state's major ski resorts are found in this region: Ski Hawksnest, Appalachian Ski Mountain, Hound Ears, Sugar Mountain and Ski Beech. The rivers are not only popular for fishing, they are ideal for canoeing and white-water rafting. The mountains lure hikers and horseback riders. There are even llama treks into the Blue Ridge Mountain wilderness areas.

During the winter months the High Country becomes a skier's playground. Each of the region's **ski** resorts offers instruction for all levels of skiers. The season begins around Thanksgiving and

In winter the mountains of the northwest are a skier's playground. In summer the region is vacationland to fishermen, canoeists, hikers, rafters and horseback riders.

extends until mid-March. Here are the addresses and phone numbers:

Ski Hawksnest, ten miles south of Boone in Seven Devils, has several slopes with a peak elevation of 4,819 feet and a 619-foot vertical drop (1605 Skyland Dr., Banner Elk, NC 28604, (704)963-6561; snow report, (704)963-6563).

Appalachian Ski Mountain between Boone and Blowing Rock has eight slopes with a peak elevation of 4,000 feet and a vertical drop of 365 feet (P.O. Box 106, Blowing Rock, NC 28605, (800)322-2372, snow report, (704)295-7828).

Hound Ears has two slopes with a peak elevation of 3,300 feet and a vertical drop of 107 feet. The slopes (open to the public on weekends only, except around Christmas week) are excellent for beginners. (P.O. Box 188, Blowing Rock, NC 28605, (704)963-4321; snow report same number, extension 275).

Sugar Mountain just south of Banner Elk, has 18 slopes with a peak elevation of 5,300 feet and a 1,200-foot vertical drop. There is a slope-side lodge (P.O. Box 369, Banner Elk, NC 28604, (704)898-4521; snow report, (704)898-5256).

Ski Beech in Banner Elk has 15 slopes with a peak elevation of 5,500 feet and a 830-foot vertical drop (P.O. Box 1118, Beech Mountain, Banner Elk, NC 28604, (704)387-2011; snow report, (800)222-2293; out of NC (800)438-2093.

As soon as the ice begins to melt fishermen start planning trips to the mountains. Most fishermen want to head off on their own, but High Country Fly Fishing offers guided **fishing** trips for the experienced fly-fisherman. They have half-day and full-day trips as well as a fishing school for beginners, which provides a one-day course on fly selection, stream tactics and casting practice. For information on these programs call (704)963-7431, or write High Country Fly Fishing, P.O. Box 2956, Boone, NC 28607.

A growing band of enthusiasts are not interested in what's in the rivers, but what to do on them. They favor **canoeing, inner-tubing** (many of the canoe outfitters rent innertubes), and **white-water rafting** on four rivers in the High Country. The New River is basically a calm Class I river, with a few Class II easy-to-negotiate rapids. Congress designated the New a wild and scenic river. Over 23 species of plants and animals found in and around the river are unique to this region of the United States. The Watauga River, ranked Class I and II, is scenically splendid with rugged terrain and huge boulders. This area was used as the background in two Mountain Dew commercials. The Toe River, a fast-running river with Class II and III rapids, is noted for the overhanging rock formations that make for a scenic treat. You can also canoe the North Fork of the Catawba River, which has Class II and III rapids. Wilson Creek too has Class II and III rapids. On its lower section there is a dramatic plunge into a gorge— recommended only for advanced paddlers. There are a number of outfitters that supply equipment and arrange guided river trips on the region's five rivers:

Edge of the World Outfitters, P.O. Box 1137, Banner Elk, NC 28604, (704)898-9550.

New River Outfitters, Inc., P.O. Box 433, Jefferson, NC 28640, (919)982-9192.

Wahoo's Outdoor Adventures, P.O. Box 1915, Boone, NC 28607, (704)262-5774.

Zaloo's Canoes, Route 1, Box 852, Jefferson, NC 28640, (919)246-3066.

White-water adventurers who go for Class III to Class V rapids have four major rivers in the High Country to choose from (the Toe, the Nolichucky, the Ocoee and the Nantahalla. The primarily Class II Nantahala River is ideal for families and first-timers. It affords excitement without requiring expertise (see Nantahala Outdoor Center selection). The calmer Toe River flows into one of the best white-water rivers in eastern America, the Nolichucky. Running through the Pisgah and Cherokee National

Forest, the Nolichucky has cut a gorge with walls more than 2,000 feet high, creating one of the most beautiful wilderness canyons in the east. The Nolichucky has 18 rapids over a nine-mile segment, with rankings from III to V. On the dam-controlled Ocoee there is a 5.5-mile white-water run that is one of the most challenging in the southeast with big waves and giant holes; rapids are ranked Class IV and V. The French Broad, winding through a rugged mountain terrain, has Class II and IV rapids. Rafting companies in the High Country also run trips on the New, Gauley, Cheat and Rio Grande rivers. Major rafting companies in the High Country are:

Wahoo's Outdoor Adventures (see above).

High Mountain Expeditions, Box 1299, Blowing Rock, NC 28605, (704)295-4200.

Also operating in these waters:

Cherokee Adventures, P.O. Box 605, Erwin, TN 37650, (615)743-8666.

Expeditions, Inc., P.O. Box 460, Erwin, TN 37650, (800)346-RAFT or (800)USA-RAFT.

USA Whitewater, Inc., P.O. Box 277, Rowlesburg, WV 26425, (800)624-8060.

This region has five major **horseback riding** stables. Two of the stables are in Banner Elk: the Sugar Mountain Stables and Banner Elk Riding Stables. Sugar Mountain, off Route 184 north opposite Blue Ridge Village/Peppertree Resort on Rough Ridge Road, also arranges hay rides, barn dances and cookouts. The stables are open from mid-May through Labor Day; call (704)898-9233 for information.

Banner Elk Riding Stables is on Shoemaker Road off Route 194. This stable is open year-round, daily from June through October and on weekends from November through May. For information on hourly rates and their moonlight rides and over-night camping rides call (704)898-5424.

The Blowing Rock Stables, on Laurel Lane, off Route 221 south in Blowing Rock, has more than 25 miles of riding trails on the Moses Cone Estate (see Blowing Rock selection). It is open daily 9:00 A.M. to 5:00 P.M. from May through November. Blowing Rock also offers pony rides for children under nine.

The Whispering Pine Appaloosa Stables in Spruce Pine is on Dale Road. It provides supervised rides for groups of two to 12 on more than 65 miles of trails in the area. It is open May to December 9:00 A.M. to 6:00 P.M., Sundays by appointment only; call (704)765-6663.

The Springmaid Mountain Stables, off the Blue Ridge Parkway and McKinney Gap Road in Mitchell County, also provides supervised rides from mid-April through October; call (704)765-2353.

You don't ride **llamas**, but they are nonetheless a big draw among those who want to get out on the mountain trails. In 1984, Noah Llama Treks, Inc. began offering the first such treks east of the Rockies. You can take to the high mountain trails for two to six days with a white, wooly llama carrying your camping supplies. These walking luggage racks are friendly, curious creatures, and part of the fun is getting to know them. The company, operating out of Rolling Thunder Farm in Valle Crucis, organizes treks for groups of six to ten. Costs vary depending on whether you supply your own food and camping gear and on the number of days and quantity of supplies. From May through October the treks head up into the Mt. Rogers National Recreation Area and the Pisgah National Forest. You don't need to be an advanced mountain climber to enjoy this High Country experience. Women guides are available for all-women groups. For information call (704)297-2171 or write Noah Llama Treks, Inc., P.O. Box 641, Valle Crucis, NC 28691.

For additional details about High Country sports options call North Carolina High Country Host. If you are calling locally from the Boone area, the number is 264-1299; from the rest of the United States including North Carolina, (800)438-7500. You can also call this number for ski reports and ski rates at the different resorts.

Mast General Store and Valle Crucis

One Stop Shopping

A sign by the cash register at **Mast General Store** reads: "Questions Answered, Simple 50 cents, Guesses $1, Intelligent $2.50, Honest $5, Dumb Looks are Still Free." This humorous response to the influx of tourists at the rural country store reflects the easy accommodation between serving the local community and catering to the ever-increasing traveling public.

Mast General Store is not just a tourist attraction; it still meets the needs of its local customers as it has since opening in 1883. W.W. Mast bought half interest in the store in 1897 and became the sole owner in 1913. It was Mast's goal to sell everything from "cradles to caskets." His oft-repeated remark was that, "If you can't buy it here, you don't need it." A barter system was frequently used since his farm customers often could pay only in produce, not currency. The Mast General Store still has the trap door in the floor where W.W. dropped his payment of chickens into a coop below.

The potbellied stove, once the only heat source, has been supplanted by modern heaters, but the small post office in the front corner still handling neighborhood mail looks as though it has always been there. The painstaking care to retain the old look has led to the store's inclusion on the National Register of Historic Places. Charles Kuralt, CBS correspondent and enthusiastic North Carolina supporter, recently wrote, "Where shall I send you to know the soul of the South? I think I shall send you to the Mast General Store."

There's something childishly pleasing about the store's jam-packed shelves. Spilling over the old oak counters and shelves are work and play clothes, Appalachian door harps, wooden folk toys, harmonicas, jellies, jams, honey, cookbooks, weathervanes, stone and tinware, local crafts, herbs and in the candy cabinet, a temptation of treats (no longer a penny-priced, alas).

Just down the road (.2 of a mile) is the Mast Store Annex, located in the old Valle Crucis Company General Store, which dates back from 1901. This annex sells clothing and outdoor goods for backpacking, camping and other recreations. The Mast General Store is open Monday through Saturday 6:30 A.M. to 6:00 P.M. and Sunday 1:00 P.M. to 6:00 P.M. The Annex opens 10:00 A.M. to 6:00 P.M. during the week and 1:00 to 6:00 P.M. Sundays.

This valley, just west of Boone, is called **Valle Crucis** because three creeks converge to form a St. Andrew's Cross, shaped like the letter X. The valley's religious significance was increased when the Episcopal Church established its first missionary station in the North Carolina mountains in the 1840s. This mission became the first Protestant monastery established since the Reformation. The Church of the Holy Cross has a lovely stained-glass window in the shape of St. Andrew's Cross.

Valle Crucis has three picturesque inns: Mast Farm Inn (704)963-5857, The Inn at the Taylor House (704)963-5581, and Bluestone Lodge (704)963-5177. In these rustic mountain retreats, you can enjoy bounteous country meals and other country pleasures like hayrides, campfire gatherings, horseback riding, hiking, crosscountry skiing and fishing. The Mast Farm is included on the National Register of Historic Places as an example of a self-contained mountain homestead.

Directions: From I-85 take I-40 to Winston-Salem, then head north on Route 421. This will merge with Route 221 as it heads north towards Boone. Just before Boone turn south on Route 105, then bear right on State Route 1112 into Valle Crucis. The Mast General Store and Annex will be on your right.

Tweetsie Railroad

Huff n' Puff

The Eastern Tennessee and Western North Carolina Railroad, known locally as the ET&WNC, and jokingly as "Eat Taters and

At Tweetsie Railroad, a popular family theme park near Boone, passengers on this train experience a hold-up and Indian attack, among other adventures.

Wear No Clothes," was chartered in 1896. The first 34-mile run began even earlier in 1881 and went from Johnston City, Tennessee, to Cranberry, North Carolina. During the First World War the line was extended to Boone, making it a 66-mile route.

The ET&WNC had about 14 engines working this run; one built in 1917 was nicknamed Tweetsie because of the clear, piping sound of its whistle. Tweetsie and the other engines made the four-hour, one-way trip daily from Boone to Johnson City and back. Gradually the name Tweetsie came to stand for all the trains making this run.

For a time the train was the Blue Ridge mountain country's major link with other parts of the country. But by the late 30s the highway that ran alongside the track made the train obsolete. In 1940 when a flood washed away a large section of the track the route was abandoned. Locomotive #12 and a coach and observation car were saved. Railroad buffs in Virginia purchased the Tweetsie and moved it to Harrisonburg. After Hurricane Hazel washed out the Virginia tracks the train was acquired by cowboy star Gene Autry, who wanted to move it to California. There were those who wanted the Tweetsie returned to its High Country home, and Lenoir businessman Grove Robbins, Jr. purchased it from Autry and brought it back to the Boone area. He built a replica of the old Boone station and a three-mile track around Roundhouse Mountain.

Now the Tweetsie again makes daily, albeit shorter, runs at one of North Carolina's most popular family theme parks. The park is called Tweetsie Railroad, but people correctly boast "it is more than just a train." No earlier run could possibly have offered all the excitement that occurs on its current schedule. Passengers see a holdup, an Indian attack, a fire at Fort Boone and other dramatic events. (For the best view sit on the right side of the train.)

The train depot is on the park's Main Street, one of the theme park's four areas. The street looks like an original from the Wild West, and there's a western shop amid the eateries and souvenir outlets. The next area is Craft Junction, where there is a blacksmith and a leathersmith shop as well as an antique photography studio and the *Tweetsie Times* print shop. Behind the picnic pavilion, you'll find a small Railroad Museum with old black and white pictures of the ET&WNC. There are several display cases with railroad memorabilia. The park has about six shows that run daily; in Craft Junction's picnic pavilion you can take in a country music show and an end-of-the-day jamboree.

Several more shows are offered in the Country Fair area, including a gospel jubilee and a musical revue. Wandering down Country Fair Lane, with its game arcade and shooting gallery, you'll feel like a time machine has transported you to a country fair in the early 1900s. There's a carousel and merry-go-round too. From this part of the park you can catch the aerial lift up Miner's Mountain, where you take a miniature train ride through a mine, try your hand at panning for gold, watch a rainmaker or visit the petting farm. The Tweetsie Cloggers perform throughout the afternoon on the mountain top.

Tweetsie Railroad is open daily from 9:00 A.M. to 6:00 P.M. from Memorial Day to Labor Day. It continues on fall weekends through October. The admission price includes all of the activities in the park. For current rates call (704)264-9061.

Tweetsie Railroad is halfway between Boone and Blowing Rock, as is another attraction, **Mystery Hill**. Advertised extensively on billboards, Mystery Hill is essentially an amusement park crazy house. A heritage museum that was here was destroyed in a fire. Current plans are to rebuild the museum, which again will exhibit crafts and artifacts of the Appalachian Mountain region. Mystery Hill is open daily from 8:00 A.M. to 8:00 P.M. in the summer and 9:00 A.M. to 5:00 P.M. September through May.

Directions: Take I-85 to Greensboro, then go west on I-40 to Winston-Salem. Continue west on Route 421 to Boone. In Boone take Route 321 towards Blowing Rock. Tweetsie Railroad will be on your right. Mystery Hill is located at the intersection of Route 321 and 221 between Boone and Blowing Rock.

NORTH WILKESBORO VICINITY

Stone Mountain State Park and Old Wilkes Walking Tour

Folk Song and Heavy Rock

The vast expanse of Stone Mountain inspires awe and a desire to capture its imposing facade. Visitors invariably reach for their cameras. Above the tree line, the 600-foot granite expanse of Stone Mountain looks like a huge, rocky sand dune. Like its sandy counterparts it can be climbed. There is a trail that branches off the main Stone Mountain Trail, but don't veer off too soon or you'll miss the picturesque Stone Mountain Falls about a 30-minute walk down the main trail.

The trail to the falls winds along one of the many park streams, guaranteed to tantalize fishermen. These streams are, for the most part, unstocked, but rainbow and brook trout are not too elusive. You need both a North Carolina fishing license and a trout license, but one-day comprehensive permits are available. On hot summer days you can wade in these cool streams or at the base of the 200-foot cascades of Stone Mountain Falls. This undeveloped 13,411-acre state park offers 20 miles of hiking trails, 17 miles of trout streams, 37 family camp sites, six group camp sites and six primitive backpack sites. There are weekend nature study programs during the summer months at the campgrounds. The park also has six miles of bridle trails, although it is BYOH (bring your own horse).

Nearby in Wilkesboro, the county seat of Wilkes County, you can take the **Old Wilkes Walking Tour**. For fans of folk music, the high point is the **Old Wilkes Jail** where Tom Dula (Dooley) was imprisoned. As fans of the Kingston Trio remember, Tom Dooley was hanged in 1868 for the murder of his pregnant girlfriend, Laura Foster. Dooley, a womanizer, was also seeing Ann Melton. She was arrested as a conspirator and spent two years in jail. You will also see the cell for women prisoners where she was held. Their lawyer was Zebulan Vance, who was the governor of North Carolina before and after this trial.

The cell where Dooley was held still has the original bars. A drawing of Dooley before he served in the Civil War shows the curly dark hair that made him such a hit with the women. The cell contained six cots, and there were undoubtedly other prisoners incarcerated with Dooley.

It is ironic that the jail's architect and builder became its first prisoner. He had a problem holding his liquor, but the jail had a problem holding him. With his inside knowledge, he was, not surprisingly, the first to escape. Other prisoners were not that lucky. The jail's massive front door was made escape-proof by placing nails a half inch apart so the door could not be sawed open. Prisoners held in the jail during 1895, according to a list on the cell wall, included 81 arrested for larceny, 21 for assault, two for murder, one for trespassing, four for keeping a house of ill repute, one for burglary, two for disturbing the peace and one for insanity.

The downstairs portion of the jail provided the living quarters for the jailer and his family. The rooms are furnished with period pieces to reflect the years the jail was operational, 1860–1915. The jailer's wife had to prepare both her family's meals and those of the prisoners on the small fireplace in the kitchen. There are also two bedrooms. In addition to displaying old items, the rooms have antiques on sale by consignment. The jail is on the National Register of Historic Places.

This is only one of the 13 buildings on the walking tour of Old Wilkes. Another, the **Robert Cleveland House**, was moved directly behind the Old Jail. When you tour this restored 1770s gentleman-farmer's wooden frame house, keep in mind that Cleveland had 17 children, 13 by his first wife. One unusual piece of furniture is the "bumpin' chair" with the front legs shorter than the back so a colicky child could be bounced, not rocked. The upstairs portion of the log house is a roomy loft. This mountain dwelling represents the transition from log cabin to wooden house.

The rest of the houses and public buildings are usually seen only from the outside, though of course you can go into the 1849–50 Presbyterian Church on Main Street and the 1849 St. Paul's Episcopal Church which sits above the town on Cowles Street. The walking tour also passes several private houses, government buildings, the Smithey Hotel and the J.T. Ferguson Store. If you want an escorted walking tour call (919)667-3712.

Another spot you might want to visit is associated with the Cleveland family. Robert's brother, Colonel Benjamin Cleveland led patriots from this part of North Carolina to the Revolutionary War Battle of Kings Mountain. The story goes that he went up on the mountain and blew his hunting horn to call the men to battle; the mountain is now **Rendezvous Mountain State Park**. In its 147 acres the park offers hiking trails, picnicking and camping, but its most distinctive feature is the "talking trees" that have tapes with basic information on forestry. Unfortunately one of the most famous trees in Wilkes County, the Tory Oak on the Courthouse Square in Wilkesboro, was damaged in a violent storm in 1989, and it is now only a reminder of the imposing tree from which, it is said, British sympathizers were hanged during the Revolutionary War.

History buffs may want to hike a four-mile portion of the 313-mile route that has been designated the Overmountain Victory National Historic Trail. The section lies within **Warrior Creek Park** along the W. Kerr Scott Reservoir. The Wilkes County Militia gathered on September 27, 1780, near what is now the Wilkes and Surry County line. A group of 350 freedom-loving patriots defied the orders of Colonel Patrick Ferguson that they disband. Instead of ending the rebellion Ferguson's incendiary words prompted the patriots to take the war to the British at Kings Mountain. The victory won by these fierce mountain fighters was, according to Thomas Jefferson, the "turn of the tide to success" that led to eventual American victory.

Directions: From I-85 at Greensboro take I-40 west to Winston-Salem. For Stone Mountain take Route 421 west out of Winston-Salem. Then take I-77 north to Exit 83, Route 21. Take Route 21 north until you reach State Road 1002, turn left and follow the signs to the park. For Wilkesboro continue north on Route 421; this will lead into town. At the Old Jail, off Main Street on Bridge Street, you can obtain a walking tour brochure for exploring Old Wilkes. For the W. Kerr Scott Dam & Reservoir you go to Wilkesboro and take Route 268. There are numerous parks along the reservoir off Route 268 including the Damsite Park and Warrior Creek Park.

SPRUCE PINE AND VICINITY

Linville Caverns and Linville Falls

Travelers are more sophisticated and less easily impressed today than they once were, so perhaps the best way to gain an appreciation for the scenic splendor of **Linville Caverns** is to recall the enthusiasm of early explorers. The first major literary reference to the caverns was by Charles Lanman in his 1849 *Letters from the Alleghany Mountains*. He wrote: "Catawba Cave (as it was then called) . . . is reputed to be one mile in length. It has a great variety of chambers, which vary in height from six to twenty feet;. . .along the entire length flows a cold and clear stream, which varies from five to fifteen inches in depth. The cave is indeed a curious affair . . ."

In 1859 Henry E. Colton, a young travel writer and adventurer, described his visit to the caverns in his book *Mountain Scenery*:

The Scenery of the Mountains of Western North Carolina and North-Western South Carolina. His was the most eloquent description thus far: ". . . But now began the wondrous splendors of the hidden world . . . we emerged into an immense passage whose roof was far beyond the reach of the glare of our torches, except where the fantastic festoons of stalactites hang down within our touch. It looked like the arch of some grand old cathedral, yet it was too sublime, too perfect in all its beautiful proportions to be anything of human, but a model which man might attempt to imitate . . . ascending a natural stairs . . . (1) . . . entered a chamber, which, in the gorgeous splendor of its transparent drapery, the beauty and delicate look of its carpeting, surpassed any natural scene I ever witnessed . . ."

Some reports say soldiers in both the American Revolution and Civil War explored these caverns, including the Over the Mountain Men who marched from Tennessee to fight the British at the 1780 Battle of Kings Mountain. Other reports say survivors hid out in the cave. It is a documented fact that deserters from both armies in the Civil War found refuge there.

Despite all this early appreciation, the caverns were not developed as a tourist attraction until 1937. After extensive work to clear out a passage for visitors, the grand opening took place July 1, 1939. The advance word over the decades had created an interest in the caverns, and they were an immediate success. But barely a year later a flood that wiped out area homes and businesses devastated the caverns as well. In the spring of 1940, efforts were again undertaken to clear out a passage and by June the caverns reopened. Few tourists came during World War II, but in the postwar years Linville Caverns regained its popularity. In 1955, the magnificent room Colton had described opened to the public, and many visitors agreed with his enthusiastic commentary.

Exploration of the caverns continues, and it is possible that eventually new areas will be opened. In 1988 the existing cavern was registered as a state Natural Heritage Area. The caverns provide a remarkable opportunity to "see nature's creations inside a mountain."

Linville Caverns are open during the summer months from 9:00 A.M. to 6:00 P.M. They are a great escape on a hot summer's day. Even then it is cool in the subterranean depths; the temperature stays at 52 degrees year-round. During the months of April, May, September and October the caverns close at 5:00. In March and November hours are 9:00 A.M. to 4:30 P.M.; and in December, January and February they are open on weekends only. There is a gift shop at the entrance.

Not far from the caverns just off the Blue Ridge Parkway are **Linville Falls**, the most historic falls in the High Country. This was once Cherokee land, and when William Linville, his son John and a friend went hunting, camping and exploring in the area in 1766 they were killed by the Indians. The falls are called the "Great Falls of Linville" in honor of the men who explored here and lie buried along the gorge. Although settlers entered the region in 1818, the common lament was "you couldn't farm a falls."

During the Civil War a Confederate iron forge manufactured rifles just upstream from the falls. When the war ended the falls were privately purchased for $31.50. Years later the John D. Rockefeller Foundation paid considerably more, $92,000, to purchase the 1,200-acre falls tract. Although it has remained substantially unchanged for the last 200 years, the falls still increased in value 3,000 times in about 60 years.

There are seven trails. Trails #1 through #4 start at the same place and then separate. The .5-mile Upper Falls Trail (#1) leads to a view of the Upper Falls, which cascade 50 feet over rocks before disappearing through a cleft in the mountainside. Interesting though that is, you don't want to miss continuing up to Chimney View (#2) .8 mile where you will have a view of both the Upper Falls and the Lower Falls and see the river reappear and drop dramatically another 60 feet into Linville Gorge. To get a bird's-eye view of both falls, climb the higher one-mile Erwin's View Trail (#3). You can also branch out on the .9-mile Gorge Overlook Trail (#4). Proceeding in a different direction as you leave the visitor center is the .2-mile Dugger's Creek Trail. The last two trails provide yet another perspective; there is the .5-mile Plunge Overlook and the .8-mile Plunge Basin Trail. Probably the two most scenic trails are #2 and #4, but all are well worth the time.

Directions: From I-85 take I-40 to Winston-Salem, then continue north on Route 421. When 421 intersects the Blue Ridge Parkway head south for Linville. The Linville Caverns are four miles south of the Parkway at milepost Exit 317.4. Get off the Parkway and turn left on US 221.

Museum of North Carolina Minerals and Emerald Village

Mining Moved Mountains

It doesn't take a geology background to realize that the Blue Ridge Mountains are rich in native minerals, precious gems and semi-precious stones. But the extent of this mineral wealth may be underappreciated until one visits the **Museum of North Carolina**

For as little as $5 a bucket, rockhounds sift for emeralds, rubies, sapphires and other gems at Emerald Village. Lucky finders can have their stones cut and set into jewelry.

Minerals three miles north of Little Switzerland at milepost 330.9 on the Blue Ridge Parkway.

More than 300 minerals have been identified in North Carolina, of which about a quarter have economic value, and roughly 40 to 50 have been produced commercially. Museum exhibits pinpoint the location of major mineral veins, present examples and give the uses for each. The state is America's leading producer of feldspar, a mineral found in 20 counties of the state. Feldspar, the world's most abundant mineral, is used in making glass and ceramics. It was also used in homes across the country as a scouring ingredient under the trade name Bon Ami.

The Spruce Pine area where the museum is located is noted for its pure quartz, which was used to make the 200-inch Palomar Mirror on the world's largest telescope at the California Institute of Technology's Mount Palomar Observatory. The state also produces 90 percent of America's pyrophyllite and has the country's largest tungsten mine. Visitors find the fluorescent minerals with their other-worldly glow the most visually interesting.

What makes North Carolina a rockhound's paradise is its accessible gemstones. The mountains yield emeralds, rubies, golden beryls, garnets, amethysts, sapphires, aquamarines and other less well-known stones. The museum exhibits these colorful gems as well as the work of native gemsmiths who have cut, polished, faceted and turned the stones into exquisite jewelry. The role of North Carolina in America's search for gold is not neglected (see Reed Gold Mine selection). In the early 1830s North Carolina led the country in gold production. The Museum of North Carolina Minerals is open daily at no charge 9:00 A.M. to 5:00 P.M. except major holidays. During the winter months it closes for lunch from 12:00 to 1:00 P.M.

You can get a first-hand look at the Spruce Pine Mining District by visiting nearby **Emerald Village**, which includes the **North Carolina Mining Museum**, the Gemstone Mine and Discovery Mill. The entire complex reflects the vision of Robert Schabilion, lifelong rockhound and mining historian. In 1980 he acquired the old Bon Ami/McKinney Feldspar Mines and opened his museum. Part of the museum collection is exhibited in and around the cavernous feldspar mine. Looking at the walls of this old mine, you'll see natural veins of feldspar and quartz, as well as outcroppings of mica. Exhibit boards tell the story of mining in this area. Heavy equipment like the ore cart, mine cart, wagon drill, slusher scraper, electric mule and the steam engine give you an idea of how the miners once worked. The museum also has a three-story building with exhibits of miner's lamps, drills and other antique paraphernalia. Mining equipment has been gathered from around the world. There is a charge for the self-guided tour of the mining museum which is open 9:00 A.M. to 5:00 P.M. May, September and October and until 6:00 P.M. during the summer months.

After the museum tour, take a walk through the re-creation of a typical mining boom town, Main Street 1920, with its prospector's shack, company store, post office, assay office, supply store and a mine-boss's office. A sign in the post office warns

38

you to "look out for mail bag when train passes." The assay office has gold samples, but a sign in the window says "Gold Strike, Gone to Californy, Won't Be Back."

Now you're ready to do some gem mining of your own. Across the street from the museum is Emerald Village's **Gemstone Mine**, where a gem find is guaranteed every time. Rockhounds buy a bucket of "muck" and wash and sift it in the shaded flume. Everyone hopes to find a quality emerald, ruby, sapphire, amethyst or aquamarine. Staff members will help novices judge the quality of their find, and as the buckets are enriched everyone does indeed make a find. A sampler bucket costs $7, a regular bucket $5, a special bucket $25, and for $50 you can buy an enriched bucket and have one of your stones faceted without extra charge. Faceting normally costs $25 and up. Cautious treasure hunters can take heart from the realization that at one time Tiffany's, one of New York's premier jewelry stores, owned and operated an emerald mine very near this one.

Adjacent to the old mine is **Discovery Mill**, a multi-level building newly built to look like a part of an old mining operation. It houses gem shops, lapidary shops and Jerry Call's School of Faceting. Call is a master gem cutter and jewelry designer, and he teaches classes in gem faceting for both professionals and beginners. Be sure to cover all the floors of Discovery Mill because on the very top is the **Antique Music Museum**, open without charge. The museum has organs, pianos, music boxes and other instruments that date back to the mid-1800s.

Emerald Village operates mine tours of area mines that are not ordinarily open to the public. They supply the hard hats, rock hammers and mine charts and maps. Tours are given Saturday 9:00 A.M. to NOON and 1:00 to 4:30 P.M. and Sunday 1:30 to 5:30 P.M.

Directions: Take I-40 east of Asheville to the intersection with Route 226. Head north on Route 226 to Gillespie Gap, 14 miles north of Marion. Or take the Blue Ridge Parkway to the museum (exit is marked with a museum sign). For the North Carolina Mining Museum at Emerald Village take the parkway or Route 226A to Little Switzerland, then take Chestnut Grove Church Road (State Road 1100) to the church, where you turn left on McKinney Mine Road and go 2½ miles to Emerald Village.

Penland School of Crafts and Artists' Studios

State of the Art

The roots of **Penland School of Crafts**, like the John C. Campbell Folk School (see selection), go back to the 1920s and a longtime interest in encouraging local people to practice the region's folk arts. In 1923 Lucy Morgan, a primary school teacher in Penland, was traveling in Kentucky where she discovered a program designed to teach women the art of weaving. The finished cloth was purchased and resold. This seemed like an ideal project for Lucy Morgan's rural North Carolina neighborhood, so Miss Lucy purchased three looms and the Penland School of Handicrafts was born.

Her students worked in their homes at first, but they found it more interesting and educational to work together and began meeting in a small weaving cabin. When they outgrew this small building, the students, their families and friends themselves built the Craft House, the largest log building in the state. From this modest beginning, additional crafts were added to the school curriculum: pottery, spinning, metal crafts, lapidary and such mountain crafts as chair caning and bobbin lace. Today approximately 20 studios offer diverse craft studies. The studios range in size from small rooms to entire floors of barn-size buildings.

After Miss Lucy retired in 1962, the school's direction under Bill Brown changed from the teaching of traditional or folk crafts to advancing the professional skills of all types of craftsmen. It was at this time the school changed its name from the Penland School of Handicrafts to Penland School of Crafts. Previously students had paid by the week and stayed for varying lengths of time, but now Penland began to offer summer sessions of two or three weeks each and a more intensive spring and fall class. Visiting artists were also utilized, and housing and studio space were made available at a minimal cost to emerging craftspeople.

The emphasis of Verne Stanford, Penland's director from 1984 to 1989 was multidisciplinary studies, encouraging a cross-fertilization of ideas. Hunter Kariher, the present director, took the helm in July 1989. The public is welcome to eat lunch or Sunday brunch at Penland's Pines Dining Room, where the animated conversation and enthusiasm of the artists attest to Penland's success at inspiring students. Do call at least 24 hours ahead to make a reservation so the kitchen can prepare enough food (704)765-2359.

Tours of the school grounds and a few selected studios are given at no charge on Tuesday at 10:30 P.M. and Thursday at 1:30 P.M. from May–October. To prearrange a tour call (704)765-6211. You may wander around the campus at other times, but the studios are off-limits when classes are in session. Be sure to stop at the visitor center where crafts are sold. Hours are 9:00 A.M. to NOON and 1:00 to 4:00 P.M. Tuesday–Saturday and 9:00 A.M. to 1:00 P.M. and NOON to 4:00 P.M. on Sunday from May–October.

If you are interested in purchasing crafts there are approximately 100 **studio craft artists** within a 25-mile radius of Penland. A map available at the school pinpoints the location of 24 studios and several country inns. Seven out of the top ten (including the #1) glassblowers in the country are located in this area.

Directions: From I-85 take I-40 west past Hickory to the intersection with Route 226, head north on Route 226; just past Spruce Pine (the nearest town) take Penland Road to the school.

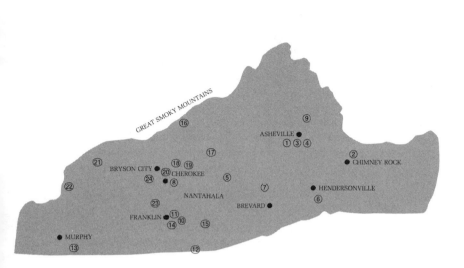

SOUTHWEST MOUNTAINS

Asheville and Vicinity
1. Biltmore Estate
2. Chimney Rock Park
3. Grove Park Inn
4. Thomas Wolfe Memorial

Blue Ridge Parkway and Vicinity
5. Blue Ridge Parkway
6. Carl Sandburg House
7. Cradle of Forestry
8. Judaculla Rock
9. Vance Birthplace

Brevard, Franklin, Murphy and Vicinity
10. Cullasaja Gorge
11. Franklin Gem Mines
12. Highlands

13. John C. Campbell Folk School
14. Perry's Water Gardens
15. Pisgah National Forest

Great Smoky Mountains and Vicinity
16. Great Smoky Mountains National Park
17. Maggie Valley
18. Museum of the Cherokee Indian
19. Oconaluftee Indian Village
20. Pioneer Farmstead and Mingus Mill

Nantahala National Forest and Vicinity
21. Fontana
22. Joyce Kilmer-Slickrock Wilderness
23. Nantahala National Forest
24. Nantahala Outdoor Center

═Southwest Mountains═

A big bonus of a one-day trip is that once you discover a new place, it is easy to return to it. Having enjoyed the delicacy of the spring wildflowers in the Nantahala National Forest or the colorful array of summer annuals at the Biltmore Gardens, you may want to re-visit these sites at a different season. Try Biltmore Estate's Christmas celebration, famous nation-wide, or drive through the mountains in autumn, an ever-changing treat.

The southwestern region of North Carolina (much of it referred to as the Highlands) bordering Tennessee, South Carolina and Georgia, is recognized as a national treasure. Large tracts of spectacular mountains, gorges, rivers and waterfalls are protected by the federal government as part of the Great Smoky Mountains National Park, Nantahala National Forest, Pisgah National Forest and the Blue Ridge Parkway.

Just as scenic spots like Chimney Rock and Judaculla Rock inspired legends among the Cherokees, so too, modern writers have found inspiration in this region. Throughout his life Thomas Wolfe wrote of his boyhood in Asheville, and Carl Sandburg spent the last 22 years of his life at his Flat Rock farm, Connemara. The Grove Park Inn hosted F. Scott Fitzgerald and other writers, and even now artists from many disciplines gather throughout the year at the John C. Campbell Folk School.

In the Southwest Mountains the long-running outdoor drama *Unto These Hills* brings the Cherokee history and culture vividly to life. The Oconaluftee Indian Village reconstructs the Cherokee way of life while the Pioneer Farmstead in the Great Smoky Mountains National Park shows how the European settlers lived.

Many of the attractions are well known far beyond the region and the state, but one little-known scenic wonder, the Cullasaja Gorge, is a guaranteed, delightful surprise. Though the area has 150 waterfalls altogether, as many as 18 small falls plus several large ones crash down the Cullasaja Gorge within a few short miles. No two are alike. You can walk behind one waterfall and drive behind another; each is splendidly unique.

ASHEVILLE AND VICINITY

Biltmore Estate

Fabled Fantasy

Many first-time visitors to George Vanderbilt's fabulous recreation of a Loire Valley chateau in Asheville get a feeling of *deja vu*. The 255-room mansion has figured prominently in the last movies made by two Hollywood luminaries, Grace Kelly in *The Swan* and Peter Sellers in *Being There*.

Only a Vanderbilt could conceive of and afford an estate on this scale. George started buying land in 1888, and by the time construction began two years later he owned 125,000 acres including Mount Pisgah (see Cradle of Forestry selection). This North Carolina mansion was designed to resemble three 16th-century-styled French chateaus: Chambord, Chenonceaux and Blois. To build his dream house he hired Richard Morris Hunt, architect for some of the grander Beaux Arts estates in Newport, Rhode Island and the architect for the base of the Statue of Liberty.

The job of making the dream a reality took hundreds of laborers five years. Many new-fangled ideas were incorporated into this mansion, the largest private home in the world. It was one of the first private residences to use Thomas Edison's filament light bulbs. It also utilized such modern ideas as central heating, plumbing, refrigeration, electricity and an elevator system.

But it is not the behind-the-scenes innovations that have fascinated visitors since the house first opened for tours in 1930 but rather the ornate and lavishly decorated living quarters. Tours include only 50 of the 255 rooms, but this is ample to grasp the scope of Vanderbilt's vision. Fabled names of artists and European royalty fill the pages of guides on the treasures found throughout the house.

Art is prominently featured in the decor of each room at Biltmore. In the marble paved Entrance Hall you'll see a bronze sculpture by Parisian artist Antoine-Louis Barye commissioned by the youngest son of King Louis Phillipe. Leading off the hall is the airy Palm Court, a flower-bower year-round. It's particularly striking at Christmas time when it is filled with bright red poinsettias and serves as a backdrop for choral groups who entertain the thousands of visitors who take the evening Candlelight Tours.

The Billiard Room is a man's retreat. Hunting trophies hang on the oak-paneled walls. Hunting and theater prints fill the walls. The pool and billiard tables were most likely made to fit this room. The medieval Banquet Hall is baronial in its size and

44

style. The room was designed to display five massive 16th-century Flemish tapestries. The vaulted 72-foot high ceiling, great stone fireplace, enormous banquet table with 68 chairs all look like a theater set for *Camelot*. Of more modest, but not much more, dimensions and design is the Family Dining Room. Here the walls are covered with leather, and the ceiling has a faux marble appearance. The intricately carved ivory chess set was used by Napoleon Bonaparte to while away the hours of his imprisonment at St. Helena.

Cornelia Vanderbilt pours tea for a friend at the Biltmore House in the early 1900s. The 250-room mansion, in the 16th-century French chateau style, was the largest private home in the world.

Art objects fill the French Renaissance style Music Room and the 75-foot long Tapestry Gallery, but it is the Library that really prompts a response from tourists. Book lovers long to curl up and enjoy the classical-baroque grandeur of this room. With 20,000 books to peruse, you could spend days just browsing through the titles. The ceiling is a magnificent painting done for the Pisani Palace in Venice by Pellegrini. The heavy, ornate black marble fireplace supports two massive sculptures by Karl Bitter.

Upstairs are the lavishly appointed bedrooms, several upstairs sitting rooms and an example of an 1890s bathroom, which made quite an impression on guests. Bathrooms were rarely installed in private homes during this era. The tour also includes a number of rooms beneath the stairs. You'll see informal gentlemen's retreats like the Smoking and Trophy Rooms as well as a gymnasium, swimming pool, bowling alley and party room. The downstairs also has work areas: the main kitchen, pantries, and servant's quarters and dining room.

But whether the rooms are humble or royal the overall impression is that America did and does have its royalty. No European monarch could live more lavishly than George Washington Vanderbilt did in this castle.

Just as no expense was spared in the design, construction and furnishing of the mansion so too the best was sought for the **gardens**. Vanderbilt commissioned Frederick Law Olmsted to lay out the gardens and parks. Olmsted's horticultural vision can be seen at New York's Central Park, Philadelphia's Fairmont Park and the Capitol grounds in Washington to name just some of his outstanding accomplishments. The gardens have both formal and informal areas. Close to the house is the Library Terrace with statuary, a tea house and jardinieres. On the lower terrace there is an Italian Garden with three formal pools, one with lotus, the second a variety of aquatic plants, and the third lilies. Down the broad stone steps is a wisteria-covered pergola particularly delightful in early spring when the delicate purple blossoms perfume the air. The Ramble, a flowering shrub-bordered gravel path leads to the English Walled Garden. This has been described as "the finest English garden in America." Within the protection of its stone walls flowers bloom from spring until late autumn. The Conservatory shares the lower half of the garden with a rose specimen area.

The **Biltmore Estate Winery** is a relatively new addition, but William A.V. Cecil, grandson of George Vanderbilt, felt it was in keeping with the avowed aim to make this a working estate in the European tradition. Grapes were planted in 1971, and in May 1985 Biltmore Estate Winery opened for tasting and tours. The winery is in a converted dairy barn that was part of the original estate. It now includes a visitors center, a theater where they show a brief film on the history of wine and on wine-making at the Biltmore Estate, tasting rooms and a sales area.

As you would expect, you can enjoy this wine at Deerpark Restaurant, the estate's charming open-air eatery. The half timbered woodwork, pebble-dash plaster and decorative brickwork remind visitors that this too was originally a series of outbuildings for the estate farm.

Just outside the gates is **Biltmore Village**, part of George Vanderbilt's vision of a European country estate. The village, he believed, would set the stage for the grand house. It would also be a cultural center where artisans could practice Old World skills. Now the village cottages have been renovated and serve as specialty shops. Like the Main House, the Village is a fairyland during the Christmas holiday season when all the cottages are outlined in twinkling lights.

Biltmore Estate ticket office is open 9:00 A.M. to 5:00 P.M.; the house stays open until 6:30 P.M.. The grounds are open until 7:00 P.M. Biltmore Estate is closed on Thanksgiving, Christmas and New Year's. Admission is charged.

Directions: From I-40 in Asheville take Exit 50 or 50B, US 25 north and travel three blocks north to the entrance to Biltmore House and Gardens.

Chimney Rock Park

Hoofing n' Puffing

The Cherokee Indians called the monolithic stone **Chimney Rock**, reputedly because smoke signals were seen rising from the summit. In 1540 in this Land of the Blue Sky the Cherokees first encountered European explorers when Hernando de Soto and his conquistadors searched the Blue Ridge Mountains for gold.

Chimney Rock offers a breath-catching view of the 14-mile long Hickory Nut Gorge, considered by many to be the most beautiful natural canyon in the eastern United States. Looking east you'll see Lake Lure where new legends were born when the cast of *Dirty Dancing* stayed at the local inn. On a clear day you can see Kings Mountain more than 75 miles away. In the opposite direction is Bat Cave. This cave for which the settlement is named is not open for tours.

The Rocky Broad River carved this gorge, washing away broken rocks and cutting the gorge deeper and deeper. The Henderson gneiss rock that forms the chimney was once a molten core, which 535 million years ago cooled and solidified deep within the earth's crust. Over time the overlying rock was eroded away, leaving the spectacular sheer exposure you see today. The chimney itself is formed by erosion cutting away weakened rock, thus leaving a gap between the chimney and the cliff face.

You should plan to spend at least two hours at Chimney Rock Park, more if you'd like to picnic or enjoy lunch in the Sky Lounge. To get the most out of your visit stop at the Nature Center on the top parking lot before you begin exploring. Exhibits will acquaint you with the geology and plants within the park.

There is a trail up to the chimney, but save your energy for the climb to Hickory Nut Falls. Besides, the 26-story elevator up the chimney is an experience in itself. In 1948 the elevator shaft was blasted out of the solid granite cliff, along with the 198-foot tunnel leading to the elevator shaft. Eight tons of dynamite were used during the 18 months of construction on this engineering marvel. The 42-second ride deposits you at the Sky Lounge. From there you'll take a foot bridge that spans the 72-foot ravine between the chimney and the cliff. After enjoying the view from Chimney Rock you'll want to see the falls, which can be reached by three hiking trails of varying difficulty.

The easiest and shortest is the .6-mile Forest Stroll to the Lower Falls, but this is a less dramatic vista than the other trails offer. The forest trail takes about 45 minutes to and from the lower falls along what was once a jeep track. There are no steps and very little incline. Secondly, the Cliff Trail leads to and from the top of Hickory Nut Falls. This is 1½ miles roundtrip and takes about two hours. For those with the time and the energy the best choice is the ¾-mile Skyline Trail up to the falls, then a return trip along the Cliff Trail. This still can be done in about two hours. It is a bit more arduous as the climb is steep, but there are steps and benches along the way. It's worth knowing as you tackle the Skyline Trail that once you reach Exclamation Point, elevation 2,480 feet, you will not have to climb any higher. At this point you will have driven and climbed 1,400 feet from the park entrance.

Along both the Cliff and Skyline Trail there are interesting rock formations. Be sure to pick up a nature trail guide so you will be aware of all there is to see. It's worth the climb to see the lovely Hickory Nut Falls, one of the highest in eastern America. At 404-feet it is twice the height of Niagara Falls. On a hot summer day hikers can't resist splashing in the upper falls, as Fall Creek cascades out of the wooded mountainside before plunging down the sheer granite cliff. Beyond the lower falls, the creek drops an additional 900 feet through dense forest to the floor of the gorge.

Chimney Rock Park is open from mid-March through November. The months of April and May are particularly appealing because the mountain laurel and rhododendron bloom profusely, and the dainty wildflowers come into their own. From mid-October until mid-November the fall foliage adds brilliant colors to Hickory Nut Gorge. But spring, summer or fall this is a scenic attraction you shouldn't miss. Hours are 8:30 A.M. to 4:30 P.M. (5:30 P.M. during the summer months). For those who arrive in the late afternoon the park remains open an hour and a half after the ticket office closes. Admission is charged.

If you want to overnight in Hickory Nut Gorge there are several historic inns. The Lake Lure Inn (704)625-2525 is a must for *Dirty Dancing* fans as this is where many of the cast stayed. Be sure to get directions to Baby's bridge and Johnny's cabin, two nearby location shoots. In the quaint town of Chimney Rock there is Esmeralda Inn (704)625-9105, an excellent spot for dinner Tuesday through Saturday and Sunday lunch. They have 13 rustic rooms. In Bat Cave there's Hickory Nut Gap Inn (704)625-9108, a mountaintop bed-and-breakfast with six rooms, all in different native woods.

Directions: From Asheville take I-40 west to I-26 south toward Hendersonville. Then take Route 64 east for 14 miles to Bat Cave, then turn right on Route 74/64 to Chimney Rock. An alternative route is to take Route 74 east from Asheville.

Grove Park Inn

A Home Away From Home

Many well-known figures have come to Asheville over the years: William H. Taft, William Jennings Bryan, Woodrow Wilson, Calvin Coolidge, Herbert Hoover, Franklin Delano Roosevelt, Dwight Eisenhower, John D. Rockefeller, Henry Ford, Thomas Edison, John Pershing, Enrico Caruso, Bela Bartok, F. Scott and Zelda Fitzgerald. The rich and famous called **Grove Park Inn** home.

Even if you do not plan to partake of the inn's legendary hospitality you should stop by to see this grand old resort hotel, now on the National Register of Historic Places. You can enjoy a meal in one of the four restaurants, have a drink at the bar in the Great Hall, or just wander around this 140-acre resort enjoying the friendly ambience. There is a walking-tour pamphlet and one on past and famous guests, who are fondly recalled in the Portrait Gallery.

Grove Park Inn is rich in history as well as ambience. The story of the inn's construction from July 9, 1912, to its dedication July 12, 1913, is one of triumph over adversity. Seven hundred and fifty men worked for 11 months and 27 days under Edwin Riley Grove's direction to build Grove Park. Grove made his fortune making Bromo Quinine and spent it building this impressive edifice. He wanted to build a hotel like Old Faithful Inn in Yellowstone National Park. After unsuccessful consultations with numerous architects, Grove turned to his son-in-law, newspaperman Fred Seeley, Sr., who designed the inn without the help of an architect and constructed it without a contractor. Wagon trains hauled massive granite boulders up Sunset Mountain. Workers hand placed these gigantic rocks to form the walls. These laborers, who were paid 10 cents an hour for their 10-hour days, were told to lay each stone weathered side out, so the giant stones were laid with moss and lichen still growing on them. The elevators, which are included in *Ripley's Believe It or Not*, are built into the cavernous fireplaces that still heat the Great Hall—the main room—during the frigid winter months.

The Great Hall is really at its best during the December holiday season when a towering live tree barely fits beneath the 24-foot ceiling and 12-foot-long logs blaze in the two fireplaces that anchor the hall. You can drop in for afternoon tea and listen to the festive concerts. This is also an excellent place to overnight if you plan to take the popular evening Christmas candlelight tours of nearby Biltmore Estate (see selection).

During the summer months you can browse through the Biltmore Homespun Shops, located on the Grove Park grounds. The shops offer a wide variety of mountain handicrafts and clothing. In the inn the Gallery of the Mountains has an excellent selection of pottery, woven goods, paintings and native crafts from talented local artists.

For information on the Grove Park Inn you can call (800)438-5800.

Directions: Take I-40 to Asheville, then get on I-240 through the city to Exit 5B, Charlotte Street. At Macon Avenue turn right. Grove Park Inn is at 290 Macon Avenue just two miles north of downtown.

Thomas Wolfe Memorial

Wolfe's Lair

When Thomas Wolfe's *Look Homeward, Angel* was published in 1929 it brought him world-wide fame and fortune, except in his hometown. The people in Asheville were enraged. They went so far as to ban his book from the shelves of the public library. But there's no question the townspeople read it, they wanted to know what he said about them. Locals remarked that they didn't mind being used as characters (he really didn't use the exact names, but he came embarrassingly close), but he could have left the telephone numbers and house numbers out of it.

In Look Homeward, Angel, *Wolfe re-created from boyhood memories his mother's boardinghouse in Asheville, now the Thomas Wolfe Memorial. For one dollar a day guests got three meals and a place to sleep.*

Thomas Wolfe began writing his great American classic in London in 1926, after abandoning his dream of becoming a dramatist. Like many American intellectuals, Wolfe had traveled to Europe for inspiration, but he found himself haunted by memories of his childhood. His total recall of the smallest details of his mother's boarding house enabled him to bring it to life even though he was a continent away.

Wolfe was disappointed in the hometown reception of his novel. As he expressed it he had "written of experience . . . which was part of the fabric of his life." It closely paralleled his days at his mother's boarding house, called Dixieland in the book but actually named the Old Kentucky Home. It is well worth reading the book before visiting this boarding house, now the **Thomas Wolfe Memorial**. The atmosphere is so redolent of Wolfe, you expect to find him rocking on the front porch.

Room after room will remind you of passages in his novel. The furnishings and personal effects were arranged by Thomas Wolfe's surviving brother and sister so that everything would look exactly as it did during the period described in Look Homeward, Angel. Wolfe was six when his mother purchased the boarding house. In spite of her husband's objections to her plan, he did loan her the money to make the deal. Young Tom was the youngest of eight children, all of whom shuttled back and forth from their mother's house to their father's home two blocks away on Woodfin Street. Thomas was later to say he had "two roofs but no home." He certainly didn't have a bedroom, his mother moved the children around her house wherever there was an empty cot and fed her family after the boarders were served.

Boarders were charged one dollar for three meals and a place to sleep. A postcard advertisement reports that the Old Kentucky Home is "Just Off the Car Line." It also advises that it does not rent to sick people. In 1916, just before Thomas turned 16, he left Asheville for the University of North Carolina. that same year his mother added a dozen rooms to her boarding house, too late for Wolfe to try to claim one as his own.

One of the upstairs bedrooms now contains the furnishings from Wolfe's last New York apartment. Even though Wolfe wrote his manuscripts out in longhand, his two typewriters are on display. Writing in longhand was a slow process, but Wolfe could churn out 10,000 words a night. Wolfe packed his voluminous manuscripts in crates and mailed them to his editor. When he was asked to take out some of his excessive verbiage, Wolfe responded, "No, I'm a putter-inner." When he died of tuberculosis at the tragically early age of 37, Wolfe left behind a prodigious amount of unpublished material. His remaining work was subsequently culled by his editors into two books, The Web and The Rock and You Can't Go Home Again plus the shorter selections collected in The Hills Beyond.

Thomas Wolfe is buried with other members of his family in Asheville's Riverside Cemetery. His grave is not marked with the "angel" mentioned in his book, as many visitors mistakenly believe. That angel can be seen in the Oakdale Cemetery in nearby Hendersonville about 25 miles from Asheville. Wolfe's grave is marked by a granite tombstone inscribed:

Tom
son of
W.O. and Julia E.
WOLFE
"A Beloved American Author"
Oct. 3, 1900 - Sept. 15, 1938
"The Last Voyage, The Longest, The Best."
. . . Look Homeward, Angel
"Death Bent To Touch His Chosen Son With Mercy, Love
and Pity,
And Put The Seal Of Honor On Him When He Died,"
. . . The Web And The Rock

You can tour the Thomas Wolfe Memorial April through October on Monday–Saturday from 9:00 A.M. to 5:00 P.M. and Sunday 1:00 to 5:00 P.M. From November through March hours are Tuesday–Saturday from 10:00 A.M. to 4:00 P.M. and Sunday 1:00 to 4:00 P.M. The Memorial is located at 48 Spruce Street.

Directions: From I-40 in Asheville take Exit 53, Route 240 around the city to Exit 5B, turning left on Charlotte Street. Make a right on College Street and a right on Spruce Street. The Thomas Wolfe Memorial will be on your right.

BLUE RIDGE PARKWAY AND VICINITY

Blue Ridge Parkway

Take a Peak!

The 470-mile **Blue Ridge Parkway** is within a day's drive of half the population in the United States. And on peak autumn weekends it seems they all choose to visit. The reason is fleeting but vivid—the burnished golds, rich russets, pumpkin oranges, brilliant scarlets and mellow yellows of fall foliage visible from mountain vistas overlooking the valleys below.

Fall color traditionally begins in early September and sometimes extends all the way into November. The color is usually at its peak around the middle of October. Variables that influence nature's palette include the amount of rainfall, the temperature and sunlight, and the varying elevation along the parkway.

The Blue Ridge Parkway stretches from Waynesboro, Virginia,

where the Shenandoah National Park and Skyline Drive end, to the Great Smoky Mountains National Park near Cherokee, North Carolina. Virginia Senator Harry F. Byrd is credited with suggesting to President Franklin D. Roosevelt that the Shenandoah and Great Smoky parks be connected. Construction of the parkway began September 11, 1935, and the last segment around Grandfather Mountain (see selection) was dedicated on September 11, 1987.

From Virginia the parkway follows the Blue Ridge Mountains south for 356 miles along the eastern ramparts of the Appalachians. For the last 114 miles the road skirts the southern end of the massive Black Mountains and wends its way through the Craggies, the Pisgahs and the Balsams (the parkway's highest elevation is 6,053 feet at Richland Balsam, milepost 431) before it reaches the Great Smoky Mountains.

At milepost 216.9 the Blue Ridge Parkway enters North Carolina. This state boundary was surveyed in 1749 by a group that included Peter Jefferson, the father of Thomas. Entering the state you'll find the first visitor center in North Carolina is at Cumberland Knob (217.5). There are hiking trails extending from this center as well as picnic tables available for visitors. Just a few miles down the parkway is Fox Hunter's Paradise. A ten-minute walk will take you to an overlook where hunters following the hounds could listen to them baying at the foxes in the valley below.

The planners of the Blue Ridge Parkway wanted to showcase the region's cultural and historical significance as well as the natural beauty of the mountains. At milepost 238.5 you'll see the cabin built around 1800 by Martin Brinegar. Another early pioneer, Daniel Boone, crossed this area when he blazed his way west. Boone's Trace is at milepost 285.1. Another old mountain cabin and church can be seen if you take one of the trails leading off the parking lot at the E.B. Jeffress Park (milepost 272). Another trail from this park leads to the Cascades, a waterfall on Falls Creek.

Several spots along the parkway offer mountain crafts. Handiwork from 11 northwestern North Carolina counties is sold at the Northwest Trading Post at milepost 258.6. The Parkway Craft Center is in the Moses H. Cone Memorial Park, milepost 292.7 to 295. Finally at The Folk Art Center, milepost 382, artists exhibit, demonstrate and sell their traditional and contemporary Appalachian region creations. Within this native stone and wood center folk singers and dancers give frequent performances.

Many of the milepost markers indicate splendid vistas. Some of the most spectacular are at Jumpinoff Rocks (260.6), Flat Rock (308.3), Chestoa View (320.7), Devil's Courthouse (422.4), Waterrock Knob (451.2), and Heintooga Ridge (458.2). At some of these stops you'll have to follow a short trail and at the last a spur road in order to appreciate the view.

In the spring there are two **garden** areas worth a stop. If you are travelling the parkway in May, Crabtree Meadows (339) is a bright pink cloud in a sea of green. There is a trail that leads to Crabtree Falls. The best time for spring blooms on the parkway is mid-June when the rhododendron, mountain laurel and azaleas come into flower. At Craggy Gardens there is a six-mile stretch of rhododendron-covered mountain. The fulsome flowers create a purple haze. A ten-minute walk along the Craggy Pinnacle Trail leads to an excellent vantage point from which to view Craggy Dome, elevation 6,085. The trail is cut through a heath bald, and the dense vegetation reminds visitors of the Scottish highlands. If you are in the area in early to mid-August sample the blueberries that grow along the trail.

One of the most scenic spots along the parkway is Linville Falls (316.3). A trail leads to an overlook where you'll see the falls tumbling into the rocky gorge.

With so much to see you may want to take advantage of the numerous campgrounds along the parkway. In North Carolina you can camp at Doughton Park (241.1), Julian Price Memorial Park (297.1), Linville Falls (316.4), Crabtree Meadows (339.5) and Mt. Pisgah (408.6). You can also stay at Bluffs Lodge (241.1) or Pisgah Inn (408.6).

For additional information write the Blue Ridge Parkway Association, P.O. Box 453, Asheville, NC 28802.

Directions· Just north of the North Carolina state line in Virginia the Blue Ridge Parkway can be reached from I-77 via US 52. In North Carolina it can be reached from I-40 via Route 70, 74 or 25, and from I-26 it can be reached via NC 191.

Carl Sandburg Home

The Write Stuff

Sh! Quiet! Genius at work—or so it appears at **Connemara**, the 240-acre mountain retreat 26 miles south of Asheville, where Carl Sandburg, poet laureate of the people, spent the last 22 years of his life. A guided tour of Sandburg's home gives visitors a glimpse into the life of this intellectual giant. His presence still permeates the rooms 20 years after his death. You almost expect to find him, his green visor perched on his thick white hair, working in his upstairs retreat. His home reflects his inquiring mind and dynamic personality. Sandburg had over 10,000 books. They spill out everywhere, and in some rooms every inch of wall space is filled with bookcases. Even the kitchen has a few books squeezed into the cabinets. The halls are filled with file cabinets, boxes of reference material, and more books.

The household revolved around Sandburg's writing. He wrote well into the night and after rising late would read or handle his correspondence. Connemara is furnished without frills, to complement a lifestyle that was long on comfort and short on time. You'll notice there are no curtains at the windows; Mrs. Sandburg preferred it this way. But Sandburg also liked to be in touch with the mountain scenery, although he did have a tendency to tell people he had moved to the Smoky Mountains at the foot of the Blue Ridge. His wife enjoyed birdwatching, and field glasses and bird books are still by the dining room window. Sandburg was also fond of birds and was particularly attached to wrens. He called them "people of the eves." These dainty brown birds still make their home in the birdhouses at Connemara.

Sandburg liked to look at pretty things, whether it be nature or the collection of pictures he hung on a bulletin board by his bed. These magazine pictures include scenic vistas, a Paul Cezanne landscape, a Matisse, and a Picasso plus a picture of himself. His daughter Helga said he had an enormous ego. There are photographs of Sandburg through the house taken by his brother-in-law, noted camera artist Edward Steichen.

The master bedroom on the first floor was his wife's, but Sandburg napped there each afternoon and frequently listened to the records he kept there in an orange crate. The Sandburgs enjoyed music and would frequently have sing-alongs in the evening with Carl playing the guitar. His musical taste from the records in his own bedroom included works by Mahler, Wagner, Bach and Prokofiev.

Mrs. Sandburg spent a great deal of her time managing her goat farm. She began raising goats when the Sandburg's lived in Michigan. Her prize-winning herd peaked at 200. Her office was filled with cabinets containing breeding records. Be sure to save about 30 minutes to wander around the farm buildings and see the goats that still live at Connemara. There are 26 points of interest on the self-guided grounds tour.

If you have a little more time you might want to explore one of the hillside nature trails. Sandburg often enjoyed an evening stroll around the grounds or into the wooded hills. There are three nature trails; two are 2.3-mile trails to the top of Big Glassy Mountain and the other a .2-mile trail up Little Glassy Mountain.

During the summer months the Vagabond Players from the adjacent Flat Rock Playhouse present *The World of Carl Sandburg* and *Rootabaga Stories.* There is no admission charge for these programs. If you are going to be in the area in the evening, consider a performance at the Playhouse, acclaimed one of the ten best summer stock theaters in the country. They perform

Broadway and London hits, both dramatic plays and musicals. For play and ticket information call (704)693-0731.

The Carl Sandburg Home is open daily from 9:00 A.M. to 5:00 P.M., except on Christmas Day. There is a nominal admission charge.

Directions: From Asheville take I-26 south to Exit 23 for E. Flat Rock. Or take Exit 64 and go to US 25 and head south for three miles to the Carl Sandburg Home.

Cradle of Forestry

Birthplace of American Forest Conservation

Up until the end of the 19th century the forests in the U.S. were plundered or ignored depending on circumstances, and there was no effort to scientifically cultivate or manage the timberlands of this country. That all changed when George Vanderbilt began building his palatial Biltmore House outside Asheville with its extensive game preserve.

In 1892 Vanderbilt hired Gifford Pinchot, a European-trained forestry expert, to manage his newly acquired forest. Pinchot, considered the father of American forestry, began the first systematic forestry work in this country. His tenure not only fostered managed growth, it also proved profitable. This inspired Vanderbilt to purchase more forested land, a 100,000-acre tract around Mt. Pisgah—the nucleus of what is now Pisgah National Forest.

Pinchot's successor, Dr. Carl Schenck, was hired in 1895. To train his apprentices this German forester established the first school of forestry. The Biltmore Forest School began operation in 1898. Winter classes were held at the Biltmore Estate and summer sessions in Pisgah Forest. Schenck invited new students to "Join us and sink or swim."

At the **Cradle of Forestry**, a national historic site in the Pisgah National Forest, you'll learn more about these forest pioneers. An 18-minute film shown on the hour and the half hour at the visitor orientation center introduces you to these forward-looking men. After the film take one or both of the two one-mile paved trails, Biltmore Campus Trail and Forest Festival Trail. You will note from the trail guide brochures that each trail presents a different aspect of the early days of forestry. You can explore on your own or join one of the six daily guided walks.

The forest school campus utilized the old cabins and farm homes that once comprised the settlement of Pink Beds, a rural mountain community. There are eight stops along the Biltmore Campus Trail. The first building you'll see is the old schoolhouse.

A sign over the fireplace indicates the students' attitude. It reads: "In Schenck we trust, in booze we bust." The Biltmore "boys" were known for playing as hard as they studied. Other stops include the community commissary, Schenck's office, blacksmith shop and student quarters. The latter was known as Hell Hole. There were four more cabins named Little Hell Hole, Rest for the Wicket, Little Bohemia and The Palace. Some students stayed with the forest ranger although newcomers were warned that the ranger's wife couldn't cook. It was said she was a "stomach robber" who "couldn't heat water, let alone cook."

After ten years Schenck wanted businessmen, politicians, educators and lumbermen to become aware of his forestry school and forest-management accomplishments so he sent out invitations to a three-day Biltmore Forest Fair. To give attendees an idea of what they were seeing Schenck provided tips. His tips are the guidepoints along the Biltmore Forest Festival Trail. They indicate areas where Schenck tried unsuccessfully to grow Norway spruce and areas where he more successfully cultivated other varieties of conifers. When he started working there were no commercial nurseries, so he and his students planted and tended seedlings. Part of his forest plan called for selective lumbering, and to aid in this work he had a portable steam-powered sawmill which you'll see. Also of interest is the 1915 Climax logging locomotive used to pull the heavy loads of logs up the steep mountain slopes.

In addition to the educational value of these trails, they are also scenic. In the fall the foliage is colorful, and in the spring the rhododendron and mountain laurel add a pink lustre to the woods. From this came the name Pink Beds.

The Cradle of Forestry in America is open for a modest fee May through October from 10:00 A.M. to 6:00 P.M. In the visitor orientation center there is a gift shop and snack bar. Just north of the Cradle of Forestry is the Pink Beds Picnic Area, which also has a loop trail.

Directions: From Asheville take the Blue Ridge Parkway southwest. Exit at milepost 412, Route 276. Take Route 276 southeast towards Brevard for four miles. The Cradle of Forestry will be on your left off Route 276.

Judaculla Rock

Don't Knock the Rock

Tourists literally travel halfway around the world to view Australia's mysterious and mammoth Uluru, more commonly known as Ayer's Rock. They also undertake a good bit of inconvenience to see the mammoth upturned faces of Easter Island's striking burial platforms. Why then is North Carolina's **Judaculla Rock** virtually unknown? Admittedly, it's not as big or as dramatic as these more well-known spots, but its origins are shrouded in mystery, and its designs also reach back in time.

Just when they were made or who made the strange markings on Judaculla Rock in Jackson County near the banks of Caney Fork Creek is unknown. They may date back to prehistoric people, but certainly predate the Cherokees who created legends to explain these ancient figures. The drawings feature six-and-seven-digit hands and feet. According to Cherokee myths, Judaculla was a giant who lived in the dark forests of Balsam Mountain. When a hunting party of Indians wandered into the Caney Creek valley, their presence angered the giant, and he sprang down from his mountaintop lair to kill the puny creatures. As he landed in the valley, he put his hand out to steady himself, and his fingers marked the huge soapstone boulder. This fanciful tale may not provide much enlightenment about the rock's origins, but it does reinforce the theory that the picture writing on the rock predates the Cherokees.

This unpretentious spot is marked only by a state historical marker that directs the curious to a "large rock covered with well-preserved Indian picture writing of unknown origin." There is no explanatory visitor center, and only recently was a roof erected over the roughly 14-foot boulder to protect the ancient drawings. In addition to the hands and feet there are stick figures, hieroglyphic-like figures, concentric circles and other symbols. For many years North Carolina's "rock" languished in a cow pasture shamefully overlooked by all but a few intrepid explorers; now it is more accessible.

This site is certainly unpretentious, and with no supporting exhibit center you'll have to use your own imagination. But it is worth seeing. It's a link with ancestors who trod the earth millenniums ago. And, since there is no acceptable explanation of who did the petroglyphs or what they represent you can create your own myth of Judaculla Rock.

Directions: Take I-40 west of Asheville to Route 74. Follow Route 74 southwest to Sylva, then take NC 107 to East Laport. At the crossroads of this small town you see the historical marker that will direct you the last 3½ miles to Judaculla Rock, which is off Caney Fork Road.

Vance Birthplace

War Governor of the South

Zebulon Baird Vance epitomized the virtues of the Appalachian mountain stock from which he sprang. The family's pioneer homestead in the high valley outside Asheville demanded self-sufficiency and resilience. The men of the Vance family proved equal to the challenge. Theirs was one of the first three settlements on the west side of the Blue Ridge Mountains. Zeb Vance's grandfather, David Vance, a former colonel in the American Revolutionary army, acquired the farm in Reems Creek Valley in 1795 but had been living on the land since the fall of 1787.

It is thought that David Vance built the two-story hand-hewn yellow pine log house for his wife and four children. One of his sons, David, served as a captain in the War of 1812, but his primary distinction is that he was the father of Zebulon B. Vance, who was born on the Reems Creek homestead on May 13, 1830. Young Vance spent only his earliest years on this remote highland farm. After one year studying law at the University of North Carolina he passed the bar at age 22. Barely two years later he was elected to the state House of Commons.

Zebulon Vance was serving in the U.S. House of Representatives when the Civil War broke out. When North Carolina seceded, he was canvassing the state in support of the Union, but after the break he sided with South Carolina and traveled to Asheville where he organized the Rough and Ready Guard. He was a colonel in the Confederate army in 1862 when he was elected to the first of his three terms as governor of North Carolina. It was Vance's untiring efforts on behalf of the people of his state that made him a well-loved political leader in the South for nearly half a century. It was this service that led to the reclaiming of his family home as a memorial to this favorite son.

The Vance farmstead was remodeled in 1894 or 1895 by the Fox family. Parts of the original house were used in the remodeling, and the fireplaces and chimney were unaltered. When the Vance homestead was reconstructed by the state in the late 1950s, the panelling, flooring and rafters that were identified as parts of the original house were saved and used in the reconstruction. Although it strikes visitors as rustic, it was considered a show place in its day, as it was larger than other cabins in the settlement. Most of the furniture that now fills the five rooms was made in this area in the early 1800s. The house resembles the way it looked when Zebulon Vance was born, although only five pieces of furniture are original.

In the sitting room, which also served as the master bedroom, there is a pewter communion service from the First Presbyterian Church Colonel David Vance helped construct. One of the communion cups was for men the other for women. The bed in the large upstairs bedroom is a family piece, and the sea star pattern coverlet belonged to Zebulon Vance's older brother, Robert. Hanging on the wall of the smaller upstairs bedroom is a bed corder, used to tighten the ropes on the bed. This gave rise to the expression "sleep tight." If the ropes were loose those sharing the bed rolled to the center.

One unusual feature of the house is that it has an inside kitchen. The farm's isolated location may explain this anomaly. The original fireplace resembles a beehive oven as it gets narrow as it reaches the ceiling. The toaster suggests the derivation of yet another expression, as the cook would turn the toaster with her foot, hence the name. The heavy trammel in the fireplace is one of the original Vance pieces.

The outbuildings were rebuilt in the general vicinity of the originals. There is a tool house, loom house, smoke house, spring house, wash area, corn crib and slave cabin. Colonel David Vance had 17 slaves housed in three cabins. In the spring and fall during Pioneer Living Days the homestead is staffed with period-attired craftsmen demonstrating old-time skills like open hearth cooking, weaving, churning, chairbottoming, woodcrafting and others.

Before taking a tour of the farm stop at the visitor center and watch the 15-minute slide presentation on the life of Zebulon B. Vance. You can visit the homestead at no charge April–October Monday–Saturday 9:00 A.M. to 5:00 P.M. and Sunday 1:00 to 5:00 P.M. From November–March hours are Tuesday–Saturday 10:00 A.M. to 4:00 P.M. and Sunday 1:00 to 4:00 P.M.

Directions: From I-40 take US 19/23 North Bypass to the New Stock Road exit near Weaverville. Follow the directional signs from the New Stock Road exit to Reems Creek Road, Route 1103. Turn right on Reems Creek Road and go about six miles and the Vance Birthplace will be on your right. The site can also be reached from the Blue Ridge Parkway, between milepost 375 and 376, north of Asheville. Just follow the directional signs from the Parkway.

BREVARD/FRANKLIN/MURPHY AND VICINITY

Cullasaja Gorge

Land of Waterfalls

By recent count the area around Highlands has 150 waterfalls, a surprisingly large number of which can be seen in one short span as you travel through the **Cullasaja Gorge**. Vacationers who are accustomed to traveling long distances to see just one picturesque waterfall will be overwhelmed by the quantity and diversity of the falls along this scenic gorge. There are 18 small falls and several larger ones along the Cullasaja River.

Traveling down the gorge from Franklin on Route 64/28, which parallels the river, you'll first pass the Lower Cullasaja Falls, where the river cascades 250 feet. Near here is Kenner Bottom picnic area, a lovely meadow with split-rail fence. Off the highway on Gold Mine Road is Dendy's Orchard. During the fall months daily except Sunday you can stop for apples and cider.

The next series of white water is known locally as "Bust-Your-Butt Falls," and it's popular with youngsters. But strong advisories are issued about attempting to climb the waterfalls. The wet, slippery rocks make for a treacherous ascent, and there have been casualties and fatal accidents. In this area you'll also find the Van Hook Glade, a small campsite. If you take a slight detour when you see the sign, you can enjoy Cliffside Lake, a one-acre trout-stocked lake.

Next is the roadside overlook for Dry Falls, which is a misnomer since the water is wide and wet, dropping over the rocky overhang about 75 feet. In the spring the river can create a tumultuous torrent. There's an easy walk down a series of stairs to the bottom of the falls. Here you can walk behind the falls, and while you won't stay completely dry, the mist that constantly permeates the air feels delightful on hot days.

If you think that's unusual wait until you arrive at the next in the series of waterfalls. At Bridal Veil Falls the water falls 120 feet, but the surprise is that you drive behind the falls. In fact at one time the main highway ran behind the falls; now the drive is an abbreviated but highly scenic detour.

The series of 18 small falls, called the Kalakaleskies, are within a ¼-mile span just below the Sequoyah Lake Dam three miles outside Highlands.

Directions: Take I-40 west past Asheville then turn left on Route 23. This will merge with Route 74 for a time. Then continue south on Route 23/441 to Franklin. At Franklin take Routes 64/28 towards Highlands.

Franklin Gem Mines

Finders, Keepers!

Don't throw away your old, worn-out clothes, not if you're planning an outing to a gem mine. This is an excursion you really have to dress down for. Come equipped with gloves to protect your hands. Panning for gems is a dirty job, as you'll get muddy from head to toe. Nevertheless, rockhounds return day after day to try their luck. What brings them back are the valuable finds uncovered every day at one of the dozen mines in the area. Be warned, panning is addictive. It always seems like the next bucket will be "the one."

The Cowee Valley area claims to be the "Gem Capital of the World," but the mines here are not deep, dark tunnels. You pan along a sloppy sluice with a bucket of dirt that you wash down to uncover potential gems. Valuable rocks found here include rubies, sapphires, garnets, rhodolite, kyanite and other semiprecious stones. At the Shuler Ruby Mine the largest ruby to be discovered was 163 carats, while the largest sapphire was 576.75 carats. The popularity of this pastime stems from the sense of anticipation. You never know what you may uncover, but you'll know you've made a lucky find when the proprietor of the mine offers to buy it. You can also establish the value of your gemstones or have them cut and faceted at the many lapidary shops in the area.

You pay a start-up fee of about $5–6, then between 25–50 cents a bucket. Regulars may wash 20 or more buckets in a day. One avid rockhound boasted he'd emptied 240 buckets in three days. Some mines have native gems only, while others are salted with gemstones from other areas.

To get an idea of what to look for stop at **The Franklin Gem and Mineral Museum** on Phillips Street right off Main Street in downtown Franklin. The museum is located in an old jail, and you'll even see one of the original cells up on the second floor. The area you'll want to concentrate on is the North Carolina room because here you'll see gems found in the mines of Cowee Valley. Another room has world-wide specimens, while a third concentrates on gems from across the United States. There is a collection of Indian artifacts and fossils as well. Perhaps the most popular room is the fluorescent room. In this darkened chamber the stones glow in the eerie light. The museum is open daily from May through October at no charge from 10:00 A.M. to 4:00 P.M. and Sunday 1:00 to 4:00 P.M.

Gem mines of the Cowee Valley (area code 704, zip code 28734); all open April–October.

1. Caler Creek Ruby Mine: 8 Cowee School Rd., Franklin, NC, 524-7271. Native gems only. Stones found here include rubies, sapphires, rhodolite, garnet, pyrope garnet, others. Monday–Saturday, 8:00 A.M. to 5:00 P.M. Digging allowed.

2. Cherokee Ruby Mine: 310 Ruby Mine Rd., Franklin, NC, 524-5684. Native stones only. Monday–Sunday, 8:00 A.M. to 5:00 P.M.

3. Dale & Denko Gem Mine: 94 Ruby Mine Rd., Franklin, NC, 524-4310. Native gems and others. Free gem checking. Open daily until dark.

4. Gibson's Ruby Mine: Ruby Mine Rd., Franklin, NC, 524-4914. Native stones only. Stones found include rubies, sapphires, rhodolite and others. Daily, 8:00 A.M. to 5:00 P.M..

5. Gregory Ruby Mine & Campgrounds: 402 Ruby Mine Rd., Franklin, NC, 524-3552. Native gems only. Daily.

6. Holbrook Ruby Mine: 3 Ruby Mine Rd, Franklin, NC, 524-3540. Native gem stones. Stones found here include rubies, sapphires and others. Daily 8:00 A.M. to 5:00 P.M.

7. Jacob's Ruby Mine: 70 Allen Rd, Franklin, NC, 524-7022. Native stones only. Daily 8:00 A.M. to 5:00 P.M.

8. Jones Ruby Mine: 52 Lloyd Tallent Rd., Franklin, NC, 524-5946. Native NC stones. Monday–Saturday, 8:00 A.M. to 5:00 P.M.

9. Laurel Valley Mine: 16 Trailer Park Rd., Franklin, NC, 524-4689. Native and enriched stones. Daily 9:00 A.M. to 6:00 P.M.

10. Mason's Ruby & Sapphire Mine: 583 Upper Burnington Rd., Franklin, NC, 369-9742. Native stones only. Daily 9:00 A.M. to 5:00 P.M. Digging allowed.

11. Rocky Face Mine: 30 Sanderstown Rd., Franklin, NC, 524-3148. Gem checking provided. Open daily.

12. Rose Creek Mine & Campground: 28 Lyle Downs Rd., Franklin, NC, 524-3225. Native and enriched stones. Daily 8:00 A.M. to 5:00 P.M.

13. Shuler Ruby Mine: 245 Ruby Mine Rd., Franklin, NC, 524-3551. Native stones only. Stones found include rubies, sapphire, rhodolite and red garnet. Daily 8:00 A.M. to 5:00 P.M.

14. The Old Cardinal Gem Mine: PO Box 1668, Mason Branch Rd., Franklin, NC, 369-7534. Native and enriched stones. Open daily. Gem checking.

15. Yukon Ruby Mine: 11 Allen Rd., Franklin, NC, 524-6186. Native and enriched stones. Daily 8:00 A.M. to 5:00 P.M.

Highlands

A Perennial Brigadoon

Brigadoon was a mythical Scottish village that appeared one day every century. That way it could never be spoiled by the follies of man. In North Carolina's **Highlands** the problem has been solved with less Draconian measures. The charming village of Highlands, nestled in the Blue Ridge Mountains, combines natural beauty with the beauty created by scores of artists and artisans who have discovered the area.

The Scottish link is suggested by more than the misty mountain backdrop. Highlands is the home of the **Scottish Tartans Museum**, the American extension of a museum operated by the Scottish Tartans Society in Comrie, Scotland. Displayed here are more than 200 tartans, each representing a different clan. They also have an index of the sett (that's the unique pattern of checks and stripes in each tartan), colors and history of more than 1,500 tartans. You'll see weapons, banners and examples of Highland dress both old and new. The museum is open daily from 10:00 A.M. to 5:00 P.M.

The population of Highlands swells during the summer months from just under 1,000 to between 12,000 and 20,000. Many seasonal residents come not only for the breeze-cooled mountain air but also for the cultural activities. Highlands boasts a 50-year-old summer stock playhouse, a studio for the arts which presents evening programs and has a children's theater, a chamber music festival and an active art league. Work by regional artists is exhibited at the Bascom-Louise Gallery located in The Hudson Library.

The fashions found in the one-of-a-kind boutiques are tempting as are the hand-crafted jewelry and decorative household items. Antique lovers have discovered Highlands also. At last count there were 15 antique shops in town.

But visitors shouldn't neglect the area's natural attractions. The best place to start exploring is the Highlands Nature Center on E. Main Street. Exhibits here deal with the flora and fauna of the region, and behind the center is a botanical garden you can visit daily from June through Labor Day weekend. Across from the center a trail leads to Sunset Rock, a picturesque overlook that provides an excellent vista of scenic Horse Cove. The trail takes about 20 minutes to hike, and you will be climbing a moderately steep incline.

After your bird's-eye view, you might want to drive through **Horse Cove**. Continue on E. Main Street, which becomes Horse Cove Road. After successfully negotiating 37 curves you will come to Wilson Gap Road on your right. Turn and head up 37 yards for a look at the second largest poplar tree in the state and one of the three largest in the country. Retrace your steps and resume your progress up Horse Cove Road until you come to a fork. Veering off to the right is Bull Pen Road. The reward for persevering up this single-track gravel road is the sight of the Chattooga River at Iron Bridge. The potent power of the river is evident here as it has worn basins in the rocks along the bank. Some of the basins seem like river-formed hot tubs, or in this case cold tubs, while others are only dime-size. From there return to the fork and take the left route, Whiteside Cove Road. From Whiteside Cove you will have a splendid view up Whiteside Mountain. This road will intersect Route 107. Turn left and you will head into Cashiers. At the traffic light turn left on US 64 W to return to Highlands. This route will take you past Whiteside Overlook, so you'll have a view from both top and bottom.

If you turn right on Route 107 and head away from Cashiers for about eight miles to the North/South Carolina border, you can see one of the most splendid falls in the area. It is actually one mile over the line on the left in the Chattachoochee National Forest off Whitewater Road. **Whitewater Falls** are 411 feet high. The hike down to see the falls is steep, and it is approximately 1½ miles, so be prepared. If you have more time there is another challenging hike down to Glen Falls. These are reached by heading south out of Highlands on Route 106. After traveling three miles you will come to a dirt road marked by a United States Forest sign. This road leads to the parking area where you'll begin your descent. The one-mile hike down is extremely steep, and coming back up is even tougher. But if you are in shape it's worth the effort. Glen Falls has a series of three large falls each dropping roughly 60 feet. Even if you skip the falls you might want to drive out on Route 106 to Blue Valley Overlook, about ½ mile past the Glen Falls Turnoff. The shifting blues and greens of the endless line of mountains make this a breathtaking vista. One additional scenic drive you won't want to miss is through the Cullasaja Gorge (see selection) where you will pass one splendid waterfall after another.

Directions: Take I-26 south of Asheville to Route 64. Turn right (west) on Route 64 and continue to Highlands.

John C. Campbell Folk School

Crafty Retreat

In 1844 Danish religious leader, Bishop Brundtvig, founded the Danish Folk School. He was inspired by the ancient Greek culture, and he in turn inspired the founders of the John C. Campbell Folk School, the nation's oldest school of traditional crafts. The school was a dream of John Campbell who wanted creative young people to stay in their rural mountain homes practicing the folk arts of the region. Campbell died before he could carry out his ambitious plans.

His dream, however, did not die. It was realized by his wife, Olive Dame Campbell, and educator, Marguerite Butler Bidstrup. They traveled to Denmark, Ireland and England gathering information on folk schools. Then in 1925, after searching five states for the ideal location these educational pioneers decided to establish their school in the southern Appalachian region of North Carolina. The community of Brasstown was so enthusiastic about the project they donated 25 acres to the school. So the school was built outside of Murphy, not far from the Georgia state line. The objective was to teach "not just how to make a living, but how to live."

The first session in 1927–28 had an enrollment of 16. But over the years the school grew. Today the **John C. Campbell Folk School** has a 365-acre campus offering 344 courses to an estimated 3,000 students a year. Courses include weaving, woodcarving (for which the school is noted), enameling, pottery, jewelry making, photography, blacksmithing, rag rug weaving, quilting, folk dancing and folk music. This is a student-friendly school. There are no examinations, no grades, and no degrees for the one or two-week intensive courses. What students come away with is the satisfaction of learning a new skill. The classes are taught by gifted artists who instruct by doing.

While most of those who find their way to the John C. Campbell Folk School come to study, visitors are welcome to tour the grounds. A booklet available at the Craft Shop, *A Walk Through the History, Buildings and Programs*, will not only help you find your way around, it will also apprise you of the significance of all you see. The campus is an historic district on the National Register of Historic Places. Visitors are welcome in the studios to observe the students at work.

The **Folk Museum** was established almost as soon as the school opened. It serves as a repository for the vanishing artifacts of bygone days. The museum is actually two log cabins filled with typical rural North Carolina furnishings from the late 19th and early 20th centuries. Nearby a Conestoga wagon reminds visitors how settlers once reached this area.

Don't miss the school's **Craft Shop** where more than 300 artists market their wares. This cottage-industry craft outlet showcases not only work by the school's guest teachers but by other local artisans.

The John C. Campbell Folk School operates year-round, but during the spring, summer and fall there are special weekend musical programs, craft festivals and two-day workshops. For more information call (800)562-2440.

Directions: Take I-40 to Asheville. From there take Route 19/129 south. At Murphy turn left on Route 64. Then follow the directional signs for the John C. Campbell Folk School.

Perry's Water Gardens

Lotusland

In the Cowee Valley most tourists spend their time elbow-deep in mud, washing buckets of dirt and rocks, earnestly searching for gemstones at the area's many mines. But at another Franklin attraction, **Perry's Water Gardens**, the beauty of nature shines unhidden above the murky water. More than 2,500 lilies and lotus in just about every color you can imagine bloom in the 39 shallow ponds of this 3½-acre garden.

Perry D. Slocum established the gardens about ten years ago. Gardening was his avocational interest before it became his business. The hybrid lotus he named in honor of his wife has been called the most beautiful lotus in the world. He was given the first patents ever granted for lotus. The leaves of a lotus plant are from six inches to 36 inches in diameter and grow up to seven feet high. The basketball-size blossoms bloom for about six weeks during the middle of the summer. Mr. Slocum and current owner Ben Gibson also have had considerable success with lilies. The Giant Victoria Lily has pads more than six feet in diameter, which look like giant stepping stones. This variety opens with a white flower that changes the next day to a pink hue. Other lily blossoms have deeper colors, that glitter like the iridescent jewels rock hunters search for at the nearby gem mines.

Aquatic plants are best seen in the early morning when they first open and their heady fragrance permeates the air. If you walk quietly you're apt to spot frogs sunning themselves on the lily pads or see an occasional turtle. Birds find the colorful pool fish delectable. If you want to enjoy your lunch while watching the birds scavenge for theirs, picnic tables are available.

Perry's Water Gardens are open at no charge from late May through Labor Day on Monday through Saturday 9:00 A.M. to 5:00 P.M. and on Sundays 1:00 to 5:00 P.M.

Directions: From I-40 west of Asheville take Route 74 southwest then pick up Route 23/441 to Franklin. In Franklin proceed north on Route 28 to the Cowee Baptist Church. Just beyond the church turn right on Cowee Creek Road. Go two miles then turn left on Leatherman Gap Road. The gardens are just 2½ miles from the church.

Pisgah National Forest

Pst . . . It's a Winner!

Pisgah National Forest's 495,000 acres makes it the second largest of the state's four national forests. Within this immense acreage in the mountains of western North Carolina there are 30 recreation areas offering a diversity of outdoor fun. For boating there's the Murray Branch, for swimming Lake Powhatan. Nineteen areas are designated for fishing, and an impressive 23 areas have hiking trails. There are also campgrounds and picnic areas.

Pisgah National Forest has something for everyone—kids love Sliding Rock, a natural water park; gardeners are entranced by the abundant rhododendron in Roan Gardens; fishermen like to check out next year's catch at the State Fish Hatchery; history buffs enjoy the Cradle of Forestry (see selection); and you can't beat the scenic appeal of Looking Glass Falls.

Remember as you search for these forest fun spots, that they are usually only marked by a small sign. If you miss that one marker you will travel miles out of your way, so obtain a national forest map before you start exploring. That is the case with **Sliding Rock** a spot that looks ideally suited for a Norman Rockwell drawing. This natural water slide offers some chilling fun. It's not that it's high, it's just cold. Even on the hottest days the water rarely gets above 50 degrees. On cooler spring and fall days determined swimmers emerge not black and blue but decidedly blue. The water flows over the wide, smooth granite stone just fast enough to buoy you up but not fast enough to put you under. There is a bathhouse and an observation deck where you can watch the fun along the 60-foot rocky sliding board. The area is open Memorial Day through Labor Day for sliding. If you drive past at other times, just stop for a look. The Sliding Rock Recreation Area is 12 miles west of Brevard on Route 276.

A different kind of scenic appeal awaits at **Roan Gardens** 12 miles from Bakersville, near the Tennessee border. The 6,286-foot bald summit of Roan Mountain is the western tip of a chain of knobs and balds called the Highlands of Roan. The 600 acres are ablaze with brilliant purple rhododendrons during June, with the last two weeks generally being the peak blooming period. Blossoms range from light red and pink to a variety of purple shades. Botanists have studied the mountain top garden for years; one noted that it was "without doubt, the most beautiful mountain east of the Rockies."

A rare Scotch heather is spreading over many acres atop Roan Mountain, and surrounding the tip is a collar of large Fraser fir. Roughly 850 acres of Fraser fir and spruce are now part of the Pisgah National Forest. A curious natural phenomenon periodically occurs on this exposed tip. Visitors comment on what sounds like the humming of thousands of bees. Nature's eerie music is believed to be created by the electrically-charged air currents swirling by each other near the peak.

If you are in the area during the winter months keep in mind that Roan Mountain's hiking trails are used by cross-country skiers. Sledders and snowshoers are also welcome. Heavy snows usually arrive in December and remain through March. For more information on this area you can write the U.S. Forest Service, P.O. Box 128, Burnsville, NC 28714 or call (714)682-6146.

Pisgah National Forest also has one of the largest trout hatcheries in the east, six miles above the Pisgah District Visitor Center on the Davidson River Road. **The State Fish Hatchery** is open to visitors at no charge from 8:00 A.M. to 4:00 P.M. daily. North Carolina has 4,000 miles of mountain trout streams, more than any other state in the southeast. The hatchery loses about 35 percent of the trout before they reach ten inches. If you visit in September through November you might be able to watch hatchery personnel artificially inseminating the trout. This process has been done in the U.S. since the Civil War, and in North Carolina since 1922. In a two-step procedure, the female fish is first milked to get the eggs; then the male is held over the eggs to fertilize them. Once the fish are born they are allowed to reach a good size before they are taken to stock the state's streams.

One of the mountain streams in Pisgah National Forest creates **Looking Glass Falls**. The cascading white water runs 30 feet wide before dropping more than 60 feet down a sheer rock into the pool below. This is one of the best-known falls in the eastern United States. A massive overhanging shelf of rock tower above the falls gives it a rugged beauty. The falls are 9.4 miles west of Brevard on US 276.

Along this same route just two miles outside of Brevard is the Pisgah District Visitor Center where you can obtain information on all the recreational areas in the forest. Behind this station is the Pisgah Ecology Trail. It takes about 45 minutes to hike this self-guided .6-mile trail. Be sure to pick up the trail guide brochure before starting out. There are 11 points of natural interest along the trail.

Directions: Take I-40 to Asheville, then head south on Route 280 towards Brevard; just before reaching this town turn right on Route 276. The Pisgah District Visitor Center is two miles ahead on the right.

GREAT SMOKY MOUNTAINS AND VICINITY

Great Smoky Mountains National Park

Holy Smoke!

Vistas in the **Great Smoky Mountains National Park** conjure up images of rolling ocean waves as the mountains undulate beneath frothy white clouds. More than a half million acres are protected in this wildlands sanctuary, preserving one of the world's finest examples of temperate deciduous forest. Recognized as having a unique environment the park is now established as both a World Heritage Site and an International Biosphere Reserve.

Traveling along the park's 170 miles of paved roads or on the more than 100 miles of gravel roads you will see forest like that encountered by early explorers and pioneers—although less lush and smaller since most of the forest has been reclaimed from early logging incursions. Most of the roads provide a number of hiking trail options, but you can see a great deal of the park from your automobile. Stop and pick up maps for auto and hiking information and brochures at one of the park's visitor centers. Two of these centers are in Tennessee, one at Sugarlands two miles south of Gatlinburg and the other in Cades Cove. Three miles north of Cherokee is the visitor center at Oconaluftee (see selection on Pioneer Farmstead), the best place to begin exploring the Great Smoky Mountains National Park.

Some routes, like **Cades Cove Loop Road** and **Roaring Fork Motor Natural Trail**, have auto-tour booklets to enhance your enjoyment of the park's special attractions. Booklets are available at the start of each of these special routes. Legend has it that Cades Cove Loop Road was named in honor of the wife of a Cherokee chief. This picturesque Cades Cove valley has reminders of pioneer times. A gristmill operates at the Cable Mill area where pioneer living-history vignettes are presented during the summer months. The five-mile Roaring Fork Motor Nature Trail also across the border in Tennessee follows the cascading and aptly named Roaring Fork River down the mountain. Other interesting routes across the North Carolina state line include Newfound Gap, Greenbrier, Rich Mountain, Parson Branch, Laurel Creek and Little River Road.

One auto-tour route in North Carolina is Cataloochee Road leading to a remote sheltered valley settled in the early 1800s. An old cemetery and some homes remain. Along the state boundary line Clingmans Dome Road offers some spectacular crestline views of the Smokies. To really experience the spruce-fir forest through which you are traveling, stop and take the Spruce-Fir Self-Guiding Nature Trail. At the end of this road park in the lot and take the ½-mile trail to the observation tower. Clingmans Dome is 6,642 feet, the highest peak in the Smokies and on a clear day you'll have a grand view of the Smoky Mountains.

Along the main roads you'll notice pull-offs for Quiet Walkways. These are short, ½-mile trails that give an opportunity to get out, explore and observe some of the 1,500 flowering plants identified in the park. These pull-offs have limited parking space to insure the trails are not overcrowded. In all there are over 900 miles of trails in the park—from these short hikes to long extended trails that take days to hike. In addition to Spruce-Fir Trail there are ten other self-guiding trails. All but two of these are in Tennessee. The two North Carolina trails are Balsam Mountain Trail through a former logging area reclaimed by the forest and Smokemont, which also shows man's earlier encroachment on the forest. Ranger stations and visitor centers in the park schedule walks conducted by naturalists so check the calendar of events.

Most visitors to the Great Smoky Mountains National Park seek trails that lead to the numerous waterfalls within the park. There are ten major falls along trails and three along the roadway. Four falls are in North Carolina, three close to each other. These are **Indian Creek Falls, Juneywhank Falls** and **Toms Branch Falls**—all on trails beginning off Deep Creek Road. The shortest trail is the easy half-hour, ¼-mile hike to Toms Branch Falls, best seen in early spring or late fall when the leaves are off the trees. It's also an easy though longer hike (roughly two hours, two miles round trip) to the 30-foot Indian Creek Falls. Here the water drops precipitously over a rocky ledge into a deep pool. Care must be taken when swimming beneath the falls as some pools have strong undertows. It takes roughly an hour to negotiate the moderately difficult 1½-mile trail to the cascading Juneywhank Falls. In an area within the Cherokee Indian Reservation (see Museum of the Cherokee Indians selection), you can hike to Mingo Falls. The ½ mile, moderately difficult, round trip begins off Big Cove Road on Pigeon Creek Trail out of Mingo Falls Campground. There is a longer trail branching off this one that takes you to the top of the 120-foot falls. Signs will indicate detour.

There are ten national park campgrounds, nine picnic areas, wayside exhibits and historic buildings throughout the park. Fishing is permitted year-round with a state license. The streams in the park are not stocked. Streams in the Cherokee Indian Reservation are stocked with trout.

Directions: From I-40 at Asheville take Route 74W, then take Route 19N through Maggie to Cherokee. Turn right on Route 441 to the Oconaluftee visitor center.

Maggie Valley

Stompin' n' Strollin'

Picturesque **Maggie Valley** leads into the Smoky Mountains National Park. This verdant 2.7-mile valley offers a variety of diversions. For one thing it's the clogging capital of the world. Every weekend from May through October the Stompin' Ground resounds to the foot-tapping beat of bluegrass and country music. Burton and Becky Edwards, the children of Stompin' Ground owner Kyle Edwards, started dancing at a tender age. Burton began clogging when he was four and Becky at the ripe old age of seven. The Edwards are now U.S. and World Champion cloggers. As you would expect, these two are crowd pleasers. They take part in the 8:00 P.M. weekend performance of the Magnum Cloggers, a group featured on the Nashville Network.

The **Stompin' Ground** is one of the sites for the popular Folkmoot USA, held each summer in late July and early August. The Southeast Tourism Society includes this international festival on their list of the top 20 events in the region. Folkmoot means a meeting of the people, and that's exactly what this festival is all about—a chance for you to meet and enjoy dancers, singers and musicians from around the world. The costumes, pageantry and unusual musical accompaniment make this an educational as well as entertaining festival. Performers share the heritage of China, Turkey, Italy, Poland, Germany, Korea, Yugoslavia, Costa Rica, Scotland, in fact countries all across the globe. As part of the festival there is an International Festival Day that fills Main Street in Waynesville with hundreds of booths featuring crafts and cuisine from around the world. For information about this year's festival call (704)452-2997.

When folks hear about the **Opry House**, they think of Nashville, but Maggie Valley boasts its own mini-version. Bluegrass and country music can be enjoyed at this unpretentious music hall located in Maggie Valley off US 19.

For daytime fun take a drive up to **Big Cataloochie Valley**. It's not uncommon to spot deer grazing in this scenic valley. You can hike the nature trails, fish in a trout stream that inspires even novices to try their luck, and explore an old chapel and school. Palmer Chapel dates back to 1902 and is set in a meadow with the mountains as a backdrop. Just up the road is the 1903 Beech Grove School. Its rustic surroundings are a testimony to the miles children had to cover in order to attend classes. These are quiet, low-keyed pleasures.

Maggie Valley also offers more commercial pastimes. First there is **Ghost Town in the Sky**. This theme park literally scales the heights. It's accessible by chairlift (a 13-minute ride), cable car (seven minutes), or you can just drive up to the gates. They've re-created the Old West on this mountaintop with gunfights, American Indian dances at Fort Cherokee, high steppin' dancers and honky-tonk piano at the old saloon, and western and country music. Over 30 rides and shows add to the fun. This is a single admission park. It's open daily 9:00 A.M. to 7:00 P.M. from May through October.

For the very young there is **Soco Gardens Zoo**. More sophisticated youngsters may find this too small, but if there is not a large zoo in your hometown this is an excellent opportunity to introduce the kids to a wide variety of wild animals—leopards, jaguars, brown bears, coatimundis, lemurs, emus, alligators and others. There are snake demonstrations and a petting zoo. Hours are 10:00 A.M. to 6:00 P.M. in May, September and October; 9:00 A.M. to dark June, July and August. Admission is charged.

If you prefer the new West to the old, you might want to consider stopping for a night or two at the **Cataloochie Ranch** high above Maggie Valley in the Southern Highlands. This easygoing mountaintop ranch offers horseback riding, tennis, hiking and fishing. You can stay in rooms at the main ranch house, the Silverbell Lodge, or rent one of their seven cabins. For accommodation information call (704)926-1401. During the winter guests like to try their skills at the nearby Cataloochee ski area, which has two easy trails, four trails for the modestly skilled and two difficult trails for the experts. For information call (704)926-0285. If you are outside North Carolina call (800)THE-IMTN.

Directions: Take I-40 west out of Asheville to Exit 27, then follow US 19, the main road through Maggie Valley. You will see the visitors center in Stallard Mall on your left as you head up the valley. Stop there for maps and information of the area.

Museum of the Cherokee Indian

Myth Keepers

The Cherokee Nation may be an ancient culture, but its history is told in a thoroughly modern way at the state-of-the-art **Museum of the Cherokee Indian**, located just outside the Great Smoky Mountains National Park.

Cherokees have lived in south Appalachia for thousands of years and the museum's six mini-theaters offer a dramatic overview of the formation of this Indian nation. You will learn that over 3,500 years ago the Cherokees separated from the Northern Iroquois, their nearest linguistic relatives. Another presentation deals with Cherokee culture at the time of their first contact with European settlers, which led to a drastic diminishing of tribal land. Cherokee tribes once spread out over parts of eight southern states, but now the Eastern Band of the Cherokee Nation is concentrated in western North Carolina.

But the stories of the Cherokees reach even farther back in time as you will discover from the museum's exhibits on Cherokee mythology. You'll hear the ancient sacred stories that speak about the origin of the mountains and valleys, the first fire and how plants and animals came to be. These stories were passed down for generations as oral history because the Cherokees did not have a written alphabet until 1821 when Sequoyah developed a system of writing. Sequoyah, a silversmith and soldier in the War of 1812, is considered a genius because he single handedly established an entire syllabary for the Cherokee nation. His work enabled the Cherokee to translate familiar English stories into Cherokee, as well as print books in the Cherokee language. You'll be able to hear the Cherokee language on the museum's headphones.

As you might expect the museum contains a fine collection of Cherokee craftsmanship. There is a regal feather cape with an ornamental trim of white feathers around the collar. Silver ornaments are adorned with colorful stones, and clothes are decorated with bright beadwork.

Anyone who has ever found an arrowhead in the woods will be interested in the comprehensive array of arrowheads dating back to the Paleo-Indian period. Methods of making arrowheads are detailed and other stone tools exhibited.

Additional displays focus on pottery, basketry, pipes, weapons, dance masks and portraits of noted members of the Cherokee tribe. The Museum of the Cherokee Indian is open mid-June through August, Monday–Saturday 9:00 A.M. to 8:00 P.M. and Sunday 9:00 A.M. to 5:00 P.M. Hours September until mid-June are daily 9:00 A.M. to 5:00 P.M. Closed Thanksgiving, Christmas and New Year's Day. Admission is charged.

If the exhibits on Cherokee crafts make you wish you could purchase the colorful jewelry or intricately decorated pottery, when you leave the museum head directly across the street to the **Qualla Arts and Crafts Mutual Coop**. This Indian owned and operated cooperative is one of the best places to purchase Cherokee crafts. You won't find any poorly made souvenir quality work here, the work is done by artists. Delicate pottery, intricate finger-woven sashes, multi-colored beadwork, white oak baskets, soapstone sculpture, soft sculpture dolls, statues, jewelry and more can be found here.

If you are going to spend more than a day in the area consider fishing; the Indian land has more than 30 miles of streams and three ponds which are stocked twice weekly. Each year more than ¼ million rainbow, brook and brown trout from the tribe's hatchery are added to the tribal waters. You will need a Tribal Fishing Permit, obtainable at a nominal cost at roughly two dozen spots throughout the reservation (mainly campgrounds and tackle stores). For information call (800)438-1601; if you are out of NC call (800)438-1601. No permit however is needed at the Cherokee Trout Farms located on Big Cove Road just ten miles north of Cherokee.

Directions: Take I-40 west past Asheville to Exit 27, Route 19, which will take you directly into the Cherokee Reservation.

Oconaluftee Indian Village

Path to the Past

If you have time for only one stop on your visit to the Cherokee Indian Reservation, make it the **Oconaluftee Indian Village**. Plan to spend about two hours exploring this replica of a 1750 Cherokee community and adjacent botanical garden.

Here in the forested mountains of western North Carolina the Eastern Band of the Cherokee Nation has been living for centuries. You'll walk along a woodland trail that leads into the past. Children raised on cowboy movies may expect to see teepees, but those were unique to Indian tribes in the west. The Cherokees were an agrarian tribe, and they lived in wooden cabins similar to those built by the settlers.

You will see the Indian forerunner of today's sauna, the sweathouse, a windowless cabin used to sweat out ailments. Another interesting structure is the seven-sided Council House. Clay was added over a wooden frame to create the multiple sides for this meeting house.

What adds life to the village are the many Cherokees you will see still practicing the old arts. You can watch while they work on a dugout canoe, form colorful beaded jewelry, hand weave belts, chip arrowheads, weave baskets and mold pottery with native clay. As your guide escorts you through the village you'll learn about the history, rituals, culture and lifestyle of the Cherokees. Before concluding your visit there is a question and answer session.

Just outside the village there is a path through the **Cherokee Botanical Garden**, open without charge. You'll see a profusion of flowers and shrubs along the forest trail. A mountain cabin is surrounded by a vegetable and herb garden.

The Oconaluftee Indian Village is open daily mid-May to late October from 9:00 A.M. to 5:30 P.M. Admission is charged.

Adjacent to the village is the **Mountainside Theatre** where *Unto These Hills* is presented nightly except Sundays from mid-June through late August. The outdoor amphitheater is the ideal setting for the dramatic story of the Cherokee Nation. The drama begins in 1540 with the arrival of Spanish explorer, Hernando DeSoto, the first white man to cross the path of the Cherokees. The story of the Cherokees continues through the colonial period. The gallant fight waged by the Cherokees under Chief Junaluska alongside Andrew Jackson against the Creek Indians in the Battle of Horseshoe Bend during the War of 1812 is brought to life. Despite their contribution the Cherokees were to suffer drastic reversals under the Jackson administration. The tragic relocation of the Cherokees along the Trail of Tears reminds viewers that more than 25 percent of those setting off for Oklahoma did not

Basket weaving is one of many crafts demonstrated at Ocona-luftee Indian Village, replica of a 1750 Cherokee community.

survive. Even those who conquered disease and exposure were set upon by earlier settlers already in the western territory. These bitter days make the Cherokee story a tragic one, but the evening is uplifted by the traditional dances including the world famous Eagle Dance.

The cast of 130 includes descendants of those Cherokees who actually lived the past that is being told. This drama begins nightly except Sunday at 8:45 P.M. from mid-June until late July and at 8:30 P.M. from late July through late August. You can purchase either general admission or reserved seats. Call (704)497-2111 for information or write: *Unto These Hills*, P.O. Box 398, Cherokee, NC 28719. If you arrive early you can enjoy the pre-performance mountain folk music concert.

Directions: Take I-40 past Asheville to Exit 27, Route 19. This will take you directly into the Cherokee Reservation via Maggie Valley (see selection) and Soco Mountain.

Pioneer Farmstead and Mingus Mill

Smoky Mountain High

Despite their enormous differences and their inevitable enmity the Scotch-Irish adventurers who settled the western mountains of North Carolina and the Cherokee Indians who inhabited this vast wilderness had one strong bond—they both knew they had to work with their natural environment in order to survive.

It wasn't enough for these pioneers to simply build a home, they had to build a total farmstead to insure their survival. From the forests settlers found the means to improve their daily life— berries to eat and use for coloring, medicinal plants, bark and wood for weaving and building their houses, animals to hunt, and new crops to plant. The **Pioneer Farmstead** in the Oconaluftee Valley is a collection of authentic farm buildings relocated from various locations in the Great Smoky Mountains National Park. Authentically garbed staff perform a wide variety of farm and household chores at the farmstead during the summer and fall such as planting, cooking, and the making and repairing of household tools.

The farm house is a particularly fine example of a pioneer home. John E. Davis, a master craftsman, built this cabin in 1901. His painstaking care is evident in the matched log walls. Davis took the time to split each tree trunk in half, then took corresponding logs from each half to build the walls. His sons, age eight and four, were responsible for gathering stones to build the two chimneys, often pulling a stone-laden sled long distances from a supply source.

Near enough to the house to make a winter's run bearable are the outhouse, meat house and woodshed. These pioneers carefully chose which trees they burned. Poplar didn't heat sufficiently, while chestnut was too volatile, popping so much they feared it would burn their house instead of heat it. The best and longest fire was from hickory or oak.

Most visitors can't identify the bee gum stand. These hollow pieces of black gum logs housed a colony of bees. Honey was a mainstay of the pioneer's diet, serving as a sweetening and, when mixed with corn whiskey, as an effective cough remedy.

Not all pioneer farmsteads had a chicken house like the one you'll see here. Some farmers let the chickens and turkeys roast in nearby trees. These barnyard fowl served several functions, providing feathers, eggs and Sunday dinner. Another building reserved for food, was the apple house; its thick rock walls prevented rotting. The apples had many uses, being made into cider, vinegar, sauces and pies.

Perhaps the greatest boon to the European settlers from their early contact with the Indians was the introduction of corn to their diet. Corn not only fed their families, it also fed the livestock, and was a major ingredient in moonshine, a mountain favorite. The corncrib was thus an important part of any farm. So vital was this daily staple farmers often allowed black snakes to live in the corncrib to keep it rodent free.

Food was a paramount concern to the farmers, but equally essential was their water source. The settlers built springhouses on their farms to serve as a primitive refrigerator where they kept melons, milk and other dairy products.

Several buildings you'll see at the farmstead indicate a permanence and prosperity. These include the barn, pigpen, sorghum mill and blacksmith shop. The farmstead also maintains a garden with vegetables and herbs.

At the farmstead you're likely to wonder why pioneers chose to eke out a rough existence in this wilderness valley. What did they find that made it worth their effort? Take your time, walk the dirt paths, look around the Oconaluftee Valley and the answer may become apparent. The Oconaluftee visitor center is open daily year round.

Just a half mile from the visitor center and Pioneer Farmstead is **Mingus Mill**, another pioneer mainstay. The Mingus family moved to this valley in the 1790s. Their first mill was an overshot waterwheel. The mill you see today was built in 1886 by a Virginian named Sion T. Early. His initials can still be seen on the front gables just under the eaves. The mill building was constructed of yellow-poplar. There are even a few decorative touches to indicate Early's craftsmanship: beaded lumber, chamfered posts, trimmed latches and moldings.

The Mingus Mill, powered by a cast iron turbine, was a custom mill, one that ground grain to each customer's taste. You can still watch this old mill grin cornmeal from mid-April through October. Take time to walk along the 200-yard wooden millrace to the main channel of Mingus Creek.

Mills such as this provided one of the few opportunities for socializing. When farmers came to this common meeting spot they had a chance to catch up on the news with their far-flung neighbors.

Directions: From I-40 at Asheville take Route 74W, then take Route 29S through Maggie to Cherokee. Turn right on Route 441 to the Oconaluftee visitor center and Pioneer Farmstead.

NANTAHALA NATIONAL FOREST AND VICINITY

Fontana

Dam It All!

Most visitors to western North Carolina delight in the wonders of nature, but at **Fontana** it is a wonder of man that is impressive.

One of the largest and most time-efficient engineering feats in our history was the construction of the **Fontana Dam** on the Little Tennessee River in the Great Smoky Mountains.

Fontana Dam towers 480 feet above the 29-mile long Fontana Lake, making it the highest dam east of the Mississippi River. When TVA started work on this dam the remote mountain mining village of Fontana was transformed from a sleepy community to a bustling town, for a time the second largest in the state. A railroad was built to transport supplies. Houses, schools, a hospital, post office, bank and library were built. The roughly 5,000 workers, motivated by the war-time emergency, labored with patriotic fervor. They worked in three shifts, round-the-clock, seven days a week. The workers set the world record for the most cubic yards of concrete poured in a 24-hour period. The dam was actually built in half the time it would have taken in peacetime. Construction began on January 1, 1942, and the first power was generated on January 20, 1945.

It is fascinating to tour this impressive TVA project. The statistics alone are overwhelming—2,815,300 cubic yards of concrete and 727,200 cubic yards of earth and rockfill were needed to complete this structure. Fontana Dam's three generating units can produce 238,500 kilowatts of electricity. Most of those who stop at the visitor center at the top of the dam are not entirely sure how the process works, but they leave with some interesting insights into the generation of electricity. A 20-minute film about the construction of Fontana Dam is also instructive.

Be sure to take the time to see the dam from the overlook before driving to the bottom to go inside the control room of the powerhouse. From a balcony in the powerhouse you will be able to look down on the powerful generators below. In order to generate 80 megawatts it requires around 3,000 cubic feet of water a second to keep the shaft rotating at 150 RPM. To grasp what this means consider that a good-size swimming pool holds around 20,000 gallons of water. The volume of water needed to generate at full power would be the equivalent of draining this pool every couple of seconds.

If you have time you might want to hike along the Lake Trail that extends for 30 miles along Fontana Lake from the dam to Bryson City. Another option is to get out on the lake. Fontana Marina rents a wide variety of boats, from canoes and paddleboats to big 17-foot bass boats. The marina also maintains a full stock of fishing supplies.

Fishing on **Fontana Lake** varies with the seasons. January, February and March you will catch smallmouth bass, largemouth bass and walleye. Your best bet is to stay along the shoreline. According to knowledgeable locals the best months for casual fishermen are April, May and June. Head out in the early morning or late evening and you're likely to catch smallmouth bass, largemouth, bass, walleye and bream. In July and August the big fish swim deeper in cooler water. You may have to troll 50 to 80 feet deep to catch big trout and walleye. In August and November the white bass run in large schools. Fishermen should also keep in mind that within 25 miles of Fontana there is the largest concentration of trout streams in the country. Hazel Creek and Eagle Creek are two popular and productive fishing haunts.

Many visitors come to Peppertree Fontana Village for a week and return the next year for a longer stay. About 40–50 percent of the guests at Fontana are returnees. There is an inn, with cabana units around the pool, modern condo units, cottages of varying sizes and a campground. This is an old-fashioned family style resort. They organize volleyball and softball games, have horseback riding, hayrides, lake cruises, guided hikes, craft instruction, bonfires and country dancing plus the swimming, fishing, hiking and tennis. For information on Fontana Village Resort call (704)498-2211. For reservations call (800)438-8050.

Directions: From Asheville take I-40 west, then take Route 74 to Bryson City. Continue north on Route 28 to Fontana Village. The village is two miles from Fontana Dam.

Joyce Kilmer-Slickrock Wilderness

"Only God Can Make a Tree"

The 1964 Congressional Wilderness Act defined wilderness as an area untrammeled by man, a place where man's influence is either nonexistent or very slight and you can enjoy solitude and a primitive and unconfined recreational experience. The wilderness experience is not for everyone; the trails are merely blazed, if that, and there are no restrooms, water spigots, shelters or campgrounds.

Like the Cherokee Indians, who once hunted in the North Carolina wilderness, today's visitors have to depend on their path-finding skills. They must also be prepared to be self-sufficient while in the wilderness. Ten essentials you should take on any trip into the wilderness are a map, compass, whistle (if you need help three blasts is the universal signal), flashlight, sharp knife, candle (or other fire starter), waterproof matches, first aid kit, food, and you should wear or carry warm clothing.

The 17,013-acre **Joyce Kilmer-Slickrock Wilderness Area** is within the Nantahala National Forest. It encompasses the headwaters and watersheds of Little Santeetlah and Slickrock Creek. Elevation in these steep basins ranges from 1,086 at the mouth of Slickrock Creek to over 5,300 feet on Stratton Bald. There are splendid views from the high ridges and cascading streams that dissect the steep mountainsides. Much of the area is virgin forest, one of the few such remaining tracts in the east. One small section of this area was logged back in 1915, but time and protective management have erased all but a few indications of this activity.

Within the wilderness area, 3,800 acres have been dedicated as a living monument to the poet and naturalist Joyce Kilmer. One of the few easy trails within this wilderness is the two-mile Joyce Kilmer National Recreation Trail that leads to a bronze plaque in the heart of the Memorial Forest. Kilmer was killed in action in France during World War I. His most memorable legacy is the poem "Trees." The opening lines, "I think that I shall never see, A poem lovely as a tree," are oft-quoted by nature lovers. It only takes an hour and a half to hike this trail, and it is an easy way to experience the virgin forested wilderness. Trees here are hundreds of years old, some more than 20 feet in circumference and over 100 feet high. The ancient trees include yellow-poplar, hemlock, sycamore, basswood, oak and other hardwoods.

All in all there are 60 miles of hiking trails in this wilderness area. Another easy and short trail is the .6-mile Wolf Laurel Trail that takes about an hour to hike. You may not want to take the entire trail, but the **Slickrock Creek Trail**, 12.9 miles total length, is an easy to moderate trail. During the spring more than 90 varieties of wildflowers have been found along this trail. If you park near Cheoah Dam and hike along Calderwood Lake to Slickrock Creek, a distance of about two miles, you should be able to spot these harbingers of spring. One thing to keep in mind, particularly after heavy rains, is that there are no footlogs or bridges over the creek, and the trail crosses the creek on numerous occasions.

Along with these easy trails several others are highly popular with wilderness visitors. The 5.6-mile **Naked Ground Trail** starts with a nice easy walk then becomes steeper for the last quarter. It takes about 4 to 4½ hours to hike up this trail and 3½ hours to come back down. Although it is a difficult hike the 5.2-mile **Hangover Lead Trail** is a winner because of its fantastic views. It is a seven-hour climb one way.

In the moderately difficult category you can enjoy beautiful waterfalls on the 1.9-mile Ike Branch Trail, a two-hour hike each way. Also plan at least two hours each way for the 2.8-mile Nichols Cove Trail. Another trail of equal difficulty is the 1.7-mile Yellowhammer Gap Trail that takes 1½ hours in and 2½ hours to hike out. Finally four trails—Haoc, Stratton Bald, Deep Creek and Big Fat Trail—are in the difficult category and should only be attempted by experienced wilderness hikers.

You will need to obtain a topographic map if you intend to

hike any of these trails, except the Joyce Kilmer National Recreation Trail. To purchase a map write: Cheoah Ranger District,
Route 1, Box 16A, Robbinsville, NC 28771.

Directions: From Asheville take I-40 west, then head southwest
on Route 74. At Sylva take Route 74 west to Bryson City. Continue
west on Route 28. Turn left on Route 143 to Robbinsville. Then
turn right on Route 129. Drive about 1.5 miles and you will see
a sign for Cheoah Ranger Station–Joyce Kilmer. Turn left at sign
and follow until you come to a dead-end. Turn right and drive
13 miles; then make a left at the Joyce Kilmer Memorial Forest
Picnic Area sign. The trail begins at the map display shelter.

Nantahala National Forest

Land of the Noonday Sun

The Cherokees, whose land this once was, called it Nantahala,
meaning Land of the Noonday Sun, because the sun only pen-
etrates the deep gorges when it is directly overhead. The highest
elevation within this half million acre reserve is at Lone Bald in
Jackson County where the mountain tops out at 5,800 feet. Located in the southwestern corner of the state, **Nantahala** is the
largest of North Carolina's four national forests.

Within Nantahala there are three wilderness areas (Ellicott
Rock, Southern Nantahala and Joyce Kilmer-Slickrock), two wild
and scenic rivers (Chattooga and Horsepasture Rivers), and numerous waterfalls (primarily around Highlands, Cashiers and
Sapphire). Many of these appealing attractions have been covered in other selections (see Highlands, Cullasaja Gorge and the
Joyce Kilmer-Slickrock Wilderness). Four ranger districts have
jurisdiction in this forest, and it is at these stations that you can
obtain additional information on the many points of interest
within the forest.

Stop at the **Highlands Ranger District Station** on Route 64 just
four miles east of Highlands on weekdays from 8:00 A.M. to 4:30
P.M. to get a map showing the waterfalls in this district. Their
accessibility ranges from easy to difficult. There are five beautiful
falls along the wild Horsepasture River. Hiking trails crisscross
the district. One particularly striking trail is the two-mile loop
along the ridge of Whiteside Mountain. The mountain is steep
with sheer cliffs ranging from 400 to 750 feet. Caution is advised
with younger children and pets.

The Tusquitee Ranger District covers 158,579 acres and is
headquartered in Murphy off Route 64. Just northwest of Murphy
along the Tusquitee River is a chain of lakes created by three
picturesque reservoirs: Hiwassee, Chatuge and Appalachia
Lakes. On Hiwassee Lake you'll find the Hanging Dog Recreation

Area with a large campground, picnic areas and a network of trails along the 180-mile shoreline. The lake is popular for swimming, water skiing, boating and fishing. On Chategu Lake the Jackrabbit Mountain Recreation Area offers similar activities. Naturalists may be interested in stopping at the Beech Creek Seed Orchard just west of Murphy off Forest Road 307. White, shortleaf and Virginia pine are grown here for reforestation. Also within this ranger district is the 25-mile Rim Trail along Fires Creek. If you park at the Leatherwood Falls Picnic Area off Forest Road 442 just northwest of Hayesville you will find a trail accessible to the handicapped.

The **Cheoah Ranger Station**, with headquarters adjacent to Lake Santeetlah off Route 129 two miles north of Robbinsville, is considered a special secret by knowledgeable nature lovers. From this district you can head into the **Great Smoky Mountains National Park**. The Joyce Kilmer Memorial Forest is in this district, as is Fontana (see selection). Cable Cove Recreation Area is four miles from Fontana Dam. It is one of five campgrounds in the district. This region is popular with both trout fishermen and hunters. Game include black bear, wild boar, grouse, wild turkey and other smaller animals.

Adjacent to the Cherokee Indian Reservation is the Wayah (that is a Cherokee word meaning wolf) Ranger District with offices south of Franklin on Route 64 Bypass. At the 5,200-foot Wayah Bald two famous national trails intersect, the Appalachian Trail and the Bartram Trail. The latter, less well-known trail, is named in honor of William Bartram, the first American-born naturalist. Bartram was an internationally acclaimed botanist who is credited with identifying many plants unique to this area. Wayah Bald is worth exploring, even if you are not going to hike one of these trails. There is an old Civilian Conservation Corps fire tower with a magnificent view of the southern Appalachian mountain chain. Scenic Standing Indian Basin off Forest Road 67 at Rainbow Springs has campgrounds, hiking trails, blue ribbon trout streams, horse trails and waterfalls. Finally, the Nantahala Gorge, popular with white-water enthusiasts, is in this area (see Nantahala Outdoor Center). If you are interested in forest management, don't miss the chance to visit the Coweeta Experimental Forest. The Forest Service established this study area to determine the effects of human use on forest growth and ecology. A brochure for self-guided hikes is available at the Forest Service Office south of Franklin on Route 441, open weekdays 7:30 A.M. to 4:00 P.M.

Because it is spread out with various sub-units you can reach the forest from various adjacent towns, like Highlands, Murphy, Franklin and Bryson City.

Nantahala Outdoor Center

Chill Thrill

It's probably a misnomer to speak of a one-day trip to the **Nantahala Outdoor Center** (NCO) because those who discover the enthusiastic staff at this outdoor adventure center return again and again. At Nantahala you not only get in touch with the natural world, you frequently get in touch with your internal world—both can be exciting adventures. The experiences NOC offers challenge both the novice and the experienced outdoor sportsman, ranging from white-water rafting on five of the best rivers in the southeast to rock climbing, cross country bicycling, backpacking, fly-fishing and corporate team-building courses.

In 1972 Payson and Aurelia Kennedy, a young couple from Atlanta, Georgia, wanted a different lifestyle, one where the work they did was more in tune with their avocational interests. They moved to the Nantahala Gorge in the Great Smoky Mountains and established the Nantahala Outdoor Center. Over the years the center has grown to more than 300 employees during the busiest season and has won countless honors for its outstanding programs. Those who work at NCO give the impression they would be on the river for fun if they weren't on the job. They love what they do, and they enjoy sharing it with first-timers and return visitors.

NOC's staff knows the rivers they run. On the difficult rivers they put a guide in each boat, and where the rapids are easily negotiated a guide accompanies each trip. Departing from the center, you can run the **Nantahala River** either in guided rafts, or on your own in rental rafts or kayaks. The Nantahala River falls 38 feet per mile as it winds through the section NOC runs trips on. The Nantahala gorge has elevations varying from 1,800 to a spectacular 5,700 feet. The guided trip takes about 3½ hours to travel eight miles. The rapids are Class II and III. This is ideal for novices, exciting enough to make an impression yet manageable to those just learning the technique. It's amazing how disoriented you can get as your river guide delivers staccato directions to pull right.

Rivers vary in difficulty depending on the season and the water level. If spring has brought heavy rains, the **French Broad River** is far more challenging than it is in late summer when temperatures rise and the water falls. NOC offers full and half-day trips down the French Broad for those ten and over. Again you will encounter Class II and III rapids as you raft through the Pisgah National Forest. For a real thrill during the summer you can even take a "ducky" trip in an inflatable one-person boat. Guides lead these solo voyages, instructing navigators as they tackle the river's challenges. These trips leave from the NOC outpost in Hot Springs.

From the moment you put in on the **Ocoee River** you know you are in for an adventure. This fast flowing river has Class III and IV rapids as it cascades through the Cherokee National Forest. Because it is dam-controlled it moves swiftly even during the driest months. For some the 4½ hour trip seems to take a lifetime, for others it is over far too soon. This is not viewed as an introductory river but should be done after you have tried calmer water. Rapids along this river have names like Broken Nose, Double Trouble, Tablesaw and Hell Hole. They plan a swim stop along the river, but many passengers get wet before the scheduled stop. Even if you don't fall out, you will get soaked, so it is advisable to bring a full change of clothes. During the colder autumn months you might want to rent a wet suit, or bring a wool sweater, hat and socks you don't mind being river washed. The minimum age on the Ocoee is 12, and trips leave from an outpost on US 64, ten miles east of Cleveland, Tennessee.

The **Chattooga** has both an introductory level trip and a more advanced section. Both leave from the NOC outpost four miles east of Longcreek, South Carolina on SC Route 37/196. Flowing through Chattahoochee and Sumter National Forests this river gained fame when it was featured in the movie *Deliverance*. Section 3 of the river has Class II, III and IV rapids, and some may feel this is too advanced for absolute beginners. You will be expected to paddle hard as you negotiate the river on the five to 13-mile trip that takes about six hours. The Class III, IV and V rapids on Section 4 challenge even the experts. It is considered by many to be one of the most difficult and exciting of all white-water rivers. There are big drops as you go over the Seven Foot Falls and Five Falls. Considerable expertise is required to successfully negotiate Woodall Shoals and Ravens Rock. You will work hard during the seven-hour trip.

In the spring NOC also rafts the **Nolichucky River**, a relatively undiscovered challenge with Class III and IV rapids. The 8½-mile trip takes about six hours and runs through one of the steepest gorges in the east. This trip begins south of Erwin, Tennessee, off US 19/23.

NOC has one-day as well as week-long clinics on canoeing and kayaking. They also sponsor trips to exciting rivers around the world. Bicycling, backpacking and rock climbing trips are also scheduled. For information on NOC programs write Nantahala Outdoor Center, US 19W, Box 41, Bryson City, NC 28713 or call (704)488-6900.

Either before or after your day's adventure treat yourself to a meal in Relia's Garden, a picturesque restaurant perched above the hillside garden of NOC co-founder Aurelia Kennedy. The freshly baked rolls and muffins add to the country breakfasts while the herbs and vegetables fresh-picked each day make the lunch and dinner offerings something special. Overnight accommodations are available at the Nantahala Outdoor Center's motel, their hostel-style basecamp, or their mountain-side vacation homes. There is even a day-care center for young children. For rates call (704)488-2175.

If you are interested in joining a white-water raft trip it is advisable to make a reservation well in advance. Call (704)488-6900 for information seven days a week year-round. Reservations must be paid for in advance and trips go rain or shine.

Directions: From I-40 west of Asheville take US 74W. The Nantahala Outdoor Center is 13 miles southwest of Bryson City on US 19S/74W.

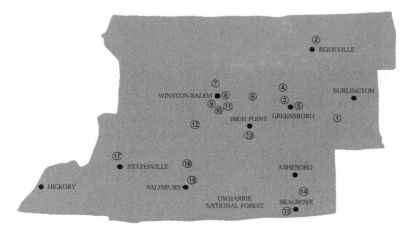

NORTHERN FOOTHILLS

Greensboro, Burlington and Reidsville Vicinity

1. Alamance Battleground, Alamance County Historical Museum and *Sword of Peace*
2. Chinqua-Penn
3. Greensboro Historical Museum
4. Guilford Courthouse National Military Park
5. Natural Science Center of Greensboro
6. Tannenbaum Park

Winston-Salem

7. Bethabara Park
8. Museum of Early Southern Decorative Arts
9. Old Salem
10. Reynolda House, Southeastern Center for Contemporary Art and Nature Science Center
11. R.J. Reynolds Tobacco Company and Stroh Brewery
12. Tanglewood

High Point

13. High Point Museum and Historical Park, Peterson Doll and Miniature Museum and Market Square

Asheboro and Vicinity

14. North Carolina Zoological Park
15. Seagrove Pottery

Hickory, Statesville and Salisbury Vicinity

16. Boone's Cave State Park, Duke Power State Park and Pilot Mountain State Park
17. Fort Dobbs
18. Spencer Shops

Northern Foothills

Encompassing the area around Winston-Salem, Greensboro and High Point, the Northern Foothills boasts world-class attractions. The vast natural habitats of the North Carolina Zoological Park near Asheboro are so impressive they would merit highest ratings in any guidebook. Chinqua-Penn, a 27-room mansion outside Reidsville, is far less well known than Asheville's Biltmore Estate, but by no means less interesting. A sophisticated collection of art from all over the world is displayed here, yet the big house retains a sense of homey comfort and suggests the owners knew how to have fun.

Arts from the American past are exhibited at Reynolda House and the Museum of Early Southern Decorative Arts; modern works make up the shows at the Southeastern Center for Contemporary Art. History comes alive when you visit the Alamance Battleground and see the drama *Sword of Peace*. Other battles are remembered at Guilford Courthouse National Military Park and Fort Dobbs. Regional parks emphasize nature and athletic activities, and Tanglewood is considered one of the top 25 public golf courses in the country. There are science museums in both Greensboro and Winston-Salem. Pick your pleasure: tour the Stroh Brewery and see hops turned to beer or watch cigarettes being made at the R.J. Reynolds Tobacco Company.

Travel back in time at Old Salem, a re-creation of a town of the 1760s, complete with private homes, shops and taverns. On Tuesday evenings in the summer the Salem Band (the oldest mixed-wind ensemble in the country) performs on the town square. Old Salem Tavern offers fine dining, and traditional baked goods are available at the Winkler Bakery.

The past is brought to life most vividly, as we all know, through personal experiences. At Spencer Shops, north of Salisbury, you get a feel for the age of steam trains. Spencer, once a significant North Carolina railroad repair facility, is once again running steam and diesel trains on the old tracks, rekindling the romance of the rails.

GREENSBORO, BURLINGTON AND REIDSVILLE VICINITY

Alamance Battleground, Alamance County Historical Museum and the *Sword of Peace*

Triple Treat

In Alamance County you can cover the virtually unknown War of Regulation by visiting the site of the **Battle of Alamance**, stopping to see a collection of artifacts at the county museum and ending your day with the *Sword of Peace*, a historical drama that brings the years before the American Revolution vividly to life.

Long before the Declaration of Independence was drafted and British troops fired on colonists at Lexington and Concord there was dissatisfaction with British rule in the colonies. Excessive taxes, dishonest sheriffs and illegal fees led to unrest. No where was this more apparent than in the western part of North Carolina. The isolated settlers here organized a movement known as the Regulation and fomented a rebellion that began with minor clashes in 1768.

Loyalists viewed these activities as mob action, and it is true that no outstanding leader appeared to organize the Regulators. The movement did foster violence, lawlessness and terrorism. Members refused to pay fines, terrorized those who tried to administer British law and disrupted court proceedings. That is where matters stood in March 1771, when Royal Governor William Tryon called out the militia and marched against the Regulators.

The 2,000-man-strong Regulators met the 1,000-man force under Governor Tryon near Alamance Creek deep in Regulator territory. The battle began on May 16, after Tryon gave the westerners the choice of returning to their homes or being fired on. The answer was "Fire and be damned!" Tryon's troops were reluctant to open fire and only did so when Tryon ordered them to fire on the Regulators or at him.

Tryon's militia may have been outnumbered, but they were better trained, better supplied and better led. The battle had barely commenced before some of the Regulators deserted the fray. It took two hours for Tryon to crush the Regulators. Both sides lost nine men, but Tryon took 15 prisoners and executed six. Those Regulators who stayed in North Carolina were given pardons if they pledged an oath of allegiance to the royal government.

The courage of those who fought against British rule was a lesson that would be remembered. The War of Regulation ended with the Battle of Alamance, but the dissatisfaction that prompted it remained.

Today a granite monument marks the field of battle, and another marker gives a map of the battle and a brief history of the Regulators. In the visitor center a short audiovisual program is shown. An 18th-century loghouse has been moved to the Alamance Battleground from Snow Camp. This house was built in 1780 by John Allen. John's sister, Amy, was married to Hermon Husband, a leading Regulator who wrote pamphlets agitating against British misrule. (Twenty years later Husband was involved in the Whiskey Rebellion in Pennsylvania.) The Allen House provides a look at a typical home found in the backcountry of colonial North Carolina.

There is no charge to visit Alamance Battleground, open from April through October, Monday–Saturday 9:00 A.M. to 5:00 P.M. and Sunday 1:00 to 5:00 P.M. From November through March hours are Tuesday–Saturday 10:00 A.M. to 4:00 P.M. and Sunday 1:00 to 4:00 P.M. This state historic site also has a half-mile nature trail that takes about 30 to 45 minutes to explore. A booklet points out various piedmont plants.

Approximately one mile from the battleground is the L. Banks Holt House, built in 1790. This house serves as the **County Historical Museum** and is the birthplace of Edwin Michael Holt, a North Carolina textile pioneer. E.M. Holt established the Alamance Cotton Factory on Big Alamance Creek in 1837. He popularized the Alamance plaids, the first commercially dyed cotton plaids made in the South. In the house's textile history room you can see examples of this colorful dress fabric. L. Banks Holt remodeled the family home in the 1870s in the fashionable Italianate Revival style.

The eight-room house is furnished with pieces from the 1870s and 1880s, when E.M.'s sixth son, Lynn Banks Holt inherited the property. Several family heirlooms have been furnished by Holt descendants. A portrait of E.M. hangs in the parlor. In the dining room is a Tiffany soup tureen that belonged to the family. The table is hand-carved, solid walnut. The bedroom upstairs is also furnished with High Victorian pieces.

The museum frequently mounts exhibits of 19th-century military artifacts, as well as Native American artifacts and regional crafts. The house is open at no charge Tuesday–Friday 9:00 A.M. to 5:00 P.M., Saturday 10:30 A.M. to 5:00 P.M., and Sunday 1:00 to 5:00 P.M. Annual events sponsored by the museum include a Fiddler's Convention, held in early summer, and a Christmas Tour of Homes and Candlelight Tea.

You will enjoy the *Sword of Peace* historical drama more if you visit the Alamance Battleground before seeing the performance. The play brings to life the Quaker settlers' peaceful resistance to the war so many of the western settlers fought against the British. The drama encompasses the action at Alamance and Guilford Courthouse (see selection). A cast of 75 presents the show on Thursday, Friday and Saturday from late June through mid-August.

This show tells a story all too often missing in history books, that of patriotic but pacifistic colonists. To get the most out of the performance, try to sit near the front because this is one outdoor drama that is not miked. You might also want to bring a bug repellent and a warm sweater or jacket. Even in the hot summer it gets cool when night falls. The amphitheater is part of the historic Snow Camp village. This settlement on the north bank of Cane Creek became known as Snow Camp by the mid-1700s. The name derives from the Pennsylvania hunters who camped here and cut the trees level with the two to three feet of snow that blanketed the camp. When they returned they recognized their earlier campsite from the tall stumps. The village now contains a post office museum (circa 1830), two Quaker Meeting Houses, cane mill, school house for blacks, old log cabin and log kitchen, herb garden, natural spring and a craft display area and gallery. Ye Old Country Kitchen restaurant is open year-round, Wednesday–Sunday 11:00 A.M. to 9:00 P.M. Try to arrive about an hour before the 8:30 P.M. show and explore the camp. For ticket information call (919)376-6948 or write *Sword of Peace*, P.O. Box 535, Snow Camp, NC 27349.

If you are traveling with children be sure to detour and include a stop at the **Dentzel Carousel** in the 55-acre Burlington City Park. This is one of only 12 intricately carved wooden carousels in the country (another in North Carolina is in Raleigh's Pullen Park, see selection). It was painstakingly restored at a cost of $86,000. The four-year effort, from 1981 to 1985, has resulted in a sparkling evocation of yesteryear. The colors are as bright as when the carousel was made sometime between 1906 and 1910. There are 46 hand-carved wooden animals and two chariots. The Dentzel carvers were noted for their realism, and the veins and muscles of the animals seem to strain with movement. The glass eyes almost move, and the tails are fashioned of real horsehair. The carousel operates from Easter to mid-June on Saturday 11:00 A.M. to 9:00 P.M. and Sunday 1:00 to 7:00 P.M. From mid-June to mid-August it runs Tuesday and Thursday 1:00 to 8:00 P.M., Friday 1:00 to 9:00 P.M., Saturday 11:00 A.M. to 9:00 P.M. and Sunday 1:00 to 7:00 P.M. From mid-August to Halloween weekend it reverts to the weekend schedule.

Directions: Take I-85 to Burlington, then head south on Route 62 for four miles to the Alamance County Historical Museum on the right. Continue two more miles to the Alamance Battleground site. For Snow Camp take Route 49 for 15 miles south of Burlington. Follow the brown Snow Camp Historic Site sign as you turn left onto Chapel Hill Road. Then turn left into the historic site. For Burlington City Park take Burlington/Alamance Exit, Highway 62, off I-85. Follow Highway 62 south for four miles and turn right on Overbrook Drive. The park will be on your left.

Chinqua-Penn

Welcoming Home

When a mansion is filled with treasures from around the world, it often takes on the ambience of a museum. **Chinqua-Penn** manages to balance an outstanding array of acquisitions with a strong sense of comfort, charm and a genuine homey atmosphere. Visitors immediately feel that this would be a fabulous place to live; it certainly is a fascinating place to visit.

Chinqua-Penn was the home of Thomas Jefferson Penn and his wife Betsy Schoellkopf Penn. His father founded Penn Tobacco Company, which was sold to the American Tobacco Company, and her family developed Niagara Falls as a power source. When they married in 1923, Jeff Penn wanted to build their home in the area where he grew up and built in the rolling country three miles north of the small town of Reidsville.

The Penns built a 27-room English country-style house of gray stone and oak logs. Penn explained how the estate was named in a 1962 interview: "The chinquapin bush grew on this hill. The nut, like a miniature chestnut, was delicious. We thought it appropriate to spell the name Chinqua-Penn."

With Chinqua-Penn as home base, the wealthy couple traveled around the world collecting fabulous art treasures for their North Carolina estate. Jeff Penn felt that "Places as well as people must have an appealing personality if they would carry on to some permanent influence." Their home does just that, artfully combining unique pieces in an eclectic mix of styles and origins.

Elaborately scrolled wrought-iron entrance gates are decorated with owls, squirrels and ornamental clusters of chinquapin nuts. As you drive through the gates and up to the parking lot you will see that the Penns collected plants, bushes and trees from around the world. On the way to the house you'll pass a four-story Tuscan fieldstone clock tower. Directly in front of the house is a fountain the Penns acquired in Versailles. Two marble dogs from Italy guard the door. The Penns' initials "J" and "B" are built into the stone wall over the door, a permanent part of Chinqua-Penn. The initials also appear in the entrance gate, patio mosaic and elsewhere.

When you enter the house, you see off the entry hall on the left an exact replica of Marie Antoinette's powder room at Ver-

Built from gray stone and oak logs, and designed in the English country style, Chinqua-Penn houses art treasures from all over the world. The 27-room estate is named after the local chestnut.

sailles. The ceiling and walls are covered with plate glass panels painted with flowers and intricate designs. The furnishings are French and the ceiling light is of alabaster. The reception hall is paneled with oak paneling acquired from an English estate. Japanese ivory statues stand on the 17th-century Jacobean mantelpiece. Japanese plank paintings flank the mantle. The most interesting piece is a rare copy of the Golden Chair of Tutankhamen. Jeff Penn tried to buy the original throne of the Egyptian pharaoh, but when that proved impossible he had it copied. It is one of only two exact copies, in design and dimension, outside Egypt.

The living room is the house's crowning jewel, a baronial creation with upstairs balconies, huge beams, timbered ceiling, oversized windows, enormous Persian carpets and elaborate tapestries. There is a china and enamel painting that belonged to Francois I of France. The objets d'art in this wide-ranging collection, purchased over many years and in many countries, blend harmoniously. The room is overpowering in its wealth of treasures, but absolutely delightful.

Each room is a work of art: the airy, multi-windowed breakfast room with wall paintings styled after murals in the villas at Pompeii, the oval pine dining room with carved chinquapins on the ceiling, the field-stone floored mud room, and the cozy comfort of the sitting room where Betsy Penn lovingly placed many of her own favorite pieces like the Italian and Russian crucifixes. The master bedroom is also on the first floor providing access to the gardens that both Penns loved so much.

The main staircase has antique oak paneling from the same English country home as the reception hall paneling. The wrought-iron stair rail has the "JB" monogram. The upstairs library overlooks the living room. The Penns did a great deal of entertaining and frequently accommodated house guests. There is a series of guest rooms each with a decorating theme: the Italian, Empire, French and Chinese rooms.

Throughout the house Mrs. Penn traditionally placed exquisite vases of cut flowers from the greenhouses and cutting garden. This practice is continued, and when you explore the grounds you can visit the five greenhouses. There is an exotic rose garden, a formal garden just off the reception hall, which in the spring displays some of the 10,000 tulips planted on the estate, an herb garden and a Chinese pagoda that faces the house across the length of a pool. The red-trimmed pagoda houses a statue of Buddha. The inscription on the pagoda captures the welcoming spirit of Chinqua-Penn: "Come, and you may find meditation for the mind, some solace for the soul, some harmony for the heart. Anyhow, come!"

Chinqua-Penn is open Wednesday–Saturday 10:00 A.M.–4:00 P.M. and Sunday 1:30–4:30 P.M. In December hours are Tuesday–Saturday 10:00 A.M.–4:00 P.M. and Sunday 1:30–4:30 P.M., with candlelight tours 6:30–9:00 P.M. on Friday evenings. The estate closes after the Christmas tours and reopens in March. The house is operated by the North Carolina State University.

Directions: From the east take I-85 to Route 87 north to Reidsville. Continue through the town, then following signs turn right on Parkland Road and right on Wentworth Road. Chinqua-Penn will be on your left. From the north or south take Highway 29, then take the first Reidsville exit you come to and follow the Chinqua-Penn signs.

Greensboro Historical Museum

Hometown Heroes

The well-remembered scene in Gone With The Wind in which Scarlett O'Hara cut down the green velvet drapes of Tara to fashion a ball gown has an historic precedent. In the early 1800s, according to a fascinating but inaccurate legend, Dolley Madison, the only First Lady born in North Carolina, took the red velvet drapes from the White House and fashioned a gown. The brownish-red velvet dress is part of the **Greensboro Historical Museum**'s extensive Dolley Madison exhibit. Dolley was born in a Quaker community, not far from what is now Guilford College. A treasure trove of 450 artifacts including portraits, letters and clothes was discovered in the refuse-filled Allentown, Pennsylvania home of Dolley's nephew-in-law, James Causlen. The find included a letter from Lafayette, the family Bible, a Mathew Brady daguerreotype of Dolley taken a year before she died, some of her trend-setting turbans (these popularized a fad in the 1800s like that prompted by Jacqueline Kennedy's pillbox hats), and a fishing lure an Indian chief had presented to James Madison.

Another Guilford County resident honored at the museum is short-story writer William Sidney Porter, widely known as O. Henry. The writer spent the first 20 years of his life in Greensboro before moving to Austin, Texas. Displayed (but part of the museum currently closed and scheduled to reopen in 1991–92) are family photographs, furniture, his school desk, letters and first-edition books. Porter started writing while in prison serving over three years for embezzling $5,654.20—a crime he insisted he did not commit.

In one of the largest local history museums in the southeast, you can follow the participation of Guilford County residents in seven of our country's wars. The Hall of Military History has weapons, equipment and uniforms, but it is the small items that are most poignant. There is a knit cap worn by Arthur Forbes who, legend has it, fired the first shot at the Battle of Guilford Courthouse and died three weeks later. An iron dumbbell is here that Major Patrick Ferguson used to strengthen his arm, injured at the Battle of Brandywine in 1777. His injuries at the Battle of Kings Mountain claimed his life in 1780. The oldest complete uniform in the museum was worn by Mark Iddings in the War of 1812. The Civil War collection includes the Second National Flag adopted by the Confederacy but abandoned because it looked too much like an all-white surrender flag when there was no wind to unfurl it. There are also mementos of the Guilford Grays, a local Civil War regiment. There are posters and equipment from both World Wars. Local hero George Preddy, who shot down six German fighter planes in a single mission, is honored. The Vietnam Medal of Honor from a later hero, Phil McDonald, is also displayed.

Displays by 13 local companies are in a Hall of Industry including those by Burlington, Wrangler, Cone Mills and Guilford Mills. There are Indian artifacts, old cars, a display tracing the ethnic contributions of the many immigrants that settled this area, and furnished rooms from numerous historical houses in the area. A section called Greensborough Village (which will be closed until 1992) includes a general store, law office, old post office, schoolhouse and several residential buildings.

The Greensboro Historical Museum is open at no charge Tuesday–Saturday 10:00 A.M. and Sunday 2:00–5:00 P.M. It is closed on major holidays. The museum is located in the First Presbyterian Church, which served the community in the 1920s and opened as a museum in 1939. The turn-of-the-century church buildings are listed on the National Register of Historic Places. A large part of Greensboro's downtown area was added to the register in 1982. Elm Street is a typical scene from America's past, a preserved small-town Main Street. Many of the commercial buildings have survived from the 1880s. A self-guided walking tour map of the historic district is available at the museum.

While in the area try to see **Blandwood Mansion and Carriage House**, Greensboro's only house museum. Blandwood was originally an 18th-century farmhouse, but in 1844 when Governor John Motley Morehead was finishing his second term, he invited the architect Alexander Jackson Davis to restructure his farm. Davis, who designed the state Capitol in Raleigh, transformed Morehead's farm into an elegant manor in the popular Italian Villa style. The house and dependencies have been restored and furnished. Tours are given Tuesday–Friday 11:00 A.M.–2:00 P.M. and Sunday 2:00–5:00 P.M.

Directions: From I-85 take S. Elm-Eugene Street into Greensboro. Turn right on Bellemeade Street and follow approximately four blocks. The museum will be on your right. For Blandwood follow S. Elm-Eugene Street into Goldsboro. Turn left on West Washington. Blandwood is visible on your left.

Guilford Courthouse National Military Park

America's First Revolutionary War National Park

The Continental Army snatched their victory at Yorktown from the jaws of their defeat at Guilford Courthouse. The cost of the North Carolina victory for General Cornwallis, in terms of men lost, was overwhelming. Fully one-quarter of Cornwallis's forces, roughly 500 men, were wounded or killed. The Battle of Guilford Courthouse set the stage for the final collapse of British control in the South seven months later.

For two hours on March 15, 1781, the armies of Nathanael Greene and Lord Charles Cornwallis fought. At stake was the control of North Carolina. By late 1780 the British had managed to gain control in Georgia and South Carolina. General Greene described the strategy of the Southern Campaign, "We fight, get beat, rise, and fight again."

The Continentals, who outnumbered the British 4,000 to 1,900, made a stand at Guilford Courthouse. The best way to understand the course of the battle is to take the 2¼-mile self-guiding auto tour route that starts at the park's visitor center. There are seven tour stops. At each one foot trails lead to monuments and graves you would miss if you limited your visit to a drive-through.

Stop #1 is the American First Line, the position held by untested North Carolina militia. The Americans chose the ground and fired the first round, but when the British regrouped and rushed the line, the militia fled. Lighthorse Harry Lee subsequently described the scene: "To our infinite distress and mortification, the North Carolina militia took to flight . . . so thoroughly confounded were these unhappy men that, throwing away arms, knapsacks, and even canteens, they rushed like a headlong torrent through the woods."

There are 11 monuments centered around the First Line area. One honors Lee's bugler, 14-year-old James Gillies. His horse was commandeered by Isaac Wright, a local farmer who had brought the Continental forces information on the British position. Wright needed a horse to ride with the troops to verify intelligence and borrowed young Gillies's. The bugler's only weapon, a pistol, was sheathed in his saddle and he neglected to reclaim it. Later in a clash with the British, the weaponless Gillies was slain. Another monument honors nationalism and unity—the No North No South Monument.

Stop #2 is at the American Second Line where General Edward Stevens's brigade of Virginia militia held the line, making the British pay for every bit of ground they gained. These veteran fighters were at last forced to give ground and the British broke through the line. Monuments #12 through #21 are found in this area. Of these probably the most significant in terms of this battle is the huge equestrian statue of Nathanael Greene. His parents were Quaker, but Nathanael was expelled from the church in 1773 for attending a military parade. Greene started the war as a private, and by 1775 he was a brigadier general commanding three regiments. For a time Greene served as quartermaster general but resigned after his work was criticized and Congress refused him a vote of confidence. Washington then named Greene commanding general of the Southern Theater. Greene survived the war, only to die of a sunstroke in 1786.

Auto route stop #3 marks the spot where the last shot was fired by an American rifleman. Major Joseph Winston led a group of Surry County riflemen who fought under Lighthorse Harry Lee. One of Winston's men, Richard Taliaferro, was likely the last American killed.

The site of Colonel William Washington's cavalry charge is stop #4. Colonel Washington (a cousin of George Washington) led a mounted military charge on the British. After their initial sortie, they turned and rode through once more, scattering those they didn't slay. One of the heroes of this encounter was Peter Francisco, over six feet tall and about 260 pounds. Fighting with a five-foot saber, this giant killed 11 British Guardsmen before he was felled by a bayonet wound in the leg. The Cavalry Monument commemorates the charge of Colonel Washington's dragoons. Inscribed on the monument are the names Washington, Francisco and the Marquis of Bretigny, who, like Lafayette, left his native France to fight for the cause of independence. The Marquis led 40 North Carolina cavalrymen in the American Third Line charge. At the end of the day Bretigny's unit had only one casualty and one man wounded.

The courthouse for which the battle is named is no longer standing, but stop #5 takes you past the site of the courthouse and the community which surrounded it. The courthouse was finished in 1776 and abandoned in 1808 when the county seat was moved.

The American Third Line is stop #6. The fighting along this line was intense as the British Guards were stopped by the First Maryland Regiment. Cornwallis was forced to fire his three-pounders into the middle of the fighting, killing both the enemy and his own men, in order to force the Continentals to retreat. This harsh decision enabled him to save the Guards; otherwise they would have been annihilated. Monuments #22 to #28 are in this area, including the Cavalry Monument, which can also be reached by a foot trail from stop #4. The last stop, #7, is another approach to the Greene Monument. The most impressive monument in the park, it can also be reached from a trail at stop #2.

Before you begin your drive, see the exhibits and 20-minute film Guilford Letters at the visitors center. Although the film does not cover the Battle of Guilford in detail, it does place the battle in perspective in terms of the Southern Campaign, which is described in the words of an American soldier. A battle diorama will give you an overall view of the action before you cover it stop-by-stop. Guilford Courthouse National Military Park is open daily at no charge from 8:30 A.M. to 5:00 P.M. You should also stop at the Hoskins House in the adjacent Tannenbaum Park. The house served as General Cornwallis's headquarters during the battle (see selection).

Directions: From I-85 exit at Greensboro on Route 220 north. The park is in northwest Greensboro off Route 220 about six miles from the center of the city. The visitor center is ½ mile east of Route 220 on New Garden Road.

Natural Science Center of Greensboro

The Greening of Greensboro

In Greensboro you are invited to "Wonder at the World, Walk into the Wild, and Gaze into the Beyond" at the **Natural Science Center**. Nature is in a constant state of change, so it seems appropriate that this natural science center is also changing. It's in the last stages of a major expansion.

The new wing adds exciting dimensions to this active, hands-on natural science facility. Astronomy is explored in the Edward R. Zane Planetarium, zoology at the feeding and petting zoo, and still other disciplines in the exhibit area.

Between the planetarium's multi-media space programs and the center's solar observatory you can gain new insights into the solar system. You're offered three views of the sun: a magnified view of the white light only, a second view of only the hydrogen light and a third view of the flame-like prominences along the sun's outer edge. At the solar observatory you can look directly at enormous sunspots measuring 100,000 miles or more across. In addition to the changing sky shows, there are regular programs

A young visitor shares a snack at the Natural Science Center of Greensboro. The new wing houses a planetarium and multi-media programs on space explorations.

like the Grand Tour, which gives you an overview of the planets, and the Starquest program narrated by Leonard Nimoy, which focuses on space exploration. Weekday planetarium shows for walk-in visitors are at 11:00 A.M. and NOON. On weekends there is a show at 2:00, 3:00 and 4:00 P.M. There is a nominal charge for these shows. For a planetarium schedule call (919)288-3769.

Enclosures along a scenic forest trail contain animals and birds from North and South America. In 1989 a jaguar exhibit was added. There are also cougars, bison, bobcats and black bears. A large animal contact area offers the chance to pet domesticated animals like goats, rabbits, calves and chickens. Under the supervision of the staff there are other animals that can be approached—skunks, ferrets, opossums and other small creatures. The zoo is open Monday–Saturday 10:00 A.M. to 4:30 P.M. and Sunday 1:00 to 4:30 P.M.

Geology is just one of the disciplines covered at this center, which has an extensive gem collection including the largest geode on display in the United States. You can appreciate the scope of the state's natural wealth when you see the collection of North Carolina gemstones (see Museum of North Carolina Minerals selection). As part of the center's health exhibit there is a transparent anatomical mannequin to instruct visitors on anatomy. Paleontology is another major focus. A lifesize model of a Tyrannosaurus towers over visitors, and fiberglass casts of Stegosaurus and Triceratops skeletons make modern day men look like pygmies. A projected re-creation of the jaw of an ancient shark will make the shark in Jaws look like a minnow. These creatures inhabited the earth during a far distant time, as the 63-87 million-year-old dinosaur egg from Aix-en-Provence reminds visitors. Fans of Jean Auel's Clan of the Cave Bear will appreciate the skull and claw from the Ursus spelaeus. The new lobby will have a series of dinosaur tracks.

The focal point in the lobby, however, is the Foucault pendulum, which solved the dilemma of proving Copernicus's theory of a sun-centered solar system. Foucault (pronounced Fooco) was a French physicist who in 1851 developed a pendulum that demonstrated the rotation of the earth. The pendulum in the museum's lobby extends from the ceiling to the basement area. Note its position when you arrive, check again before you leave, and you will have seen the earth's movement demonstrated. In the new wing there is a reptile gallery, a marine gallery with a touch tank, electronic rooms with presentations on drugs and on nutrition, plus a special programs room. Discovery labs feature physics, birds, biology and geology.

The Natural Science Center of Greensboro is open Monday–Saturday 8:00 A.M. to 5:00 P.M. and Sunday 1:00 to 5:00 P.M. Admission charge includes the center and the zoo; to see the planetarium costs a small amount more. The Center is next to Country Park where there are picnic tables, a playground area and a large lake.

Directions: From I-85 take Exit #128, Route 6 west. Then exit onto Route 29 north. From Route 29 take Cone Boulevard west and turn on Lawndale Drive heading north. The Natural Science Center is at 4301 Lawndale Road. From I-40 turn right onto Wendover Avenue. Then exit on Benjamin Parkway heading north. From the parkway take Lawndale Drive north.

Tannenbaum Park

Oh, History . . .

Tannenbaum Park stands on the site of the British battle line during the Battle of Guilford Courthouse. The only surviving structure on the battleground is the Hoskins House, used by General Cornwallis as his headquarters while he planned his assault on the American forces positioned around Guilford County's courthouse (see Guilford Courthouse National Military Park selection). Cornwallis in his written account termed the farm "a considerable plantation." After the battle the house served as a hospital for both British and American wounded.

This 1781 farmstead is the focal spot of the 7.5-acre Tannenbaum Park. The oldest structure in the county still standing on its original site, the main two-story portion of the **Hoskins House** is built of large chestnut, poplar and oak logs. The house remained in the Hoskins family until 1925. This continuous ownership facilitated restoration of the house to its 18th-century appearance since it had not fallen into total disrepair. The outkitchen was reconstructed from the ground up to look as it did when the battle was fought here. The 1830 Coble Barn, a double-pen log barn, was relocated on this site.

Throughout the year the park sponsors living history weekends giving visitors a look at what farm life was like in 1781. Guides dressed in 18th-century clothes give musket demonstrations, establish a Revolutionary War encampment, prepare food using colonial methods, operate the authentic blacksmith forge, and demonstrate other skills of the period. A colonial kitchen garden and grape arbor let visitors see what vegetables, herbs and fruits were grown in the 18th century.

The park plans to expand with the addition of the North Carolina Colonial Heritage Center. Living history demonstrations will be a big part of this discovery place designed to explore the cultural and ethnic heritage of the North Carolina colonists. Until this dream is realized, the visitor center and Guilford Sutler Gift Shop occupy the site. The shop sells 18th-century reproductions and limited edition prints of the painting of Hoskins House and the battlefield. The center has exhibits and a pamphlet on the park.

Tannenbaum Park is open Monday–Saturday 9:00 A.M. to 5:00 P.M. and Sunday 1:00 to 5:00 P.M., but the Hoskins House and kitchen are open only on weekends and by appointment; call (919)288-8259. The visitor center and gift shop are open Saturday 10:00 A.M. to 5:00 P.M. and Sunday 12:00 to 4:00 P.M. If you plan to visit during a living history weekend, be aware that many of the volunteers who establish the encampments travel great distances and have to depart in the early afternoon on Sunday.

The Tannenbaum Park kitchen garden is strictly utilitarian, but down the road is the 7½-acre **Bicentennial Garden**, adjacent to the David Caldwell Memorial Park. The Bicentennial Garden has seven specialized gardens: day lily, fragrance, rose, wildflower and rock gardens, a sundial area with bulbs and annuals and an azalea and camellia garden. In the adjacent park a life-size bronze statue of a typical 18th-century male student reminds visitors of David Caldwell's Log College, a home-school he began in 1767. Five governors were educated in Caldwell's preparatory school. Caldwell taught that freedom from English rule was the right course. So incensed was General Cornwallis by this attitude, he offered a reward of 200 pounds (that was approximately $1,000) for Caldwell's capture. At age 89 Caldwell again spoke against the British, urging North Carolinians to volunteer during the War of 1812. There is a monument to Caldwell at Guilford Courthouse National Military Park (see selection).

Another reminder of colonial days is the **Old Mill** of Guilford, a short drive from Tannenbaum Park. The British took possession of this 1764 gristmill during the Guilford Courthouse engagement. The mill was built by David Dillon from Hopewell, Virginia. Legend says that the night before the British seized his mill Dillon had a dream that his toe was on fire. The next day as Dillon attempted to drive the British off he was shot in the toe. The mill is a heavy timber frame construction on a field-stone foundation. The wide floor planks of oak and pine are original, as is the interior weatherboarding. This working gristmill, listed on the National Register of Historic Places, is open daily 9:00 A.M. to 6:00 P.M. There is a gift shop selling North Carolina crafts and a variety of stone-ground meals.

Directions: Take I-85 west past Durham to the Greensboro area, then take I-40 west towards Winston-Salem. Take the Jamestown/ Guilford College exit off I-40 and turn right onto Guilford College Road. Make another right on New Garden Road and go through the Battleground Ave./New Garden Road intersection. Tannenbaum Park will be on your right almost immediately. For the Bicentennial Garden turn south on Battleground Avenue to Holden Road and make a right. Turn left on Cornwallis Drive and right onto Hobbs Road, and the garden parking lot is on your right. For the Old Mill of Guilford, turn right onto Hobbs Road, then right onto W. Friendly Avenue. Continue to the dead end and turn right onto W. Market Street, Route 421. Then turn onto Route 68 north. The Old Mill is on Route 68 approximately five miles north on the right, past the airport.

WINSTON-SALEM

Bethabara Park

Moravians' Wachovia

Persecution of the Moravians, one of the earliest Protestant groups, prompted their frequent relocation. The church, called Unitas Fratrum, began in the states of Bohemia and Moravia, now part of Czechoslovakia, in the early 15th century. The Counter-Reformation drastically reduced its ranks, and the surviving members left for Germany in the early 1700s.

The first American settlement was established in Savannah, Georgia in 1735. It failed because the Moravians did not want to get involved in the struggle between the Spanish in Florida and the English settlers in the Carolinas. Also the weather conditions did not please them. The Moravians moved to Pennsylvania in 1740 and established Bethlehem, Lititz and other communities. In 1753 the group purchased 100,000 acres in the North Carolina Piedmont from Lord Granville. The Moravians called their tract Der Wachau (in English, Wachovia). Fifteen skilled craftsmen left Pennsylvania to establish the Carolina settlement. They arrived on November 17, 1753. Four men returned to Pennsylvania almost at once, leaving 11 to form the nucleus of the new community.

Establishing themselves in an abandoned log cabin, the 11 men started building the town they called Bethabara, meaning House of Passage. Within three years their thriving community was selling crockery and food as well as providing medical services to settlers on the frontier. In 1756 the French and Indian War prompted the Moravians to build a palisade enclosing 15 buildings in their community. More than 200 settlers from the surrounding area moved close to the fort's protective walls. They were not allowed to settle within the palisade itself due to the religious tenets of the Moravians. Most settled along the Manorcas Creek and their community was called Milltown. Because the Moravians provided medical treatment to the Indians, their fort was never attacked.

104

Thirteen years after the group arrived they began building their central town a few miles away. By 1772 the essential buildings of Salem were ready and most of Bethabara's residents had moved in. Over the years the 75 buildings of Bethabara crumbled. About 50 to 60 people remained to keep Bethabara alive as a small farming community. Years later the land was sold to a farmer who filled in the open cellars to level his farm land.

But like buried treasure, the past has been recovered at **Historic Bethabara Park**. In 1964 when archaeological excavation started, the foundations and cellars were revealed. The cellars yielded pottery, kitchen utensils and household tools now displayed in the Brewer's House, restored and used as a museum. The Potter's House is the other early home at the park. The variety and delicacy of the pottery made here was extraordinary. The surviving examples are considered a rare discovery by archaeologists. The ditch for the palisade wall was also uncovered, revealing the exact locations of the corner bastions and gate openings and allowing accurate reconstruction.

The most significant restored building is the Gemeinhaus, the community's church. The rear section of the meeting house was used as the pastor's living quarters, and some original furniture from the period fills the rooms including a tile stove made by a local potter. The meeting hall, or Saal, is once again filled with backless benches, reproduced to match the originals. An old German Bible rests on the reading table.

Ten years before the community relocated in Salem, a botanist from Philadelphia had visited Bethabara. When he saw the medical gardens on the slopes below God's Acre, the Moravian cemetery, he called them a treasure of rare herbs and wildflowers. A well-marked nature walk lets visitors follow in the botanist's footsteps. There are four additional trails that give you a variety of opportunities to explore this early Moravian community.

The park's visitor center has a 13-minute slide program that gives the history of the Moravian Church and the establishment of Bethabara. You can visit at no charge from April through mid-December, Monday–Friday 9:30 A.M. to 4:30 P.M. and on weekends from 1:30 to 4:30 P.M. The grounds and trails are open all day, all year.

Directions: From I-85 at Greensboro, take I-40 west to Winston-Salem. Exit off I-40 on Cherry Street. After you pass Coliseum Drive bear left on University Parkway. After the traffic light at Long Drive turn left on Bethabara Road. Historic Bethabara Park will be on your right at 2147 Bethabara Road.

Museum of Early Southern Decorative Arts

A Little South in the House

In the colonial era, craftsmen made doll-size samples of their furniture both to interest prospective customers and to make sure a piece was satisfactory before a full-size work was undertaken. At the **Museum of Early Southern Decorative Arts (MESDA)** you get full-size samples of the architecture and furniture from Maryland, Virginia, the Carolinas, Georgia, Kentucky and Tennessee from 1690 through 1820. You can consider MESDA a life-size, historically accurate doll house with more than 15 period rooms, some of which have the very walls of old homes that were removed and installed, complete with furnishings.

The region composed of these seven states is divided into three culturally distinct areas: the Chesapeake, the Carolina Low Country and the Back Country. All three regions are well represented in MESDA's extensive collection. The guided tours cater to the interests of those on the tour. Upon request the interpretative staff can focus on selective aspects of the art and architecture.

To help orient visitors to each room there is a watercolor drawing of the home from which it was taken or copied. The first room is a dimly lit reproduction of the main room, or hall, in Crisscross House, New Kent County, Virginia. This 1690 period setting is the oldest in the museum. The most impressive piece of furniture is the 1645 court cupboard with an open section where the owner could display his silver and imported ceramics.

Next is the Pocomoke Room from a home near the Pocomoke River along the eastern shore of Maryland, circa 1700–1725. This room represents the entire lower floor of the house. Lord Baltimore dismissed such houses as "very meane and Little, and generally after the manner of the meanest farm house in England." The furnishings are 18th-century William and Mary pieces, which while not native to the house are from the correct era and location.

The third room is the Chowan Room from a house built in 1755, or perhaps earlier, in northeastern North Carolina. This appears more spacious than the Maryland room, perhaps due to the larger windows and smaller fireplace. By this time the cooking was not done in the parlor but in separate kitchens. Four pastel portraits in the room were painted by Henrietta Johnston, considered the first woman artist in America and the first artist in the country to use pastels.

The Cherry Grove rooms are taken from a dwelling built on the Eastern shore of Virginia in the 1760s. A passage, parlor and bedroom contain furniture made in eastern Virginia, North Carolina and Maryland. The increasingly stable economy of the 18th-century South is reflected in the elegant "neat and plain" lines of the furnishings of these rooms such as the late baroque desk and bookcase from Maryland, or the bedstead from coastal North Carolina, or the sleek lines of the side table from Williamsburg, Virginia.

A gallery devoted to metals produced in the South exhibits southern silver, long rifles and cast iron. The chronological display of silver shows the earliest surviving piece of southern hollowware, a standing cup made in 1711, and an impressive 1824 gold medal made in Baltimore for General Lafayette.

MESDA's recently-installed Charleston parlor, bed chamber and gallery contain many of the finest examples known of the work of Charleston cabinetmakers. The elegant dark mahogany, which was a major import in Charleston, provided the perfect raw material for the work of Charleston's many artisans.

The Edgecombe House is also from northeastern North Carolina, circa 1760–1780. Represented is the dining room, one of two downstairs rooms. The table is set and the side table has some additional ceramic items.

Three rooms are re-created from the 1766 Blair-Pollock House in Edenton, North Carolina. The parlor, hall and bedroom do not contain pieces from the house but are furnished in the mid-18th-century style fashionable in this region. The painted red and white blocks on the parlor floor are meant to suggest the grandeur of marble halls. The gaming table indicates the popular pastime of cards, which was an important diversion for the colonial gentry. Several of MESDA's finest paintings grace the Edenton house walls, including a portrait by John Hesselius who gave Charles Wilson Peale his first painting lesson. The bedroom is wallpapered and serves as both sitting room and bedchamber.

The same year that George Blair's house was built in Edenton, John McLean's Piedmont house was built in Guilford County, North Carolina. This solid timber dwelling is typical of frontier homes. The room represents the downstairs portion of the house furnished with Back Country pieces. The dower chest, an Old World tradition that was brought to this region by German immigrants, is a painted wooden blanket chest given to young girls to hold their new household belongings. There are several chests on display. Also from western North Carolina is the Catawba bedroom and dining room from a brick house completed in 1811. Representing a more affluent period, the furnishings are in the neoclassical style. The bedroom contains a mix of patterns from the bed rug to the carpet and the curtains and bed linen. The dining room boasts marbleized fluted pilasters framing carved urns and swags over the fireplace. The room has Windsor pieces including a settee made in Virginia.

If the Catawba dining room represents a folk version of the

Federal style, the parlor and bedroom from a 19th-century Oxford house represent a more sophisticated Federal style. The parlor decor is still busy with competing patterns on wallpaper and rug. Four painted cane chairs exemplify the fancy furniture popular in America after 1790. Two paintings in the parlor were done by Joshua Johnson, the earliest known black American portrait painter. A small, rear, first-floor room from the Oxford house is used to display Federal style bedroom furniture. Again there are fancy chairs as well as a lady's desk and pouch sewing table.

From South Carolina comes a dining room out of the White Hall plantation built in the Santee-Cooper River Valley in 1818. This elegant room has an inlaid dining table and an elaborate sideboard. Many of the decorative items in the room are embellished with an eagle design, a popular Federal motif. There are several fine paintings in the room and MESDA's galleries are filled with additional paintings, silver work, furniture and pottery.

It is advisable to make reservations to tour MESDA as tours are given in small groups. You may call the Old Salem Visitor Center, (919)721-7300 or MESDA (919)721-7360. Tours are given Monday–Saturday 10:30 A.M. to 4:30 P.M. and Sunday 1:30 to 4:30 P.M. There is a separate admission to MESDA or you may tour it on an Old Salem admission ticket (see Old Salem selection).

If visiting these exquisitely decorated rooms has awakened your taste for old style elegance you should try an overnight stay at the Brookstown Inn where each room is individually decorated with early American furniture. The inn was built as a textile mill in 1837, and the original architecture has been incorporated into the high-ceilinged rooms. From your quilt-covered four poster bed you look up at exposed pipes and beams. But the inn is far from old fashioned; some of the rooms have working fireplaces and whirlpool baths. Wine and cheese are served in the evening in the parlor before a roaring fireplace and in the morning there is a complimentary light breakfast including homemade Moravian pastries. The inn is at 200 Brookstown Avenue within easy walking distance of Old Salem. For information call (919)725-1120.

If you have lunch at Salem Tavern and want to dine in a historic reminder of early Winston try the Zevely House for dinner. This house was built in 1815–16 by Van Neman Zevely, a Moravian cabinetmaker. Today it is the oldest dwelling still standing in what was Winston Township. The menu changes daily but the quality is consistent; it is an excellent eatery. The Zevely House was moved to 901 West Fourth Street in 1974 from its original location on a 160-acre plantation. For reservations call (919)725-6666.

Directions: From I-85 at Greensboro travel west on I-40 to Winston-Salem. Follow directional markers from I-40 to Old Salem.

Old Salem

Steps in Time

Strolling the brick sidewalks of **Old Salem** evokes the same "you are there" feeling that visitors get in colonial Williamsburg. There is the same formidable collection of old homes, gardens, businesses and public buildings faithfully restored to bring to life the colonial era. You might wonder why Salem is not as well known as its larger Virginia counterpart. Williamsburg was restored in the 1930s, whereas the Salem restoration was only begun in 1950. Also the Rockefeller Foundation underwrote the Williamsburg project and its subsequent promotion as a tourist attraction.

In Salem the local community mobilized when the old district was threatened by plans to erect a grocery store in the historic area. Realizing the threat to an irreplaceable heritage, the local citizens organized a non-profit corporation that has restored or reconstructed 66 buildings in the historic district. Most of these are still private residences. In all, the district has 91 historic buildings. For a real feel of the past you should take an evening stroll through this historic district. With the windows shuttered or curtained over, you can imagine that people inside are living in the late 1760s.

Salem was founded in 1766 by Moravians from the nearby Bethabara settlement (see selection). Like most communities established by this religious group, Salem was a closed congregation town in which all the economic and spiritual activities were directed by the church. The residents were divided into choirs based on age, sex and marital status. Daily life revolved around worship service, work and music. By the middle of the 19th century, Salem was no longer a church-owned town. In 1913 it merged with adjoining Winston, which was established in 1849.

Most of the Old Salem museum buildings are on Main Street, and a five-block walk will cover all the spots of interest on the self-guided walking tour map. If, as you look in the windows of the homes along Main Street, you long to drop in for a visit, then don't miss the two family homes open to the public: the **Vierling House** and the **John Vogler House**.

The imposing brick home of Dr. Benjamin Vierling reflected

Relive colonial life at restored Old Salem, established by the Moravians in 1766. Cakes, cookies and bread are still being made and sold at the bakery operated since 1800.

his imposing stature in the community. Dr. Vierling was an accomplished physician; his achievements included mastectomies, skull trepans, cataract surgery, and diagnosing the dangers of excessive salt in the diet. In 1804, Dr. Vierling married for the second time. His new wife was Martha Elizabeth Miksch, daughter of the tobacconist Matthew Miksch. With eight children (one by his first marriage), the Vierlings needed the space this house offered. The Vierling House is one of the largest in Salem. An inventory taken at the time of Dr. Vierling's death enabled curators to return the house to its original appearance. A desk that may have belonged to the doctor is in the parlor as are a few of his more than 200 books. His apothecary has been fully restocked. An exhibit on medicine in Wachovia (the region in which Salem was located) from 1750–1820 includes some daunting devices. Behind the house the wash-bake, where clothes were washed and food baked, has also been restored.

The second family house, the **John Vogler House**, circa 1819, was used as home and shop by Salem's best known silversmith. The Voglers, one of the wealthiest families in town, had their home designed in the popular Pennsylvania Federal style. The majority of the furnishings are family pieces and represent excellent examples of Moravian craftsmanship. In Vogler's silversmith shop there are examples of his work including spoons, soup ladles and snuff boxes. He also made clocks and drew silhouettes. You'll see a physiognotrace, a device Vogler made to get precise profiles of his subjects.

Straddling the line between residence and public building is the **Single Brothers House** built in 1769 (with a 1786 addition). This two-story, half-timbered structure was home to the unmarried males in the community, who would generally move there at age 14 to begin learning a trade. The building houses a meeting hall and a wide range of shops for woodworking, pottery, tailoring, gunmaking, cooperage and weaving. Workers still employ old methods and tools in these workshops.

Until the boys moved into the Single Brothers House, they lived with their parents or roomed at the Boys School, now the Wachovia Museum. Boys attended from age 6 to 14 studying Latin, German, English grammar, geometry, geography, history and penmanship. The days began early, at 5:15 in the summer and 6:30 in winter, and were filled with unremitting study. You'll see a typical schoolroom. Exhibits cover the history of the Moravian religion, the economy of Old Salem, the waterworks system that was one of the nation's first municipal waterworks, childhood in Salem and music of the period. An art gallery on the top floor displays portraits of sons of the town's leading citizens.

When a man married he left the Single Brothers House and established a shop in his home like that of Matthew Miksch. The weather-boarded log house Miksch built in 1771 was the first privately-owned house in town. It is also the oldest tobacco shop still standing in its original location in the country. His wife and daughter helped out until the latter wed Dr. Vierling. Originally .the shop was only three rooms, but another room was added in 1785. Although the shop sold primarily tobacco, other things were available including vegetables, seeds and homemade gingerbread. Mrs. Miksch was the only one in Salem permitted by the church to sell gingerbread.

By the early 19th century shops were no longer a part of the craftsman's home. This was the case with the Shultz Shoemaker Shop, a one-room, one-story workshop built in 1827. Samuel Shultz made shoes and sold readymade footwear from Philadelphia. His work was pegged instead of sewn. In the early days shoes were not always made for left and right feet, but were rotated like tires. One curious tool is the shoemaker's window, a four-globed device that magnified the light of a candle ten to 15 times.

The most popular shop with visitors and still operational is

Winkler Bakery built in 1800 and enlarged in 1827. The wood-fired oven is heated daily except Sunday and the shop is open 9:00 A.M. to 5:00 P.M. White, honey-wheat and dark breads as well as Moravian sugar cake and sugar cookies are made and sold here. The street floor exterior of the shop is plastered while the top is of brick. Inside you will find that although the workers are busy baking they gladly take time to explain how they laid the wood for the fire the day before and lit it in the morning, and how they mix the dough in a large trough. They make 60 to 80 pounds of dough at a time.

For a much wider sampling of Moravian and other styles of cooking stop for lunch or dinner at the **Old Salem Tavern Annex**. Chicken potpie may not be a dish you would ordinarily order but here it is a marvelous treat. Other luncheon specialties include ragout, and sauerkraut stew. At dinner there is venison, rack of lamb, deviled duck, and cheese spaetzle to name just a few of the entrees. Their pumpkin muffins are mouth-watering and the desserts almost sinfully tempting. The tavern museum next door, first opened in 1772, was operated by the church. When a fire leveled the tavern in 1784, a new one was completed within the year. The building now serving as a restaurant was added in 1816 as an annex to handle guest overflow. George Washington spent two nights at the Salem Tavern in 1791. Before or after your meal, you may tour the tavern next door. There is a gentlemen's room where men of quality ate and the publick room where the ordinary citizens were served. The tavern is furnished with period pieces.

Every other Tuesday evening during the summer there is a band concert on the town square. Visitors are welcome to picnic while they listen to the Salem Band, which has the distinction of being the oldest continuing mixed-wind ensemble in the country. Most of the trees on the square were uprooted by a violent storm in the summer of 1989; since then a major replanting has been completed. On the Main Street side of the town square is the Market-Fire House. This was totally reconstructed, but it is exactly like the structure built in 1803 to house the town's fire equipment and to serve as the town's meat market. While strolling around Old Salem don't neglect the gardens, many of which are open to the public. Ten garden spots are located on the visitor guide to Old Salem. When the town was established each lot had a garden plot. This was maintained year-round and provided the primary source of food. A typical garden was divided into four or six squares bound by walkways of grass. Vegetables, herbs, flowers and fruit trees were grown.

Brochures and maps are available at the visitor center, which, along with the exhibit buildings, is open daily except Thanksgiving, Christmas Eve and Christmas Day. Hours are 9:30 A.M. to

4:30 P.M. and Sunday 1:30 to 4:30 P.M. There are two shops operated by Old Salem within the historic district. On Church Street you will see the Home Moravian Church, which has the largest congregation of any Moravian Church in North America, and the campus of Salem College. The Museum of Early Southern Decorative Arts (see selection) is also part of Old Salem.

Directions: Take I-85 to Greensboro, then travel west on I-40 to Winston-Salem. Turn left off I-40 and follow direction signs to the Old Salem parking lot and visitor center.

Reynolda House, Southeastern Center for Contemporary Art and Nature Science Center

Art Find—Fine Art

It has all the ingredients of a Hollywood movie. Richard J. Reynolds was 30 years older than his bride, Katharine Smith. She was his cousin and executive secretary. When she was growing up in Mt. Airy, just outside Winston-Salem, she used to ask why he wasn't married, and he would always tell her that he was waiting until she grew up—and he did!

In 1904, a year before they married, Katharine won a company prize of a thousand dollars for the best letter advertising one of the Reynolds tobacco products. She always teased her husband about marrying her to get his prize money back.

Mrs. Reynolds was instrumental in building the country estate on the outskirts of Winston-Salem after the birth of four children made their townhouse less practical. The house was started in 1912. The war interrupted the work, but construction resumed in 1914 and was finished in 1917. Charles Barton Keen was one of the Philadelphia architects who specialized in the newly popular country-house design. He had designed numerous estates on the Main Line of Philadelphia. Mrs. Reynolds was interested in all aspects of Keen's designs for **Reynolda**. She was so much a part of the planning that the name of the estate is derived from the Latin feminine form of Reynolds.

The low rambling house, with verandas and overhanging eaves, was deliberately designed in a comfortable and informal manner. Architectural historian Brendan Gill wrote, "Reynolda House marks an unprecedented development in American domestic architecture. It is perhaps the first of an entirely new genre—a house on a grand scale that yet assumes an exterior demeanor almost as modest as that of a bungalow. We are not in the presence of wealth made formidably manifest . . . the intention here is plainly not to show off but to be happy among

113

friends—a pleasing novelty in the first decades of the twentieth century."

The elaborate Georgian Revival details in the interior are far more formal than the exterior. There are 100 rooms, with a total of 25 bathrooms, one off each bedroom. The grand two-story living room is surrounded by a cantilevered balcony, with a finely crafted wrought-iron balustrade done by the era's finest ironmaster, Samuel Yellin of Philadelphia. Everything was made new for the house rather than acquired from European estates, and all the work was done by the finest craftsmen available.

A sad note is struck with the realization that Mr. Reynolds died a year after the house was finished. Mrs. Reynolds died in 1924. The house remained a family home until 1963. Reynolda, on the National Register of Historic Places, opened as a museum house, not a home, in 1967. The art collection represents works of major American artists from 1755 to the present. The only non-American art are the wedding portraits of Katharine Smith and Richard Joshua Reynolds done in Paris.

The art is displayed in rooms filled with Reynolds family furniture, providing a natural setting unlike the starkness of many museum galleries. The colonial period is represented by fine portraits by Jeremiah Theus and John Singleton Copley. Vibrant landscapes from the Hudson River School are typified by Frederic E. Church's light-charged *Andes of Ecuador* and Worthington Whittredge's *The Old Hunting Grounds*. American artists of the late 19th century included in the collection are William Merritt Chase, Mary Cassatt and Thomas Eakins. Cubism, pop art, black artists, American pottery, Tiffany glass and a complete collection of American birds created by Dorothy Doughty for England's Royal Worcester Porcelain Co. are displayed. John Wilerding, deputy director of the National Gallery of Art, says this is "the finest concentration of American art in a public collection south of Washington . . ."

The Reynolda Foundation sponsors a continuing series of educational programs. During your visit you may see works of fiction and poetry beneath paintings of the same period, tying together the visual and written arts. On Sunday afternoons from 1:00 to 4:30 P.M. there are organ concerts on the 2,498-pipe Aeolian organ installed when the house was built.

The third floor rooms of this museum house are filled with Reynolds family clothes dating back to 1892, including elegant evening wear, wedding clothes, children's outfits and toys and delicate undergarments. The basement is equally interesting; when the house was remodeled in 1934 as the family home of Mary Reynolds Babcock, daughter of the original owners, she added a recreational area on this level. There are squash courts, an indoor swimming pool, bowling alley, shooting gallery and an art deco bar.

The grounds are also worth exploring. Although there is a floriferous formal garden, the landscaping was done according to the English tradition of pastoral design. The natural look was retained, and the grounds incorporate the 18 springs, woodlands and rolling hills on the over 1,000-acre estate. Only 20 acres are still owned by the foundation that operates Reynolds House, but the adjoining natural area is owned by Wake Forest University and nature trails meander through their grounds. In the spring thousands of daffodils are planted, and during the Christmas season the greenhouse has a two-story tree formed of poinsettia plants.

When the house was built, Mrs. Reynolds planned it so that none of the servants would live in the house but in an adjoining village, as did those who worked on the 350 acres under cultivation. The village had a church, post office, schools and blacksmith shop. Today there are elegant boutiques and restaurants in Reynolda Village.

Reynolda is open Tuesday–Saturday from 9:30 A.M. to 4:30 P.M. and Sunday 1:30 to 4:30 P.M. It is closed on major holidays. Admission is charged for the house tour, but the gardens are open until 5:00 P.M. at no charge.

In the same neighborhood, a few blocks away is the **Southeastern Center for Contemporary Art (SECCA)**. This exciting museum, scheduled to open a spacious new wing in May 1990, does not have a permanent collection but instead mounts 45 to 50 different exhibits each year. All the work exhibited is by living artists of the Southeast. It is interesting that the current census reveals that the South has the largest number of working artists in the country.

SECCA is located in the 1929 English-style home of the late industrialist James G. Hanes. The addition is harmoniously blended with this baronial estate and uses a great deal of glass to bring the outdoors into the museum. Contemporary art is displayed in an informal arrangement of rooms. The new space effectively doubles the exhibit area and adds a sculpture court. It should herald exciting times for the center.

SECCA is open at no charge Tuesday–Saturday 10:00 A.M. to 5:00 P.M. and Sunday 2:00 to 5:00 P.M. It is closed on national holidays. The center sponsors workshops, lectures, children's programs and artistic evenings with music, dance and drama.

While exploring Winston-Salem's museums and galleries, you might want to include a stop at the **Nature Science Center**, one of seven such facilities in the state. The science center was first located in a barn on the Reynolda estate. It was moved to its current location in 1974. An expansion program is underway that will double the exhibit space. The project will be completed in stages and current plans are for all the work to be done by late 1992.

This hands-on science center invites adults and children alike to get involved with the exhibits on the human body and the five senses, as well as with those on light, sound and motion. The center has several rooms devoted to space including the Hanes Planetarium, the Planet Earth exhibit and the 3-dimensional solar system in the Man and Space exhibit. There are live animals like a skunk, screech owls and a giant Indian rock python (called Monty Python), as well as information on endangered species and dinosaurs. The most popular exhibit is the tidal pool, a 650-gallon salt water tank. Another crowd pleaser is the model railroad layout with 18 separate trains in the transportation exhibit. Visitors can operate one train by pushing a button. Each week the center presents 40 science-oriented presentations for the general public including planetarium shows, programs dealing with kitchen chemistry, live animals, electricity and tidal pool feedings. On the 30-acre grounds there is a barnyard with farm animals, plus nature trails and picnic areas.

The Nature Science Center is open Monday–Saturday 10:00 A.M. to 5:00 P.M. and Sunday 1:00 to 5:00 P.M. It is closed Thanksgiving, Christmas and New Year's. Admission is charged.

Directions: From I-85 take I-40 at Greensboro, then follow I-40 Business in the Winston-Salem area. Turn right on Cherry Street, which becomes University Parkway. Go 2.3 miles then turn left on Coliseum Drive for 1.2 miles, and at the intersection of Coliseum and Reynolda Road take a right on Reynolda Road. The entrance to Reynolda House will be on your right. To reach SECCA, turn left off Reynolda Road onto Marguerite Drive. The center is located in a residential community at 750 Marguerite Drive. For the Nature Science Center enter the Winston-Salem area on I-40 and turn right onto Route 52 north. Travel 7.5 miles then take the Hanes Mill Road exit, turn right off the ramp, then go .3 mile and turn left at the first stoplight onto Museum Drive.

R.J. Reynolds Tobacco Company and Stroh Brewery

Pick Your Pleasure

You can watch cigarette manufacturing machines turn out 8,000 cigarettes a minute at the R.J. Reynolds **Whitaker Park** plant, then visit Stroh Brewery to see the filler-seamer machine process 1,500 twelve-ounce cans a minute. More than 40,000 visitors annually tour the tobacco plant and 25,000 tour the brewery.

The Whitaker Park facility is one of the world's largest cigarette factories, and the tour takes visitors out on the floor for a close look at the process. R.J. Reynolds makes and markets about one-third of all the cigarettes sold in the United States. Brands they produce include Winston, Salem, Camel, Vantage, More, NOW, Century, Magna, Ritz and Doral.

As you enter the Reynolds tobacco plant you'll see Old Joe, a replica of the original model used for the Camel cigarette logo. The model is made of shredded tobacco and it sheds; every 18 months Joe gets a new coat. The exhibits cover how tobacco is grown, the history of the RJR Company, over 100 years of tobacco related advertising, plus an extensive array of tobacco memorabilia. There is a video of old commercials, various items made from cigarette packages, information on sporting events sponsored by R.J. Reynolds, and information on products manufactured by the parent company RJR Nabisco. A souvenir store sells sweatshirts and other logo-enhanced items. All tour members are given tokens to use in vending machines stocked with Nabisco products, and those over 21 are given their choice of cigarettes.

It is the opportunity to get out on the floor and get an up-close look at the manufacturing process that intrigues visitors. The plant makes 200 million cigarettes a day. You can see the filter being made from a man-made fiber that resembles gauze. The fiber comes in 1,000-pound bales that are between 45 and 90 miles long; each bale makes roughly 700,000 filters. Transparent tubes let you see the tobacco as it's blown in from the blending rooms into the hopper. It is formed into a continuous roll, which if measured would be roughly four miles long; when cut that would make approximately 95,000 individual cigarettes. A two-mile long strip of cigarette-tipping paper will make 123,000 cigarettes. This prodigious output means that Reynolds pays the federal government about four million dollars a day in taxes.

Free tours are given of the 65-acre Whitaker Park Monday through Friday from 8:15 A.M. to 10:00 P.M. It is closed on holidays, the Monday following Easter and during Christmas week. Visitors are welcome to stop at the employees cafeteria for lunch.

The **Stroh** plant in Winston-Salem encompasses 28 acres under one roof. When it was built in 1968 it was the largest brewery in the world under one roof. The 30-minute, half-mile walking tour lets you look down through large glass windows at the production floor where 5.5 million barrels (each barrel contains 31 gallons) of beer are produced annually. The plant operates 24 hours a day on three shifts.

Stroh's has five additional breweries—in Texas, Pennsylvania, Tennessee, Minnesota, Florida—and the corporate office in Michigan where the first plant opened in 1850. Stroh's makes ten standard beers and five light beers, making it the third largest brewer in the country and the seventh largest in the world. Only Stroh's, Stroh's Light and Signature are fire-brewed; all other brands made in America are steam-brewed.

The brewery tour starts with the packaging and moves backwards through the brewing process. You'll see the production line for cans and bottles first, later the aging tanks, storage cellars and the brewing department. At the conclusion of the free tour, given Monday–Friday 11:00 A.M. to 4:30 P.M., visitors are invited to enjoy the hospitality of the Strohaus, the company pub. Stroh's beers are available without charge and there are pretzels on the table. For groups in the Winston-Salem area, the Strohaus is available at no charge for evening events. Refreshments and a bartender are supplied compliments of Stroh's.

Directions: From I-85 take I-40 to Winston-Salem. Head north off I-40 on US 52 to the Akron Drive exit. Turn left on Akron Drive and follow the signs onto Reynolds Boulevard leading into Whitaker Park. For the Stroh Brewery return to US 52 heading south and exit on South Main Street. Turn left onto South Main Street and proceed to Barnes Road; then turn left and continue to Schlitz Avenue where you will again turn left. Stop at the security gate and identify yourself as a visitor. Strohaus is on the second floor of the brewery.

Tanglewood

Multiple Choices

"T'would fill a page, had I a book, To Tell the joys of Tanglewood!", wrote owner Kate B. Reynolds, in a poem she composed about her much-loved estate. Mrs. Reynolds and her husband William N. Reynolds, Chairman of the Board for R.J. Reynolds Tobacco Company, purchased the estate in 1921 from the Johnson family, who had owned the land since 1757. For a time the land cost the Johnson family "five shillings, lawful money of Great Britain in hand and a yearly rent of one peppercorn payment at the Feast of Saint Michael, the archangel."

The Reynolds lived for 30 years on their farm and horse breeding center, which they named for the tangled undergrowth on the estate grounds. In 1951, the 1,100-acre estate became the William and Kate B. Reynolds Memorial Park, better known as **Tanglewood**. The park opened to the public in 1954.

It takes more than a page to describe the diverse pleasures awaiting visitors at Tanglewood. *Golf Digest* called this "one of the ten best public parks in the United States." Mr. Reynolds bred horses, and the track he built has been used for steeplechase events since 1962. Each year on the second Saturday in May there are five races as part of the annual steeplechase. The horses bred here were so highly regarded that after Mr. Reynolds died one of his stud horses brought the highest price ever paid at the time for a harness horse. The park still has stables and a riding trail.

While Mr. Reynolds pursued his equestrian interests, Mrs. Reynolds developed the gardens around the Manor House. To carry out her plans she hired Frank Lustig, a German immigrant who arrived in 1926. Lustig continued working at the estate even after it became a park. The rose garden added in front of the house was actually an experimental garden; Jackson and Perkins sent Tanglewood their newest breeds in exchange for evaluation. Now an All-American Rose Selections Garden, it has over 800 rose bushes. Of these more than half are American Rose Society winners.

The arboretum, behind the Manor House, was planted by Lustig with help from the North Carolina Council of Garden Clubs. The gardens have Chinese Stranvaseia, oakleaf hydrangea, lilac chastetree and a host of other trees and shrubs. There is a fragrance garden for the visually handicapped, a grape arbor and a garden overlook. The estate's most impressive specimen, a stately oak, is not part of the arboretum but is found on the Manor House lawn. This oak is North Carolina's third oldest oak tree, estimated to be between 369 and 380 years old. A plaque on the tree is inscribed with Joyce Kilmer's poem, *Trees*.

If you want to enjoy the trees and natural features of the land take the park's Little Walden Nature Trail. Audio stations provide commentary on the flora and fauna. Visitors can enter fenced protected areas where deer and peacocks are kept. The trails are alive with birds not often spotted: yellow bill cuckoos, woodcocks and pileated woodpeckers. The park's population of bluebirds is thriving because of the numerous nesting boxes added to attract them. There are several lakes; Skilpot is popular with fishermen because it's stocked with bass, the Children's Center lake is stocked with bream for younger fishermen, and there is a ten-acre Mallard Lake. The latter is home to the green-headed ducks. The waterfowl population did include a swan, but the unruly bird was deported after a rampage on the golf course.

Golf is serious business at Tanglewood. The Vantage Golf Championship tournament is played here each October, and *Golf Digest* considers the Vantage course one of the top 25 public golf courses in the nation. The course was given an even greater accolade when the #5 hole was chosen as one of the most challenging golf holes in the country by *Golf Magazine*. The 1974 PGA Championship was played at Tanglewood as was the 1986 USGA Public Links Championship. Two of the park's 18-hole courses were designed by Robert Trent Jones.

Golf is but one of the sports enjoyed at Tanglewood. There is canoeing on the lakes and along the Yadkin River. As mentioned hiking and riding are other options. Additional trails are set aside for bikers, and there is a BMX race track for bicycles. A pool and waterslide are available for swimmers and both clay and hard courts for tennis players. There are also hayrides, a miniature golf course, a driving range and a concert shell where musical programs are scheduled frequently.

Tanglewood ranks third in the state for visitor attendance, after the Biltmore House and the Battleship *North Carolina*. The park has several spots of historical interest. The white-framed Mt. Pleasant Methodist Church was built on its present location in 1890; its old-fashioned charm makes it a popular spot for weddings. Some of the gravestones in the adjacent graveyard date from the 1760s, including that of William Johnson, the original owner of the Tanglewood land. The 110-ton coal-fired steam engine, Old 542, offers children the chance to play Casey Jones on this old Southern Railway locomotive.

The Manor House, whose center wing was built in 1859, is now a bed-and-breakfast; other accommodations are available at the park's motor lodge, the six vacation cottages and the campground. Tanglewood Park is open 8:00 A.M. to dusk, but for overnight guests the access roads are always open.

Directions: From I-85 take I-40 west to Winston-Salem and continue on I-40 for 12 miles past Winston-Salem. Then take the well-marked Tanglewood exit. As you reach the bottom of the exit ramp turn left on Highway 158 and go 200 yards to the park entrance on the right.

HIGH POINT

High Point Museum and Historical Park, Peterson Doll and Miniature Museum and Market Square

High Spots

North Carolina's sixth largest city was inadvertently named when the surveyor for the North Carolina Railroad Company pinpointed the area as the highest point on the proposed route between Goldsboro and Charlotte. The plank road between Fayetteville and Salem ran through this point, and the crossing of these major transportation arteries led to the development of a thriving industrial and trading center.

The history of this region from the prehistoric people who once lived here through the prosperous international and regional furniture markets established here is displayed at the **High Point Museum**. The McCall collection of Shakespearean items you see as you enter the museum reflects the town's prominence as the location of the North Carolina Shakespeare Festival held each year in August and September (call (800)672-NCSF for schedule and ticket information). Of historic interest at the entrance area are several large cases filled with long rifles.

One of the major focuses of the museum is on the industries that have led to High Point's development: the North State Telephone Company, the High Point Buggy Company, plus the numerous companies that have made this the furniture and hosiery capital of the world.

The museum's second focus is on life in the Piedmont from the days of the first settlers. The **Historical Park** adjacent to the museum helps the staff realize their objective. The **Haley House**, circa 1786, is the oldest structure in High Point still standing on its original site. The furnishings are of the period and represent pieces listed on John Haley's death inventory. This brick house, resembling homes built in the Virginia and Carolina tidewater area, was far more substantial than neighboring log cabins.

John Haley was a blacksmith as well as a sheriff, tax collector and road commissioner. Next to his 18th-century house is a restored blacksmith shop. On weekends costumed interpreters demonstrate this old skill. Weaving is demonstrated on a collection of old handlooms in a log cabin. Other crafts practiced are candlemaking, spinning, weaving and hearth cooking.

The High Point Historical Society, which operates the museum and park, also administers the Mendenhall Store and Quaker Meeting House two miles east of the museum in the High Point City Lake Park. At the store built by Richard Mendenhall in 1824 you'll find handcrafted items for sale. They are also available at the Museum Store on the museum grounds. The 1820 Jamestown Friends Meeting House, now restored, is used for public meetings.

The High Point Museum is open at no charge Tuesday–Saturday 10:00 A.M. to 4:30 P.M. and Sunday 1:00 to 4:30 P.M. The historical park is open on weekends only from 1:00 to 4:30 P.M. The Mendenhall Store is open Wednesday–Saturday 10:00 A.M. to 4:00 P.M. and the Meeting House is open by appointment.

Not far from the High Point Museum is one of the South's largest doll collections. Angela Peterson amassed more than a thousand dolls, many of which now fill the shelves of a special room at the Wesleyan Arms Retirement Center. The dolls span the globe and the centuries, dating back to the 15th century and representing more than 53 countries. There are rag dolls, portrait dolls, religious dolls, voodoo dolls and paper dolls. A collection of seven doll houses includes a replica of Mrs. Peterson's own home. The museum also displays one of the largest creches in the country. The 50 figures that make up this tableau date from the 1490s to 1820. The museum is open Tuesday, Wednesday, Thursday and Sunday from 1:30 to 4:30 P.M. It is closed on major holidays. There is no charge but donations are gratefully accepted.

Since High Point is noted for its furniture manufacturing, a visit to the showrooms of **Market Square** is a must. The old Tomlinson furniture manufacturing factory has been converted to a home-furnishing design center. In all there are more than 90,000 square feet of exhibition and convention space and more than 6,000,000 square feet devoted to permanent showrooms. Between 70 and 80 percent of these showrooms are open year-round. The public is not able to tour them during the April and October Furniture Mart held for buyers. Insiders know that the best time to visit is just after one of these furniture marts. In 1991 the Furniture Discovery Center is scheduled to open in the same building as the Visitors Bureau, 101 West Green Drive. It will showcase furniture manufacturing, color and style selection, and live demonstrations by craftsmen. Market Square includes a lively dining spot, the Boiler Room Bar & Grill, with a Gay Nineties theme and an adjoining game room complete with pool tables.

Directions: From I-85 take I-85 Business into High Point then exit on Route 311 north. To reach the museum, turn right on E. Lexington Avenue to #1805. To reach the Peterson Doll Museum from the High Point Museum, turn right on East Lexington and drive two blocks to N. Centennial Street and make a right. The Peterson Doll and Miniature Museum is on the left at 1911 N. Centennial Street in the Wesleyan Arms Administration Building. Market Square is located just off Highway 311 at 305 W. High Street.

ASHEBORO AND VICINITY

North Carolina Zoological Park

How Do You Zoo?

"When I die I don't know what animal I want to come back as, but I know I want to live at the North Carolina Zoo," exclaimed ABC's Roger Caras, the only network environmental reporter in the country, after his visit to the 1,448-acre **North Carolina Zoological Park**. This park has one of the largest land areas of any zoo in the world and is the first zoo to be developed entirely around the concept of natural habitats. There are no bars, no cages, no sense of animals being confined. It is illusion that separates visitors from the animals, although moats, rock enclosures, streams and vegetation provide natural and protective screens.

Due to this extraordinary arrangement, visitors can watch more than a dozen species of antelope including gazelle, impala, kudu and gemsbok running free across a 37-acre African Plains that duplicates their environment on the Serengeti. Four overlooks provide different views of the animals that co-exist on the plains and some ground-dwelling birds like the Masai ostrich, marabou stork and secretary bird. A display panel pictures the various animals sharing the plain, and there are telescopes to bring the action closer. Binoculars are helpful during your zoo safari, so remember to bring them.

The plains habitat is but one of seven outdoor areas in the 300-acre African exhibit. There are also two indoor habitats. Together these nine areas showcase more than 700 animals and 15,000 plants. A two-mile footpath winds through the African region, and trams make frequent circuits of the region. You are allowed to hop on and off the tram for a closer look at the animals.

Adjacent to the plains is a large watering hole from which the elephants drink their daily 30-gallons worth. When the zoo sponsored a conference for elephant specialists, it was a compliment to the park that several participants applied for jobs at the close of the meeting. The elephant is the only animal in the zoo that can't be sedated when medical attention is needed. Since the elephant is so large its lungs are likely to collapse if it falls down, elephant handlers have to train the animals to respond to commands.

Near the elephants' 3½-acre reserve is a similar watering hole for the southern white rhinoceros, the world's third largest land animal. The southern white rhinoceros was nearly hunted to extinction in Africa; only the efforts of American biologist Dr. Herbert Lang, saved a herd of 20. These few remaining examples of a vanishing breed were discovered in an isolated area of Zululand. Today in protected parks and reserves there are more than 3,500 southern whites, all descendants of that small herd.

Not far away from the elephants and rhinos, the lions bask in the sun or rest in the shadows of the towering rocks of their habitat. You can see the lions eye-to-eye at ground level or get a panoramic view of their habitat from an 18-foot-high overlook.

The first exhibit area of the zoo, the 3.2-acre Forest Edge, opened in 1979. This turf-and-tree-covered habitat is home to the long-necked giraffes and distinctive zebras, ostriches and marabou storks. Across the well-marked pathway is the half-acre wooded chimpanzee habitat. The North Carolina Zoological Park is part of Dr. Jane Goodall's project Chimpanzoo that compares chimp behavior in the wild to behavior in captive environments. It's fun to watch the antics of the chimpanzee troop. Nearby is the baboons' home. In August 1989 a new 16,200-square-foot gorilla habitat opened. This Forest Glade habitat has a garden so the gorillas can pluck their own cucumbers, watermelons, radishes, green beans and other vegetables. This habitat is connected to the African Pavilion.

The unique African Pavilion has a Teflon-coated fiberglass roof supported by three 90-foot, cupola-topped, steel masts. This design lets in the sun, illuminating the 200 animals that live in the pavilion. Four geographic regions of Africa are represented: forest, forest edge, swamp and plains.

The second indoor habitat is the R.J. Reynolds Forest Aviary housing 150 exotic birds and 1,500 tropical plants in an equatorial jungle beneath an 18,000-square-foot plexiglass dome. Having no inside beams to interrupt the birds' flight, this free-flight aviary is one of the largest of its kind in North America. The North Carolina Zoo has achieved prominence for its successful breeding program with rare and endangered birds. Even the birds appear to feel their indoor environment is a natural one.

It is easy to spend an entire day at the zoo; however, four hours will give you at least a glancing exposure to the African habitats. You'll need a full day after 1992 when the zoo plans to unveil the North American continent habitats. This 200-acre exhibit area will double the zoo's present animal collection, adding 60 exhibits with nearly 100 species of animals and 200 species of plants from the various regions of North America. Habitats will include the rocky coast, desert pavilion, streamside, great plains, cypress swamp and marsh, and a contact area. Long-range plans call for the construction of habitats from other continents—Asia, Europe, South America, Australia and a World of Seas.

The North Carolina Zoological Park is open year-round. Hours from April through October are 9:00 A.M. to 5:00 P.M. weekdays and 10:00 A.M. to 6:00 P.M. weekends and holidays. From November through March hours are 9:00 A.M. to 4:00 P.M. daily. Admission is charged and there is a nominal fee for unlimited tram rides. During the hot summer months the animals are more active in the early morning.

Directions: From I-85 take Route 64 at Lexington and head east to Asheboro. The zoo is six miles southeast of Asheboro off Route 64 on Route 159. Signs indicate the turn off Route 64.

Seagrove Pottery

All Fired Up

In Seagrove the ties of family are strong and deep, as deep as the clay from which eight to nine generations of potters have worked.

The craft of pottery making in the Seagrove area started around 1750 when the region was still part of the British empire. Some Seagrove families trace their roots back to Staffordshire, England. For a glimpse of the functional pottery made in the 1750s, visit the **Museum of North Carolina Traditional Pottery**. The museum traces the history of pottery making in North Carolina back to the Creek Indians. Here you can see the tableware, jugs and jars early potters produced. You'll also learn about the clay found in this area and how pottery is turned and glazed. However, it is not in the museum that the mystery and beauty of the craft can be experienced, but in the more than 25 pottery studios in the Seagrove area. All are open Monday through Saturday 9:00 A.M. to 5:00 P.M. unless indicated; a few do open slightly earlier.

The museum was founded in 1969 by Dorothy and Walter Auman whose pottery shop, Seagrove Pottery (Tuesday–Saturday 8:00 A.M. to 4:00 P.M.) is next door. If you arrive in Seagrove from US 220 south, this is the first shop you will see on the right. A map available at the museum and at most of the potteries will pinpoint each shop. Like so many of the potteries, the Auman's shop is a family operation. Dorothy's father, C.C. Cole, was a well-known potter, and Cole Pottery (which closes at 4:30 P.M.) is still one of the best. Nell Cole Graves, one of five family members who work in the shop, has been turning pottery since the 1930s.

Turning off US 220 onto North Carolina Route 705 you will pass nine shops, by far the largest cluster. The first you'll see will be the Turn & Burn Pottery, which specializes in utilitarian stoneware pieces and face jugs. These jugs are exactly what the name implies; like Halloween jack-o-lanterns they often are given comical features.

Next comes Old Gap Pottery where potter Phil Pollet has been working for about 15 years. His traditional pieces have a contemporary edge. His work has been exhibited at the Mint Museum in Charlotte and the North Carolina Museum of Art in Raleigh. A bit farther down the road is Phil Morgan Pottery. He is one of only a few potters in the country to work with crystalline glazes. The crystals on his one-of-a-kind vases, pots and urns reflect the sun. The pieces look like they are sprinkled with jewels. The glaze contains zinc oxide crystal nuclei that grow in the firing process in circular or fan shapes, floating on the surface of the glaze when it is molten, then freezing in place as the glaze cools.

After you pass Route 2859 on your right (which will take you to Twin Oaks Pottery and Cole Pottery located on Route 1414) and Route 1002 on your left (which leads to Whynot Pottery, Backwoods Pottery and Fork Creek Mill Pottery) you will come to the Wild Rose Pottery on your left on NC 705. Wild rose is located in a 150-year-old log cabin. The pottery here is done in traditional shapes, but surface decoration and carving make it decorative as well as functional. There are five more shops in a row along Highway 705. The next is Chrisco's Pottery where you'll find an assortment of functional pitchers and lidded pots. Down the road a short distance is Old House Pottery, a rustic studio full of ring jugs, face jugs, cake tubes and other functional shapes. Across the highway is Rock House Pottery featuring rusticware and brown saltware that suggest carved wood. Also on this side of the street is Pot Luck Pottery where you can find splatterware, (the result of colored glaze splattered over a white base glaze).

Continuing down NC 705 you'll come to Humble Mill Pottery, which opened in the Seagrove area a few years ago. Owners Jerry and Charlotte Fenberg spent 25 years studying pottery and porcelain all over the world. Their shop here is a showroom, and the work is done at a potter's shop off NC Route 42 at Asheboro. Next is Ben Owen Pottery, whose studio combines the sturdy Moore County Pottery style with Oriental influences. Benjamin Wade Owens worked with Jacques Busbee to establish Jugtown Pottery (from NC Route 705 turn left on Route 1419 and then left again on Route 1420). From 1959 until 1972, Wade worked at his own pottery studio. His son and grandson continue to turn out work in their father's well-remembered style (open until 6:00 P.M.). The last shop along NC Route 705 is the Cady Clay Works. Two potters work here producing contemporary decorated pieces.

There are numerous other shops on the small country roads around Seagrove. One that most pottery enthusiasts always include on any visit to the area is the M.L. Owens Pottery shop, which has been open since 1895. This is one of the few studios open on Sunday.

It is easy to spend a day exploring these studios; each is unique. If you do plan a long day you might want to bring a picnic lunch as there are not many restaurants nearby; the closest are in Asheboro. If you ask, you can generally picnic in the yard at Whynot Pottery noted for its functional stoneware. A quick rundown of other studios includes:

Westmore Pottery (Route 1419) featuring elaborate surface designs on redware and salt glazed stoneware;

Potter's House (Route 1405) with decorated slipware;

Oakland Pottery (NC Route 22) featuring colored glazes and face jugs from miniatures to gallon size;

King's Pottery (Route 1410) with the popular Rebecca pitchers modeled on the loopy-handled Roman pitchers;

Hickory Hill Pottery (Route 1419) with utilitarian stoneware;

Dover Pottery (Route 1405) with decorated, functional and swirled pieces.

For more information on the Seagrove Pottery shops, contact the Asheboro/Randolph Chamber of Commerce, P.O. Box 2007, Asheboro, NC 27204-2007; (919)626-2626.

Directions: From I-85 south of Greensboro, take US 220 11 miles south of Asheboro to Seagrove.

HICKORY, STATESVILLE AND SALISBURY VICINITY

Boone's Cave State Park, Duke Power State Park and Pilot Mountain State Park

Recreational Trio

Three scenic state parks in the Piedmont foothills offer such diverse recreational options as visiting historic sites, hiking, boating, caving, fishing, picnicking, canoeing, camping, swimming and studying nature.

The 110-acre **Boone's Cave State Park** is 14 miles west of Lexington. Tradition says that it was on land now included in this park that Squire Boone, Daniel's father, first settled his family in 1752 when they migrated west from Pennsylvania. Daniel was 18 years old and one of 11 children. The Boone cabin reputedly stood on a high bluff overlooking the Yadkin River. The Daniel Boone Memorial Association reconstructed a single-room cabin on the site where speculation placed the Boone family house. A .5-mile trail leads from the park entry gate to the cabin. Even if this is not the exact spot, it reflects a long association between Daniel Boone and the Yadkin River. For 17 years after his marriage, he and his wife, Rebecca, lived at several different locations along the Yadkin. There is even speculation that it was Daniel himself and his family who built a cabin on this high bluff.

Local legends hold that Daniel Boone explored and spent nights in the narrow cave located within the park and hid from Indians in its dark depths. Boone's Cave, also called Devil's Den, has an 80-foot tunnel. It is so narrow in places that explorers must crawl along the passageway. The Daniel Boone Trail leading to the cabin travels down a steep slope to a flood plain, then along the riverbank to Boone's Cave. A wooden stairway returns hikers to the parking lot.

The park trails are particularly appealing in the spring when the rhododendron and mountain laurel bloom and some 30 species of wildflowers can be spotted. The park has a picnic shelter on the bluff near the Boone cabin. An exhibit board provides information on the exploits of Boone, the Long Hunter of the Yadkin. (This exhibit is vandalized frequently; currently there is no information displayed there.) One fact of interest is that Boone never wore a coonskin cap. He was a Quaker and like his fellow Quakers wore a broad-brimmed beaver hat. You might want to emulate Daniel Boone and fish the Yadkin in hopes of catching bass, crappie, catfish and sunfish. You will need a fishing license, however. The rock outcrop beside Boone's Cave is also a rest stop for canoeists on the Yadkin River Canoe Trail. To find out more about this trail write: Yadkin River Trail Association, 280 South Liberty Street, Winston-Salem, NC 17101. Boone's Cave State Park opens at 8:00 A.M. In November and early December it closes at 5:00 P.M.; in March and October it closes at 6:00 P.M.; April, May and September closing is 7:00 P.M.; and June–August at 8:00 P.M. The park is not open from mid-December to mid-March.

Another state park, roughly an hour away, is **Duke Power State Park** located 10 miles south of Statesville. This roughly 1,500-acre park is located along the northeastern shore of Lake Norman, the largest man-made lake in the state. The park extends for 13 miles along the shore of this 32,510-acre lake, often called North Carolina's inland sea. The lake itself has a 520-mile shoreline.

Water sports are a major draw at Duke Power State Park. The swimming area has a sandy beach, a bathhouse, vending machines and a picnic shelter. Rowboats or canoes can be rented, but private boats are not permitted on the 33-acre lake within the park. Near the campground, a launching ramp provides access to Lake Norman. Near the shores of Lake Norman are 33 sites for family tent and trailer camping. No reservations are accepted for these campsites.

Lake Norman offers one of the best fresh water fishing spots in the state. From the shore the catch includes black crappies and bluegill. In open water white bass is plentiful. The lake also has channel catfish, yellow perch and largemouth bass.

The park has two nature trails: the .8-mile Alder Trail, which has a small stretch along the lake and a longer walk along several creeks, and the 5.4-mile Lakeshore Trail, which can be shortened for a less strenuous 2.5-mile hike. The longer walk takes a loop around the peninsula bordered by Lake Norman and Hicks Creek.

Duke Power State Park opens at 8:00 A.M. daily. It closes at 6:00 P.M. from November–February, at 7:00 P.M. in March and October, at 8:00 P.M. April, May and September, and at 9:00 P.M. from June- August.

Pilot Mountain State Park is 24 miles north of Winston-Salem.

This park has two sections, the 2,200-acre Pilot Mountain section and the 1,500-acre Yadkin River section, connected by a six-mile hiking corridor. The park was established to protect the unique quartzite knob, or what geologists call a monadnock, that rises 200 feet from the top of the mountain. A monadnock is a mountain of resistant rock that survived the erosion that diminished surrounding foothills. This looming sentinel dominates the countryside. The Saura Indians called the mountain, Jomeokee, meaning pilot or Great Guide. Thomas Jefferson's father, Peter Jefferson, surveyed the area in 1751. He named this high peak Ararat for the mountain on which Noah's Ark came to rest after the flood.

Pilot Mountain is crowned by two distinctive pinnacles. A trail leading from the main parking lot to Little Pinnacle has a slight grade for 100 yards. The path through a forested section of the mountain leads to a rocky overlook. On a clear day you can see over 3,000 square miles. Rappelling is popular from the rock promontories of Little Pinnacle but cannot be done from Big Pinnacle.

Adjacent to the Little Pinnacle overlook, the one-mile Jomeokee Trail leads to the base of Big Pinnacle, circles it, and returns to the overlook. This walk takes a lot of energy and about 45-minutes of time. Big Pinnacle rises 1,400 feet above the valley floor with a 200-foot knob. Another trail which begins from Little Pinnacle is the half-mile Sassafras Trail. Guide booklets are available in distribution boxes at the beginning of this trail. The roughly 30-to-40-minute walk is not strenuous. More challenging is the 2-mile Ledge Springs Trail, which climbs almost continuously along the cliffs and ledges to the west of Little Pinnacle. It is best to begin this trail at the picnic area off the parking lot at the Little Pinnacle base and end below Little Pinnacle where the Jomeokee Trail begins. Forking off Ledge Springs is the two-mile Grindstone Trail, which winds from the summit area to the campgrounds. The picnic areas are located on the lower side of the summit parking lot in a forested area. The campgrounds are located approximately one mile from the entrance. Pilot Mountain is noted as the most eastern nesting area for the common raven. A rare bird for this area, the pileated woodpecker is often sited at the park.

The Yadkin River section of the park offers hiking, horseback riding, canoeing, rafting and fishing. You have to come fully equipped. The park encompasses a two-mile segment of the Yadkin River, with two islands—one 45 acres and the other only 15 acres. Fish frequently caught include catfish and sunfish. You must have a license to fish. There are two small picnic places on each side of the river. A 12-mile bridle and hiking trail links all sections of the park, including the Pilot Mountain section and the area along the Yadkin River. Another trail, the half-mile Canal Trail, leads along the north shore of the river beginning at the Yadkin River section turnaround.

Pilot Mountain State Park opens at 8:00 A.M. daily. It closes at 6:00 P.M. November–February, at 7:00 P.M. in March and October, at 8:00 P.M. in April, May and September, and at 9:00 P.M. from June–August. There is no admission charge at any of these state parks.

Pilot Mountain, it should be noted, is in the Sauratown Mountain Range, not the Blue Ridge. The Sauratowns, for this reason, are sometimes called "the mountains away from the mountains." The second park in the Sauratowns is **Hanging Rock State Park**. Located 24 miles to the east of Pilot Mountain, it lures nature enthusiasts with lake swimming, rental boats, picnicking, hiking trails, rental cabins and 74 tent and trailer campsites. In all, 5,862 acres of great outdoors!

Directions: For Boone's Cave State Park from I-85 take Highway 150 east and travel five miles to Churchland, then turn left on Boone's Cave Road (State Route 1162) for 4.5 miles to park gate. For Duke Power State Park return to Highway 150 and go north to Highway 64 and turn left. Take Route 64 west to I-40, follow I-40 south to Statesville. At Statesville take I-77 south for ten miles to Highway 21 exit. Take Highway 21 west to Troutman. You will see a park sign. At the sign proceed west on Wagner Street (State Route 131). Then take State Park Road for four miles to the main entrance of park. To reach Pilot Mountain State Park from I-85 take I-40 west to Winston-Salem, then take Highway 52 north to the park. To reach Hanging Rock State Park from Winston-Salem, take Highway 311 north to the intersection with Highway 89. Take Route 89 northwest to the park entrance on State Route 1101.

Fort Dobbs

Lasting Impression

There are no stockade, moat, cannons—no fortifications of any kind to mark the spot on the western frontier where **Fort Dobbs** was built in 1756. The log walls of this back country earthenworks fortification offered protection to North Carolina settlers when Indian raids threatened their existence during the French and Indian War. There were approximately 2,600 Cherokee warriors in what would become the southeastern part of the United States. Rumors circulated, but were never substantiated, that there were marauding bands of Shawnees and Delawares moving into the region from the north.

You will have to use your imagination as you climb the mound on which the fort once stood. From this slight rise you have a far-reaching vista, extending to the foothills of the Blue Ridge Mountains in the distance. Provincial rangers under the command of Lieutenant Hugh Waddell built the fort on this knoll, and it was named in honor of the colony's royal governor, Arthur Dobbs. On February 27, 1760, the fort successfully withstood a direct attack by a raiding party of some 60 to 70 Cherokees.

The following year a large force of British regulars and provincials pushed the western frontier 50 miles west of Fort Dobbs. The threat of Indian attack decreased even more with the signing of the Treaty of Paris in 1763, ending the French and Indian War. A year later the colonial assembly voted to dismantle Fort Dobbs. The buildings fell into ruins, and eventually all traces disappeared. Archaeological excavations have pinpointed the exact location of the fort.

Artifacts from these digs are exhibited in the Fort Dobbs visitor center, an old log frontier dwelling that was moved to this historic site. In addition to displays uncovered from the old fort there are exhibits on daily life on the frontier.

There is a short (less than a mile) scenic nature trail you can explore. A shaded picnic area is available. Hours are April through October, Monday–Saturday 9:00 A.M. to 5:00 P.M. and Sunday 1:00 to 5:00 P.M. From November through March it is open Tuesday–Saturday 10:00 A.M. to 4:00 P.M. and Sunday 1:00 to 4:00 P.M.

Directions: Take I-40 west from Winston-Salem, and exit on Route 21 north and travel approximately one mile. Then turn left on Fort Dobbs Road, State Road 1930. The fort is roughly one mile ahead on the right.

Historic Spencer Shops

Close Railroad Ties

Historic **Spencer Shops** provides a bridge to the time when the railroad bound the country together with two rivers of steel. In its heyday in the early 1900s, the vast layout at Spencer was the pulsing heart of the Southern Railroad. Here the rolling stock and the great steam locomotives were maintained. But today Spencer is more than a link in the railroad chain that crisscrossed North Carolina. It is a living community and its retired railroad men have dedicated countless hours of unpaid labor restoring steam locomotives, passenger coaches and tracks at Spencer Shops.

Volunteers speak of the romance of the rails. For many of the old-time railroad men, the steam trains were living, breathing entities. Their hard work has brought them back to life and re-

Classics from the 1930s shine in the North Carolina Transportation Museum at Historic Spencer Shops. Exhibits span transportation methods from dugout canoes to modern airplanes.

stored a piece of history for future generations. Fortunately, there is a younger generation of volunteers the old-timers call weekend warriors, to whom they are passing their knowledge and skill.

Spencer Shops began in 1896 in answer to the Southern Railway's need for a steam locomotive repair facility. The 150-acre tract was located halfway between Atlanta and Washington, D.C. It was named for the railroad's first president, Samuel Spencer. The shops operated 365 days a year, repairing approximately 75 steam locomotives a day. The roundhouse had stalls for 37 engines, and there was a series of smaller repair shops. These shops represented 21 different unions and crafts including machinists, boilermakers, pipefitters, carpenters, oilers and engineers. At its peak in the 1920s there were 3,000 people working at Spencer Shops. When the shops closed at 11:15 P.M. on Saturday, July 30, 1960, brought down by the advent of diesel engines, only eight workers were retained.

The first diesel locomotive to arrive here was towed in by a steam locomotive. Yes, it really did arrive in that fashion. An old boilermaker took one look at it and said, "Let's take it down to the Yadkin and run it into the river." Southern Railway switched to diesel engines in 1953, and for a few years diesel repairs were done at Spencer Shops, but eventually they were switched to the Spencer Yards in nearby Linwood. In 1977 (and another section in 1979) Southern Railway donated Spencer Shops to the state as a transportation museum.

Historic Spencer Shops is one of a handful of places in the country where you can watch men working in a steam repair facility, see an old roundhouse and ride a steam locomotive. Thirteen old buildings are still standing, but as you walk through the repair shops you'll see leaky roofs, puddled floors and peeling paint. The site badly needs money for basic repairs. The volunteers can't tackle the structural problems of the buildings, although their prodigious efforts have put the tracks back in working order, restored five coaches and two baggage cars, done a cosmetic restoration on a 1922 locomotive, and put the steam locomotives back on the tracks. Despite their present run-down condition, the shops look like places where work is being done. You feel like picking up a wrench and helping with the ongoing repairs. Long-term projects in progress include the luxurious private railcars built for steel magnate Charles Schwab and for industrialist James Buchanan Duke. The Pullman car that Duke bought in 1917 was named for his daughter, Doris.

The outdoor facility on this 57-acre complex is devoted exclusively to railroading, but in the former Master Mechanic's Office Storehouse a wider world of transportation is on exhibit as part of the North Carolina Transportation Museum. The theme is "People, Places, and Times." Exhibits reach back to a prehistoric Indian dugout canoe, up through the Conestoga wagon, into the automobile era with an early Ford truck, and into the present with a Commonwealth Skyranger airplane. They even have one of the first North Carolina highway patrol cars. Exhibits feature memorabilia about the men who once worked at Spencer Shops, and there are old railroad cars both inside and out.

For children of all ages, the highlight of any visit here is the 2½-mile train ride. Volunteers restored and now operate the former Buffalo Creek and Gauley Railroad steam locomotive #4. Its identity was lost along the way, but it was reborn as Southern Railway #604, a long-scrapped Southern engine that was based at Spencer. The new #604, like the old, has an eagle proudly mounted on the locomotive's front, a visored headlight and large numbers on the tank. On weekdays and during the off-season rides are given on a Southern Railway FP-7 diesel locomotive. No rides are given January–March. Daily diesel rides run from April through Labor Day, and steam train rides on weekends. During September steam engine rides are given on weekends and there are no rides during the week. After October and until mid-

December there are no steam train rides. On weekends visitors can ride the diesel-driven train.

Spencer Shops is open November through March Tuesday–Saturday 10:00 A.M. to 4:00 P.M. and Sunday 1:00 to 4:00 P.M. From April through October hours are Monday–Saturday 9:00 A.M. to 5:00 P.M. and Sunday 1:00 to 5:00 P.M. It is closed on major holidays. There is no admission and only a nominal charge for the train rides.

Directions: From I-85 take Exit 79, Andrew Street. Head west to the intersection with Route 29/70 and turn left. Spencer Shops is down Route 29/70, Salisbury Avenue, on the left.

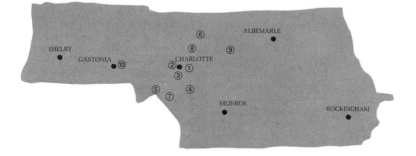

SOUTHERN FOOTHILLS

In Charlotte
1. Discovery Place
2. Hezekiah Alexander Homesite
3. Latta Place
4. Mint Museum, Nature Museum and Spirit Square

Around Charlotte
5. Carowinds
6. Fieldcrest Cannon Mills
7. James K. Polk Memorial
8. Philip Morris Cabarrus Manufacturing Center
9. Reed Gold Mine
10. Schiele Museum of Natural History and
     Planetarium

═══Southern Foothills═══

Charlotte, surrounded by the Southern Foothills, has acquired a big-city appearance while retaining its southern charm and hospitality. Although it has the largest business district in the state, the city's greenspace plan provides flowers, trees and shrubs to the downtown area. Charlotte is noted for the sophisticated exhibits at the Mint Museum as well as the bucolic charm of its Latta Plantation.

Travel options within the region are typical of the many choices one has throughout the state. In one day you can watch raw cotton transformed into bed sheets at the Fieldcrest Cannon Mills, descend at Reed into the depths of one of America's first gold mines, watch cigarettes made at Philip Morris Cabarrus Manufacturing Center and visit the birthplace of America's eleventh president, James K. Polk.

Flexibility is often the key to successful day-tripping and when planning trips in the Southern Foothills, as in the other six North Carolina geographical regions, it is easy to adjust your itinerary. If it rains on the day you had planned an outing to Carowinds, the popular theme park south of Charlotte, you needn't stay home, head instead for Discovery Place, a scientific wonderland with plenty of hands-on fun for youngsters. Or visit the Schiele Museum where anyone, young or old, can reach for the stars in the planetarium and search for the past at the pioneer site and the Catawba Indian Village. The Schiele is one of America's ten best regional museums.

IN CHARLOTTE

Discovery Place

What A Find!

A year after its 1981 opening, Charlotte's **Discovery Place** was rated by the American Association of Museums as one of the top ten science museums in the country. By 1986, the museum was selected by the Southeast Tourism Society as the Travel Attraction of the Year.

The key to success at this hands-on science wonderland is

visitor involvement. Would-be scientists can try cooking crystals at the Piedmont Natural Gas Hearth, challenging the laser pinball machine, holding sea animals in the ocean pool or exploring the human body with the Life Center's transparent anatomical model. Collectors can swap shells or rocks at the Trading Post or observe museum staff preparing exhibits in the Collections Gallery in a behind-the-scenes glimpse of museum work. Watching science films on the First Union Science Theater's two-story screen establishes a sense of direct involvement. In 1991, an Omnimax theater will be added creating an even stronger you-are-there affect.

Wednesdays are always rainy at Discovery Place. At 2:00 P.M. watch a simulated thunderstorm in the three-story Tropical Rainforest where more than 35 species of birds create the illusion of nature in the wild. Be glad museum policy calls for the confinement of some of the animals, otherwise you might have a close encounter with Monty Python and Elizabeth, the museum's exceedingly large Burmese pythons. Animal encounters are just one of the more than 70 live programs offered each week at Discovery Place.

The Science Circus is a sensory treat with exhibits that flash, buzz, zing and ring. A large whisper dish encourages you to play a variation on the old childhood game of Secret. You can whisper a secret at one end of the room and be heard at the other. Ride the Momentum Machine a few times and learn a lesson while going around in circles. At some hands-on museums the experiments require two participants. Here at Discovery Place, at least 75 percent of the exhibits can be done by one person. The science puzzles will fascinate visitors from seven to seventy.

Discovery Place is open Monday–Friday 9:00 A.M. to 5:00 P.M. from September through May and 9:00 A.M. to 6:00 P.M. from June through August. Saturday hours at 9:00 A.M. to 6:00 P.M. and Sunday 1:00 to 6:00 P.M.. Admission is less than the price of a movie.

Directions: From I-85 take Brookshire Freeway south. Take the Tryon/Church Street exit. Take a right on Church Street. Go 5 blocks and Discovery Place is on your left at 301 North Tryon Street between 6th and 7th Streets in uptown Charlotte.

Hezekiah Alexander Homesite

The Rock House

To most of us the date May 20, 1775, is not as familiar as July 4, 1776, but in Mecklenburg County school children know both dates. By issuing the Mecklenburg Declaration of Independence (also called the Mecklenburg Resolves) on that historic May day, this North Carolina Piedmont region was the first to claim independence from Great Britain. Local lore is that one of the signers was Hezekiah Alexander, a Scotch-Irish blacksmith and planter, who moved to the area in 1767.

Alexander purchased a 600-acre homesite near the Catawba River. Two years later he acquired additional land and built his **Rock House**. You can still see the original stonework on this two-story homestead. In this large but simply designed house Alexander and his wife Mary raised ten children. Education and religion were important to Alexander not only for his family but for his community. He was one of the founding trustees of Queens College, the first college south of Virginia, and an elder in the Sugaw Creek Presbyterian Church. Alexander was also active in local politics serving as a delegate to the Fifth Provincial Congress, which drafted the North Carolina Constitution and Bill of Rights.

Homesite tours include some social history. Docents provide details on the daily life of each member of the family. You'll discover how they spent their time, what their meals were like and what it was like to live in the Piedmont region in the 18th century. The furniture is of the period but did not belong to the Alexander family. Note how many of the pieces can be converted to multiple uses. Even some of the rooms had double uses, like the formal entry room Alexander used as an office while serving as a justice of the peace. One puzzling element in the architectural design is the meaning of the Masonic symbols over the door and windows.

Outside the reconstructed log kitchen is Mary Alexander's herb garden, painstakingly restored and labeled so that visitors can see the herbs she once used for her family's needs. Also restored is the old spring house, another two-story stone structure used to store dairy products. Water still flows through this 18th-century building, and it is as cool inside the building today as it was back in the late 1700s.

The homesite visitors center also serves as the History Museum for the city of Charlotte. Rotating exhibits and special programs focus on local history. The museum also houses a craft shop specializing in regional arts and crafts. The **Hezekiah Alexander Homesite** can be toured for a nominal charge Tuesday–Friday from September–May from 1:00 to 5:00 P.M. with the last tour at 3:15. From June–August weekday hours are 10:00 A.M. to 5:00 P.M. On weekends year-round hours are 2:00 to 5:00 P.M.

Directions: From I-85 take Exit 41, Sugar Creek Road. If you are traveling northbound on I-85 turn right on Sugar Creek Road; if southbound make a left on Sugar Creek Road, then continue to Eastway Drive. Turn right on Eastway and then left on Shamrock Drive. The Hezekiah Alexander Homesite is on the right at 3500 Shamrock Drive.

Latta Place

Back Country Plantation

James Latta came to America from Northern Ireland in 1785 determined to better his lot, and he did! He became a prosperous merchant, not by establishing a shop, although eventually he did have a store in South Carolina, but by peddling goods in a Conestoga wagon. Latta purchased supplies in Philadelphia and Charleston then sold them to the isolated farm families in the Carolina Piedmont.

Latta not only got his merchandise in the north, he also looked there for his architectural inspiration. In 1799 Latta purchased land along the Catawba River. He built a two-story frame house with a side entrance. Front entrances were taxed in Philadelphia. Although Latta wouldn't have been taxed in rural North Carolina, he copied the city style of design. At a time when most houses in the area were stone or rough logs this one was made with hand-beaded white clapboard siding in a Georgian/Federal transition style. This is one of the last remaining architecturally significant plantation houses of its era in this region and the only one open to the public.

Historians believe the interior woodwork was done by Hessian soldiers, German mercenaries who remained in America after the Revolution. The intricately carved dentil molding in the overhead frieze should be noted as well as the elaborate mantles, overmantles and staircase.

Latta seems to have absorbed more than just architectural ideas while in the north. He was liberal enough to send his three daughters to a girls' seminary to be educated, and in his property inventory he used the term "family Negroes," not "slaves."

The furnishings you'll see today were selected to match Latta's inventory and other family records. There are a few family pieces as well as a dress worn by Nancy Latta Reid in 1828. When Nancy died her sister, Betsy, who was recently widowed, married Rufus Reid, Nancy's husband. All three of the sisters lived in nearby plantations after they married.

Outbuildings include a slave house, barns and smokehouse. Children enjoy visiting with Miss Ella, the mule, and Chico, the burro. During the summer the kitchen garden is planted with herbs and vegetables. Extra money was made by growing cotton, which is still planted each spring. By 1816 James Latta had a cotton gin. Guided tours of Latta Place are given at 2:00, 3:00

Dating from the early 1800s, Latta Place was built of clapboard siding in a Georgian/Federal transition style. Intricate carving inside is attributed to Hessian soldiers.

and 4:00 P.M. Wednesday–Sunday. A nominal admission is charged for the house museum, but the grounds are free.

Latta Place is part of the 760-acre Latta Plantation Park on Mountain Island Lake. The park's visitor center has native wildlife displays and a gift shop. This is also the place to pick up trail maps. There are three miles of nature trails and seven miles of bridle trails. The 15-acre Latta Equestrian has two arenas for showing. The 3½-acre lake shoreline offers appealing opportunities for fishermen, or they can try their luck from the two fishing piers. There is a launching area for canoes. Families appreciate the wooded picnic sites and the children's playground. Ambitious plans call for the building of the Carolina Raptor Center in the park to rehabilitate injured birds of prey. This facility is now housed in trailers, and several hundred birds are being rehabilitated.

Directions: From I-77 take Exit 16B just north of Charlotte. You will be on Sunset Road; follow it west to Beatties Ford Road. Turn right, and head north for 4.8 miles to Hopewell Presbyterian Church. At the church turn left on Sample road. Latta Plantation Park is at the end of Sample Road.

Mint Museum, Nature Museum and Spirit Square

Newly Minted

There is a link between Conrad Reed's discovery of a 17-pound gold nugget (see Reed Gold Mine selection) and the Mint Museum of Art (known simply as the **Mint Museum**). The Piedmont region of North Carolina became the first major gold-producing area in the United States. After a slow start, gold mining around the Charlotte area gained momentum, and at one time there were between 75 and 100 gold mines in a 20-mile radius. Responding to this influx of gold, Congress in 1836 opened the first branch of the Philadelphia Mint in Charlotte. It is this old mint, relocated, reconstructed and substantially enlarged that houses the Mint Museum.

The Charlotte Mint operated until the Civil War. During that conflict it served briefly as a Confederate Army Headquarters and then a U.S. military post. By 1932 this Federal style edifice was threatened with demolition. A group of Charlotte citizens raised money to buy the materials comprising the building, and it was re-constructed on Randolph Road. In 1936 it became chartered as the Mint Museum of Art, the first such museum in the Carolinas.

At the beginning the collection consisted of borrowed work, but over the years an acquisition program and substantial donations created an impressive permanent collection. In 1985 the Dalton Wing opened; its 24 exhibition galleries (as well as libraries and other work areas) tripled the size of the museum.

Built as a mint during the peak of the Piedmont gold rush and later used as Confederate headquarters, this reconstructed building is now the Mint Museum of Art.

The donation of the Dalton Collection has enlarged every area and era of American and European art in the museum's collection.

With this new space the European and American art at the museum has been reinstalled with the unifying theme being the artist's role in society. Thematic groupings of artworks illustrate both continuity and change among artists. The way artists were viewed critically, the patron system, the training artists received and their innovative approaches to their discipline are all part of the new approach to present art to viewers on many different levels.

The Mint Museum has a noted collection of pre-Columbian art, European and American pottery and porcelain, regional crafts, as well as Piedmont historic artifacts and coins and currency of the Carolinas. Each year it hosts a series of changing exhibitions on national tour and related education programs.

The Mint Museum's galleries and Museum Shop are open 10:00 A.M. to 10:00 P.M. on Tuesday, 10:00 A.M. to 5:00 P.M. Wednesday–Friday, and 1:00 to 6:00 P.M. on Sundays (closed on Mondays and state holidays). There is an admission charge.

Another Charlotte museum that offers an educational yet fun afternoon for families with children age seven and below is the **Nature Museum** located next to Freedom Park. This hands-on natural science center has a puppet theater, an imaginative treehouse, a sea-life touch room, a center where youngsters can interact with live animals, exhibits on space science and earth science, plus a planetarium (this is not geared specifically to the younger set; it appeals to all ages). There is also a wildlife observation deck, a wildflower garden and a nature trail. You can literally spend hours for a nominal fee. The Nature Museum is open June–August on Monday–Friday 9:00 A.M. to 6:00 P.M., Saturday from 9:00 A.M. to 5:00 P.M., and Sundays 1:00 to 5:00 P.M. Closed on Thanksgiving and Christmas.

When you are in Charlotte you should also check the performance and workshop schedule at **Spirit Square**, the downtown center for the arts. They have a nine-month performance season plus a wide range of classes and workshops. Spirit Square also houses several art galleries and studios for sculptors, ceramists, weavers, painters and other artists. Spirit Square is on North Tryon Street between 6th and 7th. Directly across the street is Discovery Place (see selection).

Directions: For the Mint Museum, from I-77 take the John Belk Freeway, I-277, and exit onto Independence Boulevard. Turn right on Hawthorne Lane (first traffic light), then turn left on Fourth Street, which becomes Randolph Road. The Mint is at 2730 Randolph Road. For the Nature Museum, from I-77 take Woodlawn Road, then turn left on Park Road, right on Princeton

Road and left on Sterling Road. The Nature Museum is at 1658 Sterling Road.

AROUND CHARLOTTE

Carowinds

Winds of Whirl

Carowinds is one of 31 major theme parks in North America. This recreational concept was launched in 1955 with the opening of Disneyland. Although some parks are independently operated most are part of entertainment groups. Five park concessions— Walt Disney Productions, Six Flags Incorporated, Anheuser-Busch, Sea World Enterprises and Kings Entertainment Company—operate a total of 20 parks.

Carowinds is one of the six parks operated by Kings Entertainment Company. This 77-acre park near Charlotte straddles the state line between North and South Carolina. The park's ten theme areas present the cultural heritage of the Carolinas, but along with regional entertainment, crafts and cooking are more than 30 amusement rides. Thrill-seekers head for Thunder Road, an old wooden roller coaster, the quadruple-looping Carolina Cyclone coaster, the 360-degree looping-Frenzoid and the 45-foot drop of the popular White Water Falls. For those who like their fun a tad tamer there is the 320-foot high Carowinds Skytower, a stern-wheeler, monorail and an antique 1923 carousel with 68 hand-carved horses. Just added at Carowinds is the Riptide Reef theme area with 6-acres of water attractions including a 700,000 gallon wave pool.

There are three areas especially for young visitors—Hanna Barbera Land, Smurf Island and a mini-water play area called Waterworks. Cartoon characters greet and entertain the kids. Nine rides have been scaled down for the small set, and there are even a few like the balloon race and boat float that parents can enjoy with their children. The 1.3-acre Smurf Island is a participatory play area. Kids can climb a giant rope or try one of two huge tubular slides. There are trails beside the two waterfalls and a hidden Smurf Village.

Each year the entertainment changes, but the park regularly presents seven shows ranging from country music and bluegrass to Broadway. The cartoon characters add their own whimsical charm, and noted artists are showcased on summer weekends in the 8,200-seat outdoor Palladium amphitheater. New in 1988 was a 180-degree theater showing Omni films.

Thrill-seekers hang upside-down in the Giant "Frenzoid" at Carowinds, a 77-acre amusement park 10 miles south of Charlotte.

Within the park there are over 60 food, game and merchandise shops. Carowinds is open on weekends from mid-March to June when it opens daily except Fridays. In late August it returns to its weekend-only schedule and continues until mid-October when it closes for the season. Plan to spend the day. The park opens at 10:00 A.M. and stays open until 8:00 P.M., except summer Saturdays when it stays open until 10:00 P.M. There is a parking fee and a single price admission that includes everything except special shows in the Palladium. For information call (800)822-4428.

Directions: Take I-77 south out of Charlotte for ten miles, then take Exit 90, Carowinds Boulevard exit, to the park entrance.

Fieldcrest Cannon Mills

Not Run of the Mill

You can get a fascinating behind-the-scenes look at how **Fieldcrest Cannon Mills** turns out the bed linen we all take for granted when you tour Plant 4 at Kannapolis and watch raw cotton fiber and synthetic polyester processed into yarn then woven into fabric.

The 600 non-union employees in Plant 4 produce an average 750,000 square yards of sheeting in a seven-day work week. One of the most surprising discoveries is how much of the work is done by machines. Workers watch and make sure the machines do not malfunction.

The first step in the process is the uniflox machine which picks up and cleans small bits of cotton, removing even the smallest trace of metal. The raw cotton then travels through a tube to the second floor and the second cleaning step. This involves a beating process to remove lumps and debris. The brush rollers also eliminate impurities before the fiber feeds onto a carding machine and the straightening begins. Up to this point the raw cotton and the polyester are kept separate, but during a series of three drawings the two fibers are blended.

The repeated drawings pull the fibers, straightening and stretching them into yarn. The combing step creates a silky effect. Next the fiber is fed onto a bobbin, a step which takes roughly three hours. From the roving bobbin the fiber is taken to the spinning room. At this point the fiber is twisted to give it strength and then threaded onto another bobbin before being fed onto a cone at a rate of 1,200 yards per minute.

The warping machine is particularly interesting to observe. It looks as if it's raining sideways as the fibers are exceedingly fine and move rapidly, processing 700 yards per minute. To give the fabric strength it is put in a starch solution, although after the material has been woven the starch is washed out. At Fieldcrest Cannon weaving is state of the art. Air jet looms blow the filling back and forth across the loom. Plant 4 has two different kinds of looms, one weaving muslin sheeting and the other percale sheeting.

If you think this would be the place to find bargains in bed linens you're right. Cannon Village, a collection of manufacturing outlet stores designed to create a Williamsburg image, has a Cannon Bed & Bath Outlet. This is only one of the more than 35 shops including items from such well-known names as Manhattan, London Fog, Fostoria, Aileen, Van Heusen, Bass, Jonathan Logan, L'Eggs, Hanes, Waccamaw and others. The quaint village also has restaurants and quick-food emporiums.

To arrange a free guided tour of the factory or obtain a map of the shops of Cannon Village stop at the visitors center. Before leaving the center wander through the exhibits detailing the history of Cannon Mills which started in 1887. The Kannapolis plant opened in 1906. The shops are open Monday–Saturday from 9:00 A.M. to 8:00 P.M. and Sunday 1:00 to 6:00 P.M. Fieldcrest Cannon's

Plant 4 can be toured Monday–Friday at 9:00 and 10:15 A.M., and 1:00 P.M. This can usually be done on a walk-in basis, but if you want to make reservations call (704)938-3200. Children under 12 are not permitted to take the tour.

Directions: From I-85 take Kannapolis Exit 63 and follow signs to Cannon Village.

James K. Polk Memorial

Polk's Peak

In 1785, a year after Jane and Samuel Polk built a small rustic wooden cabin on the 250-acre Mecklenburg County farm they received as a wedding present from Jane's father, their son James Knox Polk was born. He only spent his early years on this homestead near Charlotte, as the family moved to Tennessee when he was 11. As a young man Polk returned to North Carolina to attend the state university, graduating as Latin salutatorian, excelling in both the classics and mathematics. Later Polk turned to the law and to politics.

James Polk was the first dark-horse candidate for president. His administration added 800,000 square miles to the United States with the annexation of Texas, the acquisition of the California Territory and the settlement of the Oregon boundary. Despite Polk's accomplishments few Americans know much about the country's eleventh president. A visit to his birthplace, now the **Polk Memorial**, fills in the major details of his life. At the visitor center a film on his life and museum exhibits help answer the questions "Who is Polk?"

An old two-story log house of the period was moved here from another part of Mecklenburg County. The Polk family undoubtedly started with a smaller cabin than this. The pine and walnut furniture represent the style found here in the late 1700s and early 1800s; there's even a plain wooden cradle like the one young Polk might have slept in. The authentically garbed staff shows visitors around the homestead while talking about the daily routine of the Polks, their five children and five slaves.

Outbuildings include the kitchen and an old barn. There is also a work area for country woodworking. On the first Saturday in November Polk's birthday is celebrated by a day of living history at the homestead.

There is no charge to visit the Polk Memorial, which is open April–October on Monday–Saturday from 9:00 A.M. to 5:00 P.M. and Sunday 1:00 to 5:00 P.M. Hours November–March are Tuesday–Saturday 10:00 A.M. to 4:00 P.M. and Sunday 1:00 to 4:00 P.M.

Directions: Take I-77 south of Charlotte then turn left on Route 51, then right on Route 521 to Pineville, roughly three miles south of the Charlotte city limits.

148

Philip Morris Cabarrus Manufacturing Center

They Still Call For Philip Morris

Imagine cigarettes encircling the earth not once but 120 times, and you'll have an idea just how many cigarettes are produced each year at **Philip Morris Company's Cabarrus Manufacturing Center**, the world's most technologically advanced cigarette manufacturing center. Their annual output is 60 billion cigarettes, including what is now ranked as the world's most popular cigarette brand, Marlboro.

The 1.8 million-square foot manufacturing center sprawls across the company's 2,100-acre site. The natural environment has been carefully nurtured, and the grounds are a haven for wildlife, including the Canada geese, which now stay here year-round. Much of the grounds have been kept in their natural wooded state.

Free motorized tours are given of the plant Monday through Friday, hourly from 9:00 A.M. to 3:00 P.M. You'll listen through earphones to the guides explain the manufacturing process as you travel by cart around the precision machinery that produces and packages the cigarettes. Each year the plant processes more than 120 million pounds of tobacco leaf, much of which is purchased in North Carolina. Despite the automated production process, approximately 1,600 employees work at the Cabarrus Manufacturing Center, which began production in 1983.

The Philip Morris Company has amassed an extensive collection of contemporary North Carolina folk art at the Cabarrus center. Quilters will be impressed with the world's largest hanging quilted tapestry, which was hand-stitched in Franklin. Paintings by 40 of the state's leading artists are displayed along with crafted items like baskets and pottery. Visitors frequently spend a lot of time in front of the more than 1,500 postcards from every North Carolina region trying to pick out their favorites. Art tours are given on Tuesdays and Thursdays at 9:30 A.M. and 2:30 P.M.

The Cabarrus Manufacturing Center is closed on weekends and during the Christmas and summer shutdown periods as well as other major holidays.

Directions: The Cabarrus Manufacturing Center is 20 miles north of Charlotte in Concord. From I-85 turn right on W.T. Harris Boulevard and then turn left on Route 29.

Reed Gold Mine

Gold Stones

Horace Greeley said "Go west, young man." Actually it wasn't Greeley who penned those immortal lines but rather John Soule, a reporter in Terra Haute, Indiana. Greeley then used them in a *New York Tribune* editorial, and they were forever attributed to him. But whoever the author, the advice might well have been "go south," because the first gold strike was in North Carolina not California. Today you can learn about gold mining on a tour of the **Reed Gold Mine** north of Charlotte, near Concord.

Strike is not an accurate description of the first authenticated find; a slow take might express it better. In 1799 while playing hooky from Sunday service, 12-year-old Conrad Reed found a large yellow rock. His dad, John Reed, tried to get it identified but failed. The 17-pound rock served as a doorstop for three years before Reed sold it for $3.50—one tenth of its $3,600 value. When the jeweler tried to buy more rocks the family realized their value and began searching for gold stones along the bank of Little Meadow Creek.

By 1803 Reed was ready to start the first extensive mining operation in the country. He formed a partnership with three local men who supplied the equipment and manpower to begin placer, or surface, mining. During their first season a 28-pound nugget was uncovered. The Reed Mine was a success even though it was only worked in late summer when the stream was dry and the crops were planted. By 1824 it was one of the three major mines in North Carolina, and by the late 1820s an estimated $200,000 worth of ore had been unearthed.

Reed was slow to switch from placer to hard-rock mining beneath the surface. This was a more expensive method, and Reed was reluctant to embark on it. But by 1854 there were 15 separate shafts. These shafts were connected by tunnels, some 500 feet long. When you visit you will be able to explore a restored section of one of the old mine tunnels. Be sure to wear walking shoes and bring a light sweater as it is 40–60 degrees even on hot summer days. The rock you'll see is volcanic greenstone shot with the milky white quartz. It was within the veins of quartz that the miners found flakes or specks of gold.

The miners, candles affixed to their hats, picked, shoveled and dynamited the hard rock. The rock was transported to the surface by means of ore carts and iron buckets, called "kibbles" (examples of both can be seen on your tour). While you are down in the mine look up the 150-foot Engine Shaft, Reed's second largest shaft. Once you are back above ground take a walk up to the archeological ruins of the Engine House with a 30-ton iron boiler. From this vantage point you can look down the main shaft into the mine.

To separate the gold from the quartz they first used a Chilean mill then later adopted the more efficient stamp mill. You'll see a circular Chilean mill in front of the visitors center. This procedure used huge grinding stones to crush the ore into fine particles. The stamp mill operated more rapidly than its predecessor. The ten-stamp mill you'll see at Reed Mine is the only one still in existence east of the Mississippi and duplicates the one operating at Reed in 1895.

For an overall look at mining in North Carolina and at Reed in particular watch the orientation film shown in the visitors center before you take the guided tour around the mine. The center also has descriptive displays to familiarize you with both the methods and the tools of the trade. But experience really is the best teacher, and after your tour save time for trying your hand at panning for gold. A good miner could work through a pan in about 30 seconds, but you'll find it takes you a lot longer. It's a laborious process of shaking and dipping, working out the larger stones until you're left with fine sand and possibly small nuggets of gold. There is a small charge for this activity, but you get to keep any gold you find.

The Reed Gold Mine is a state historic site encompassing 822 acres. Little Meadow Creek is a picturesque stream winding through a wooded piedmont region. There is a ¾-mile nature trail as well as a picnic area. There is no admission charge. Hours April through October are Monday–Saturday 9:00 A.M. to 5:00 P.M. and Sunday 1:00 to 5:00 P.M. From November through March hours are Tuesday–Saturday 10:00 A.M. to 4:00 P.M. and Sunday 1:00 to 4:00 P.M. The Stamp Mill and panning area operate from April through October.

Directions: From I-85, heading north out of Charlotte, turn right on Route 601 south towards Concord; continue for 5 miles to the intersection with Route 200. Turn left on Route 200 and proceed 3 miles; then turn right on Reed Mine Road for approximately 2 miles. The entrance for Reed Gold Mine will be in your left.

Schiele Museum of Natural History and Planetarium

Don't Shield Yourself From This Experience

One of the most heavily visited museums in North Carolina is the **Schiele Museum of Natural History** in Gastonia. This award-winning "museum without walls" is one of the top ten regional museums in the United States and in 1989 gained a listing in the International Guide to Tourist Attractions. There are 19 buildings to explore on 30 acres, four exhibit halls, a new Earth-Space Science Center, the most complete North American land mammal collection in the southeast, a Catawba Indian village, planetarium, a backcountry pioneer family site, nature trails, an arboretum and much more. But a mere recital of all that Schiele offers doesn't capture the zest with which it is presented. The Schiele Museum staff is enthusiastic about their museum. They want to capture the attention of their visitors, and they do!

Innovative programs, a hands-on approach to museum going, and an impressive diversity make this an enjoyable destination. There is so much here you should watch the 20-minute introductory video to decide what you want to see. Plan to spend at least two hours at the Schiele Museum. One of the museum's most interesting exhibits, the **Hall of Earth and Man**, tackles the ambitious task of telling five billion years of history. A life-size model of the American mastodon, which roamed this region 8,000 years ago, is the first thing you'll see as you enter the hall. Mankind is shown both in drawings and in actual replicated archaeological specimens from the earliest times to the modern. The mental, physical and social differences of various stages of man's development are highlighted. The displays on our planet include an exhibit showing the position of the continents 250 million years ago compared with their present location. This section of the exhibit also displays a striking collection of gems, minerals and crystals.

School groups, workshops and special monthly programs utilize the re-created **Catawba Village**. If you are fortunate to drop by the museum while one of the special Southeastern Native American Studies Programs is in progress, usually the first weekend of every month, you can wander through this fascinating village. The oldest dwelling they have built is the Bark House, in the style the Catawbas were using when the European explorers first encountered the "People of the River." The staff built this wattle and daub structure using pre-historic tools, stone flake tools and axes. This is the only authentic reconstruction of a tribal village of the southeastern Catawba Indians. The village also has a pre-Revolutionary European-style Indian home, which you can compare with the backcountry pioneer cabin.

The **backcountry farm** is viewed as an experimental laboratory for studying history. In the log cabin you might observe volunteers preparing food in the open hearth or weaving. They might be working in the fields or in the blacksmith shop. Perhaps when you visit they will be enjoying a country dance or firing their muskets on a winter's eve to ward off evil spirits, a much-practiced 18th-century custom. Living history is presented at this farm the last weekend of every month.

A short nature trail, just $7/10$ of a mile, gives you a look at the interaction between man and the environment. One of Schiele's objectives is to give visitors a sense of their place in the natural world. This trail helps to achieve that aim. You can observe the changes from old agricultural fields, through levels of developing pines, until the area becomes a hardwood habitat. An old mill, springhouse and the pioneer farm are also along this trail.

While there is no charge to visit the Schiele Museum, planetarium shows do charge admission. Each month they have a different show. In 1990 the museum opened a new Earth/Space Science addition. This has a state-of-the-art Cinema 360 planetarium, which is an advance over the IMAX system. This $7-million addition doubles the size of the museum.

The Schiele Museum of Natural History is open Monday–Friday 9:00 A.M. to 5:00 P.M., Saturday and Sunday 1:00 to 5:00 P.M, closed on all legal holidays. Planetarium shows are given at 3:00 P.M. on Saturday and at 3:00 and 4:00 P.M. on Sundays. For information on special programs call (704)866-6900.

Directions: From I-85 take Gastonia Exit south on New Hope Road (Route 279) to Garrison Boulevard. The museum is at 1500 E. Garrison Boulevard in Gastonia.

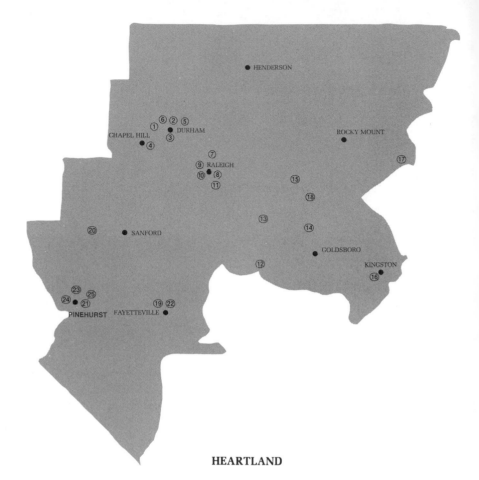

HEARTLAND

Durham and Chapel Hill Vicinity

1. Bennett Place
2. Duke Homestead
3. Duke University Chapel
4. Morehead Planetarium and The North Carolina Botanical Garden
5. Stagville Preservation Center
6. West Point on the Eno

Raleigh

7. Joel Lane House
8. Mordecai Historic Park
9. North Carolina Museum of Art, Museum of History and Museum of Natural Science
10. North Carolina State Capitol, State Legislative Building and Executive Mansion
11. Oakwood and Pullen Park

Goldsboro Vicinity

12. Bentonville Battleground
13. Carolina Pottery, Southland Estate Winery and Ava Gardner Museum
14. Charles B. Aycock Birthplace
15. Country Doctor Museum
16. Richard Caswell Memorial and CSS Ram Neuse
17. Tarboro Historic District
18. Tobacco Farm Life Museum

Fayetteville and Pinehurst Vicinity

19. Fort Bragg and Pope Air Force Base
20. House in the Horseshoe
21. Malcolm Blue Historical Farm
22. Museum of the Cape Fear
23. PGA World Golf Hall of Fame
24. Shaw House
25. Weymouth Woods Sandhills Nature Preserve and Weymouth Center

Heartland

Did you know that you can tour the Governor's Executive Mansion, study the stars from the Morehead Planetarium observatory or attend a tobacco auction on your own without the auspices of a group or organization? Individuals or families are welcome to tour these and all the other attractions in this book without traveling as part of an organized group. Traveling on your own allows you to arrange your own schedule, stop when you see a photo opportunity or quaint shop, and spend as long as you like, wherever you like.

The Heartland, which cuts a north-to-south swath through the middle of the state from border to border, is noted primarily for its importance as an historical area. The Joel Lane House, Mordecai Historical Park and the Museum of Cape Fear recall the establishment of the capital city of Raleigh and the state's early years. Homes (or memorials) of two early governors—Richard Caswell and Charles B. Aycock—and the 17th president, Andrew Johnson, are found in this region. Battlefields from both the American Revolution and the Civil War—House in the Horseshoe and Bentonville Battleground—are found here as well as Bennett Place, one of the sites where Southern troops surrendered at the end of the Civil War. The military's current strong presence is evident at Fort Bragg and Pope Air Force Base. The influence of tobacco on the whole history of the state is keenly appreciated at the Tobacco Museum of North Carolina and the Duke Homestead.

One of the region's most unexpected delights is Duke University. It looks as English as Oxford. The Chapel's soaring architectural lines lift visitors' eyes to the heavens, while the university's Morehead Planetarium literally maps the skies. Beauty is also found at your feet, in the Sarah P. Duke Gardens, a short walk from the Chapel.

DURHAM AND CHAPEL HILL VICINITY
Bennett Place

All Hope Surrendered

The largest troop surrender of the Civil War took place at the **Bennett farm** outside Durham, North Carolina on April 26, 1865.

More Confederates laid down their arms here than at Appomattox Court House, Virginia, where General Lee's army had surrendered a few weeks earlier. Nearly all the soldiers from the Carolinas, Georgia and Florida were mustered out and issued paroles after the Bennett Place surrender. Two smaller surrenders took place before the entire Confederate army was disbanded, one on May 4 in Alabama and the last on May 26 in New Orleans.

In early March, General Joseph Johnston had attempted to stop Sherman's northward march at Bentonville, North Carolina (see Bentonville Battleground selection). After General Lee surrendered, Confederate President Jefferson Davis gave his reluctant approval to Johnston's meeting with Sherman. Where they met was the Bennett farm, seven miles from the Confederate lines at Hillsborough and six miles from the Union lines at Durham Station. It was fortunate President Davis allowed the meeting as soldiers from Johnston's army were already deserting, and Sherman's army still had roughly 90,000 men.

Johnston met Sherman three times at the farm of James and Nancy Bennitt (the correct spelling of the family name). Their meetings did not always proceed smoothly. On one occasion Sherman poured himself a drink without offering one to Johnston or John C. Breckinridge, the Confederate army secretary of war and former U.S. vice president under James Buchanan from 1857 to 1861. Breckinridge, a Tennessee gentleman, said that Sherman was a "hog, yes, sir, a hog."

But despite provocation, Sherman, realizing Johnston's surrender was not necessary for the cessation of fighting, attempted to offer reasonable terms. Just before their meeting on April 17 Sherman received a telegram informing him of the assassination of President Lincoln. At the first meeting Johnston argued for political as well as military terms in the surrender agreement. When they met again the following day, Sherman did offer a liberal armistice which Jefferson Davis approved but which officials in Washington rejected.

A third meeting was not originally planned because Jefferson Davis opposed the more rigid terms under which General Lee had surrendered his army. Federal officials had ordered Sherman to impose these terms in the aftermath of Lincoln's death. Johnston, realizing the futility and tragedy of continuing the war, disobeyed Davis's orders and met with Sherman on April 26. The surrender they signed dealt exclusively with military terms and ended the war in the Carolinas, Georgia and Florida. Johnston's determination to end the now pointless struggle saved North Carolina from the devastation suffered by her neighboring southern states.

It is fortunate that Theodore Davis, an artist who traveled with the Union army, was on hand to sketch the Bennitt farm because in 1921 a fire destroyed the farmhouse and kitchen. From Davis's sketches and early photographs, the farm has been reconstructed. There is no original furniture, of course, but the pieces are of the period.

A 15-minute audiovisual program at the visitor center tells the story of the surrender. There are exhibits on the years before and during the war, showing how it affected North Carolina.

Bennett Place State Historic Site is open at no charge April through October on Monday–Saturday 9:00 A.M. to 5:00 P.M. and Sunday 1:00 to 5:00 P.M.. From November through March hours are Tuesday–Saturday 10:00 A.M. to 4:00 P.M. and Sunday 1:00 to 4:00 P.M. There is also a North Carolina wildflower trail at Bennett Place.

Directions: Take I-85 south past Durham to Exit 172 (traveling north on I-85 take Exit 170). Follow signs to site at 4409 Bennett Memorial Road.

Duke Homestead

Brightleaf-Bright Future

Though the Civil War ruined many a Confederate, Washington Duke triumphed over adversity. In his forties and twice a widower, Duke planted his first crop of tobacco shortly before the war began. His plans to begin manufacturing tobacco products were interrupted when he was conscripted into the Confederate army.

About the same time the last major Confederate force surrendered in April 1865, at a farm not far from his own (see Bennett Place selection), Duke was released from Union imprisonment. Totally without funds, he walked 135 miles to his farm near Durham. There he found the Federal troops had stolen everything but two blind miles and a wagon load of tobacco. They had also acquired a taste for the brightleaf tobacco of the area. So, at age 45, Duke started over, first growing, then processing tobacco. In a log cabin on his farm he started a factory to produce smoking tobacco he called Pro Bono Publico—"for the public good."

The public certainly thought it was good. So successful were Washington Duke and his sons that they soon expanded to three tobacco processing factories at the farm. In 1869 the eldest son, Brodie Duke, opened his own factory in Durham, and by 1874 the entire business was moved to town. In 1884 the first mechanized cigarette-rolling machine was turning out 250 cigarettes a minute compared to four a minute by hand. The Duke family business became the largest tobacco company in the world.

At the **Duke Homestead** you get a good idea of both the extent and the nature of the business. At the newly renovated visitors

Tobacco demonstration at Duke Homestead near Durham. The first cigarette-rolling machine (1884) helped to make the Duke family business the largest tobacco company in the world.

center and museum, opened in late 1989, you can see a 22-minute video on tobacco farming. From there you may explore on your own. The first factory has been reconstructed, but the original third factory still stands. You'll see a tobacco packhouse, a curing barn and the family's six-room house as it was in the 1870s.

Throughout the year special programs help bring the past alive. The homestead sponsors Farm Days that give visitors demonstrations of farming methods and household work. In July there is a curing barn party, in October a mock tobacco auction and during the Christmas season there are candlelight tours of the decorated house.

Any time of the year you can take a 45-minute guided tour of the homestead; you must be escorted to get inside the buildings. The farmhouse is furnished with simple items. The straw mattress on the downstairs bed suggests the expression "hit the hay." One of the rooms was called the old folks room as it was used by the older generation as well as for the family dining room. The kitchen is next to the dining room. Some of the utensils are folk tools, like the homemade toothbrush, a black or sweet gum twig that was chewed until frayed and then used with baking soda to clean teeth. Efforts at decoration include lace-trimmed curtains hanging from tobacco stocks and a plaster wall in the entryway to impress guests.

The Duke name is omnipresent around Durham, as the family funded churches, hospitals and colleges including Trinity, which became Duke University. At this farmstead you'll see where the Dukes got their start. The homestead is open at no charge April through October, Monday–Saturday 9:00 A.M. to 5:00 P.M. and Sunday 1:00 to 5:00 P.M. From November through March hours are 10:00 A.M. to 4:00 P.M. Tuesday–Saturday and 1:00 to 4:00 P.M. on Sundays.

Directions: Take I-85 to the Durham area then take the Guess Road, NC 157, north. Then turn right on Duke Homestead Road for the state historic site.

Duke University Chapel

Uplifting!

Tourists have a tendency to seek out churches, ancestral homes, gardens and museums when traveling far from home and to ignore enticing attractions with a foreign flavor in their own communities. If you are guilty of this lapse, then think of the **Duke University Chapel** as a little bit of Old England and go see this towering cathedral that calls up the Gothic majesty of Great Britain.

In April 1925 James Buchanan Duke was walking through the

woods around Durham searching for a suitable site on which to establish a university. Duke said, "I want the central building to be a church, a great towering church which will dominate all the surrounding buildings, because such an edifice would be bound to have a profound influence on the spiritual life of the young men and women who come here." The Chapel, built on the spot Duke selected, fulfilled his hopes; it has been the center of the university since its dedication on June 2, 1935.

It is a stunning architectural achievement. Built of North Carolina stone its soaring tower, spires, buttresses, pointed arch and ribbed, vaulted ceiling are characteristic of English Gothic design. The Chapel is not a copy of any European church, but the tower was modeled after the Bell Harry Tower at Canterbury Cathedral.

You should pick up a brochure from the chapel hostesses stationed just inside the door, then return to the outside to view the east doors of the main entrance. The massive oak doors have wrought-iron trim. Above the portal are three Indiana limestone statues of early Methodist evangelists and religious leaders. Seven additional statues in the doors' portal include both religious leaders and what have been termed "southern saints"— Thomas Jefferson, Robert E. Lee and Sidney Lanier, the "Poet of the South."

Once inside the door, you'll enter the Chapel's narthex, or vestibule. The trinity design of three circles over the exterior doors is repeated over the interior doors in stained glass. There are also six stained-glass windows in the narthex depicting women from the Old Testament. From the narthex you'll begin walking down the nave, or central corridor, of the Chapel. From this vantage point you will have a splendid perspective of the soaring lines of the interior.

Moving to the left and proceeding clockwise around the Chapel you will see the 77 stained-glass windows depicting more than 800 New Testament figures. At the end of the left aisle are the gates of the Memorial Chapel, where members of the Duke family are buried. The unusual window treatment in this small chapel is called grisaille, a French design using pastel colors on gray-white glass. Entombed in the Carrara marble sarcophagi are Washington Duke, Benjamin Newton Duke and James Buchanan Duke (see Duke Homestead selection). Note also the carved figures over the altar and two small organs.

To the right of the Memorial Chapel are steps leading to the crypt. This subterranean chamber is simply designed with lead grilles and deep purple glass windows. In addition to Duke family members, others who made Duke University their lives' work are buried here.

Climbing the stairs will lead you back up to the altar area. On the left are choir stalls, intricately carved with statues of early martyrs. Above the altar is a representation of the boy Jesus with the elders in the Temple, then Jesus before Pilate and finally Jesus entombed. This is flanked by four statues of saints. An Aeolian organ is located on either side of the chancel behind pipes and an oak screen. There are a myriad of small decorative touches to be observed. Look carefully at the lectern, pulpit and the canopy that surmounts it.

Looking back from the altar towards the Chapel entrance you'll see the Benjamin N. Duke Memorial Organ. This immense organ has 5,000 speaking pipes with five keyboards. It was built in Holland by Dirk Andries Flentrop, then dismantled and shipped to the Duke Chapel where it was rebuilt. It was dedicated on Founder's Day, December 12, 1976.

If you climb or ride the elevator to the belfry you can see the 50-bell carillon. The largest bell weighs roughly 11,200 pounds, and the smallest is only ten pounds. While you are in the Chapel's upper reaches try to visit the observation area, open during the school term weekdays 2:00 to 4:00 P.M. and some Sunday afternoons. The view of the campus from here is striking.

The Chapel is open daily at no charge from 8:00 A.M. to 11:00 P.M. during the school year and 8:00 A.M. to 5:00 P.M. at other times. It is closed on Christmas Day. There is an ecumenical worship service Sunday at 11:00 A.M. During the spring and fall terms there is a carillonneur recital weekdays at 5:00 P.M. and 3:30 P.M. on Sundays. For dates of other recitals throughout the school year or additional information call (919)684-2572.

A short path from the Chapel leads to the **Sarah P. Duke Gardens**. Sarah Duke was the wife of Benjamin, Washington Duke's middle son. She financed the gardens that Dr. Frederic M. Hanes created for Duke University's West Campus in 1934. Four years later her daughter, Mary Duke Biddle, commissioned a terraced garden as a memorial to her mother. There are 20 acres of developed garden plus another 35 acres of pine forest with plantings of Asian trees and shrubs in the meadows and around a small lake. In the spring the garden is a blaze of color with hundreds of azaleas; then in late May more than 300 rose bushes in the circular garden begin blooming. There is also a wisteria pergola, a rock garden, the Hanes iris garden, the terrace and the H.L. Blomquist garden of native plants. The gardens are open daily from 8:00 A.M. to dark.

While in the Durham area you may also want to visit the **Museum of Life and Science**, which has plenty of hands-on activities for youngsters. Attractions here include a science arcade area that makes a game out of such complex subjects as force fields and gravity, a geology and aerospace exhibit, a butterfly garden, a barnyard, a reptile collection and a wildflower trail. A small

161

train takes you around the 50-acre sanctuary sheltering bears, wolves, deer, buffalo, cougar and other North Carolina wildlife. There is also a prehistoric walking trail with life-size models of dinosaurs and a science park where children may dig in a giant sand box and climb around a fort, castle or cottage. Hours are 10:00 A.M. to 5:00 P.M. Monday–Saturday and 1:00 to 5:00 P.M. on Sunday. During the summer the museum stays open until 6:00 P.M. The museum is off I-85 at 433 Murray Avenue. Admission is charged.

Directions: From Raleigh take I-40 to Durham, or take I-85, which also takes you into the city. If you take I-40 then head north at the intersection with the East West Expressway. Then turn left on Route 15/501. If you are traveling on I-85 take the Route 15-501 exit south to Duke University Campus and follow the signs to the Chapel and garden.

Morehead Planetarium and the North Carolina Botanical Garden

Nature's Bounty

Two special facilities at Chapel Hill offer the opportunity to appreciate the wonders of nature. You can reach for the stars at **Morehead Planetarium** or stroll a wooded path amid the delicacy and beauty of native plants and wildflowers at the **North Carolina Botanical Garden**.

The planetarium was John Motley Morehead's gift to his alma mater for the children of North Carolina. Since it opened in 1949 more than three million visitors have enjoyed the planetarium's educational and entertaining astronomy programs. The planetarium shows are presented at the Star Theater, which was used as a NASA training center. Astronauts from Project Mercury through the Apollo-Soyuz mission studied celestial recognition and stellar navigation at this facility, and *Star Trek's* Captain Kirk, aka William Shatner, has visited.

The domed 330-seat Star Theater is one of only a few planetariums in the country to have a Zeiss Model VI projector and one of the few in the world to have a completely automated Zeiss system. This powerful projector can show some 8,900 stars down to magnitude 6.5. It can also show 17 star clusters and nebulae. The planetarium has Friday night "Sky Rambles," featuring the stars seen in the night sky and many special features on subjects like the planets, energy and space exploration and 35mm films such as *Genesis* and *To Fly*.

The **Morehead Observatory** at the top of the planetarium has a regular series of Friday Guest Nights. Thirty-five lucky visitors are given free tickets to observe through the 24-inch Cassegrain reflector telescope. For tickets write Guest Nights, Department of Physics and Astronomy, Phillips Hall, University of North Carolina, Chapel Hill, NC 27599-3480.

The planetarium also has a Copernican Orrery, the only one of its kind in the world. Named after Nicholaus Copernicus who conceived the theory that the sun was the center of the solar system, not the earth, this 35-foot walk-in model of the solar system shows the six closest planets in orbit around the sun. By pushing a button you can set the planets and their satellites in proper relative motion and listen to an explanation of the progress of the planets across the sky. The term "Orrery" comes from the Fourth Earl of Orrery, for whom the first precision, mechanical model of the solar system was created. The great Austrian composer Franz Joseph Haydn also had an orrery.

Morehead Planetarium is worth noting architecturally and artistically. The walnut-paneled rotunda is ringed by 16 monolithic columns of green Ozark marble. Works by Rembrandt, Gainsborough, Rembrandt Peale and other artists adorn the walls. John Motley Morehead collected clocks, and the rotunda's 13-foot pendulum model is a giant replica of his office clock. Unlike most clocks, this one ticks every two seconds and has a different English cathedral peal each day of the week. Most of the art displayed in the North Gallery are temporary exhibits, but the 1720 tapestry made by the Reydams Studio of Bruxelles is always on display. The planetarium also houses the offices and meeting rooms of the Morehead Foundation. The foundation administers scholarship programs both in the United States and England. The undergraduate program was originally patterned after the Rhodes Scholarships at Oxford.

The Morehead Planetarium is open daily except December 24 and 25. Hours are 12:30 to 5:00 P.M. and 6:30 to 9:30 P.M. Sunday through Friday and 10:00 A.M. to 5:00 P.M. and 6:30 to 9:00 P.M. on Saturday. Admission to the exhibits is free, but there is a charge for the main feature, for films, and for "Sky Rambles" programs.

As you leave be sure to see the Sundial Rose Garden in the center of the public parking lot north of the planetarium. The 35-foot diameter terrazzo dais is ringed with the words, "It is always morning somewhere in the world," and "Today is yesterday's tomorrow." Hybrid roses grow around the sundial, and a plaque has a description of roses written by Helen Keller, who overcame the twin handicaps of blindness and deafness.

Immediately east of the planetarium is the four-acre **Coker Arboretum**, a facility of the **North Carolina Botanical Garden**. The Arboretum was begun in 1903 by botany professor Dr. W.C. Coker and displays specimens of native and exotic trees and shrubs including dwarf conifers and broad-leaved evergreens.

Colorful annuals and perennials provide seasonal interest. Flower lovers will also want to visit the North Carolina Botanical Garden two miles south of the center of the University of North Carolina campus. Around the Totten Center office complex there are display gardens and special collections of wildflowers, ferns, herbs and aquatic plants. Another garden shows examples of major plant groups. The habitat collections include native plants of the mountains, coastal plains and sandhills regions of the southeastern United States presented in simulated natural settings.

The trail system across Laurel Hill Road from the display gardens has almost two miles of woodland walks and self-guided trails. The lower self-guided trail takes about 40–50 minutes to explore, the upper trail, between 60–70 minutes.

The Botanical Garden offers daily plant sales, public interest programs, trips and events. Ask for information on current activities at the entrance to the garden. The Botanical Garden display area is open Monday–Friday 8:00 A.M. to 5:00 P.M.. From mid-March to mid-November it is open 10:00 A.M. to 5:00 P.M. on Saturdays and 2:00 to 5:00 P.M. on Sundays. During this period there is a tour given every Saturday at 10:30 A.M. and Sunday at 3:00 P.M. The nature trails and Coker Arboretum are open daily during daylight hours throughout the year.

Directions: From Raleigh take I-40 west to Chapel Hill Exit 273B, Route 54. Take Route 54, Raleigh Road, to the University of North Carolina campus. Turn right on Raleigh Street, then left on E. Franklin and left again into the parking lot for the Morehead Planetarium and the Coker Arboretum. The North Carolina Botanical Garden is on Laurel Hill Road, south of its intersection with US 15/501 NC 54 Bypass.

Stagville Preservation Center

Learning to Save the Past

The **Stagville Preservation Center** is America's first state-owned facility for teaching and developing historic preservation. Its staff tries to find solutions to the technical stumbling blocks that bedevil historic preservation efforts. Workshops, lectures and preservation-related courses are offered, often in cooperation with institutions with similar goals like Colonial Williamsburg, Old Salem and Tryon Palace Restorations (see selection).

The Center offices are in the **Bennehan House**. Stagville Plantation was named for Thomas and Judith Stagg, who acquired the property in 1757. Thirty years later Richard Bennehan bought the property from widowed Judith Stagg and constructed the 1½-

story house that now forms the east wing of the Bennehan House. The two-story west wing was added in 1799.

Richard Bennehan became one of the largest landowners in the Carolina Piedmont. His estate passed to his only son who died in 1847. The land was then inherited by his grandson Paul Cameron. By 1860 the Cameron family owned almost 30,000 acres, one of the largest holdings in the state. They had nearly 900 slaves working their Piedmont plantations.

Since the house serves as a working center many of the rooms have not been furnished. But the dining room and the parlor, where Richard Bennehan's daughter, Rebecca, was married, are filled with early 19th-century pieces. The house itself is used as a teaching tool, and in some rooms the restoration is incomplete so that you can see the skeleton of the house. Upstairs you can see a model of Stagville Plantation representing the years between 1825 and 1860.

The plantation outbuildings are long gone, but you can walk up to see the old graveyard. There is also a stable and a tobacco barn. Just past these work areas are on-going excavations of old slave cabins.

A second section of the Stagville Center at nearby **Horton Grove** includes four original slave houses, a barn built in 1860 and a cottage dating from the Revolutionary era. Richard Bennehan purchased this land from William Horton in 1823, two years before Bennehan's death. The slave houses are believed to be among the few rural two-story, four-family slave houses still standing. They were built by slaves during the 1850s when there were 80 to 100 slaves working this area. Each house had four rooms, 17' x 17'. One slave family lived in each of the rooms. Some of the building practices used on these timber frame houses date back to the Middle Ages. Notice the use of wooded pegs to join the timbers and the insertion of brick infill, called nogging. The exterior has board and batten siding.

A divining rod, or forked-shaped stick, found in the walls of one of the slave cabins was used, according to West African tradition, to make sure that the guardian spirit that protected the house would not be forgotten when the family moved. A less benign discovery was that of a walking cane wedged between two sections of the wall in the west wing of the Bennehan house. The cane's east/west position may have indicated a curse put on the family by a conjurer.

Skilled slave labor was used to build what was once one of the largest agricultural buildings in North Carolina. When the barn was finished at the end of the summer in 1860, Paul Cameron called it "the best stables ever built in Orange" County. Slave crews cut huge trees to hew the timber beams for the barn, some of which are 60 feet long and nearly a foot deep. The barn has a 135-foot framework. This barn marks an end of an era. Within months of its completion the Civil War devastated the great plantations of the south.

Also at Horton Grove is **Horton Cottage**, a 1776 house typical of those built by pre-plantation yeoman farmers. It is built with wide, thick, pit-sawn, dove-tailed planks. More than a hundred years of history are encompassed at this site. The Stagville Preservation Center is open at no charge Monday–Friday from 9:00 A.M. to 4:00 P.M.

Directions: From I-85 take Business 501, Roxboro Road, northbound 1.3 miles to State Route 1004, Old Oxford Highway. Turn right on Route 1004 and drive seven miles northeast. Look for "Stagville Preservation Center" sign and turn right. Go to end of drive where Richard Bennehan House is located. To reach Horton Grove from the Bennehan House, go right on Old Oxford Highway for .6 miles. Then make a left on Jock Road for .2 miles. The Horton Cottage and Slave Houses will be on your left and **Paul Cameron's Barn** on your right.

West Point On the Eno

The Old Mill Stream

West Point on the Eno is not a Carolina military academy; in fact, it has no military association whatsoever. It is a 371-acre city park stretching for two miles along the Eno River. Its name reflects its geographic location. Situated at the most western point on the mail route from Raleigh to Roxboro, the mill, the community and the post office were called West Point.

The **West Point Mill**, which has been reconstructed and is once again operational, was the most prosperous and the longest operating of the 32 mills along the Eno. The mill became the focal point of a 300-family community six miles north of Durham at one of the best fording spots on the river. In addition to the gristmill, West Point had a saw mill, cotton gin, still, blacksmith shop and general store. The gristmill operated from 1778 to 1942, when the dam broke. After the mill building collapsed in 1973, it was rebuilt with stones, timber and equipment from other mills along the river. Today you can buy stone-ground meal and flour at the mill's store.

In the 1840s West Point Mill was owned by John Cabe McCown, who built the Greek Revival farmhouse that you can tour at West Point on the Eno. McCown lived here roughly 30 years, then Presley J. Mangum, a Durham postmaster bought the property. The Mangum family was in residence until 1968. This continued occupancy helped preserve the house and contents. Much of the original woodwork has been retained including the wide planks used for the heart-of-pine walls and the mantels. The house is interpreted from the 1890 period, and many of the furnishings belonged to the Mangum family.

The garden surrounding the house is not as extensive as it was when the Mangums lived here, but it does have perennials, herbs, roses and flowering shrubs. Like most people in this area, the Mangums also planted tobacco. In the late 1800s they built the large tobacco barn you see on the grounds. Green tobacco leaves were hung on tiers in the barn, and wood-burning fires were lit in the rock flues to dry it. To achieve the brightleaf tobacco this region was noted for, workmen had to monitor the heating of the leaves.

Near the barn is the packhouse, where the dried and cured tobacco was sorted and graded. The renovated packhouse is now the Hugh Mangum Museum of Photography. Hugh Mangum, the son of Presley J. Mangum, was 16 when his father purchased the McCown House on the Eno. For about two years they spent the summers here and the winters in town, but in 1893 they moved here permanently.

By this time Hugh Mangum was already a self-taught photographer as well as a proficient painter. He had his darkroom in the packhouse. When 500 of Mangum's glass negatives were discovered, many covered with hay and chicken manure, this museum was born. It provides a fascinating look at photographic techniques of the early 1900s, as well as photographs of the southeast. Mangum traveled throughout North Carolina, Virginia and other southern states.

His eye was always captured by a pretty face, as you'll see. His wife, Annie Carden, was said to be the most beautiful girl in East Radford, Virginia. When an influenza epidemic struck the community and the Magnum family, Hugh ordered the doctor to administer whiskey, the only known remedy, to his wife and their daughter but refused it for himself. That decision cost him his life. He died in 1922 at age 44.

In addition to the above attractions, there is an extensive network of nature trails winding through the woods that have changed little since they were used by the Shocco, Adshusheer and Eno Indians. Some trails follow the Eno River through rocky terrain with granite bluffs that come alive in the spring when the mountain laurel and rhododendron bloom. Fishing is popular in the Eno, this being one of only two rivers in the state where you can hook the redeye or Roanoke bass (the other is the Tar River). The rapids and deep water invite canoeing and rafting. There are picnic facilities at the park. West Park on the Eno is open daily 8:00 A.M. to dark. Free tours of the house, mill and museum are given 1:00 to 5:00 P.M. on weekends. Weekday tours must be arranged by calling (919)471-1623.

While in the Durham area you might want to lunch at the Weeping Radish Brewery in Brightleaf Square. You can taste the beer and German food in the outdoor beer garden or indoors and watch German brewmasters supervise each phase of the brewing process in a glassed-in microbrewery. There's often an oompah band on hand to lend a festive note to your visit. You can sit and watch or join the Bavarian dancers.

Directions: From I-85 exit on North Duke Street, Route 501 N-Bypass. Follow Route 501 N for roughly 3.5 miles, and West Point on the Eno will be on your left.

RALEIGH

Joel Lane House

Founding Father

Joel Lane was definitely a patriarch. Not only was he the father of 12 children, but due to his distinguished public service, he was called the Father of Wake County and the Father of Raleigh. Joel was one of six sons of Joseph Lane and Patience McKinnie, both members of prominent southern colonial families.

Lane was a colonial patriot who held political offices in four North Carolina counties, sometimes in several concurrently. He was high sheriff of Halifax County, a militia officer in Halifax and Wake, a justice of the county courts of Halifax, Johnson and Wake, a clerk of the court in Chatham, and a representative to the Colonial Assembly from both Johnston and Wake. He also served Wake County as senator in the General Assembly for 11 terms, as well as a myriad other posts. Both he and his son Henry attended the 1789 Constitutional Convention in Fayetteville that ratified the U.S. Constitution.

Colonel Joel Lane moved to the area that would become, largely through his efforts, North Carolina's capital in the early 1760s. In 1762 he married Martha Hinton (at her death he married her sister Mary) and soon began building Wakefield, named originally in honor of Governor Tryon's wife, Margaret Wake (it's now called the Joel Lane House). The finished house was considered one of the finest within a hundred miles. Because his dining room was one of the area's most commodious rooms, it is believed that the first session of the Wake County Court of Common Pleas and Quarter Sessions met here on June 4, 1771. Both Joel Lane and his brother Joseph served as justices on the court. It is also thought that some of the General Assembly sessions in 1781 were held at Wakefield. So many travelers stopped here that Lane eventually added an ordinary, or inn, to accommodate them.

One of the most significant meetings occurred here in 1792 when six of the nine commissioners entrusted with finding a permanent capital for North Carolina met. Joel Lane wined and dined the commissioners, and they decided to buy 1,000 acres from their host. North Carolina has the distinction of being the only one of the 13 original states to have standing the house of the colonial leader whose land was purchased for the state capital.

The house originally stood slightly northeast of its present location. It was moved and restored to its 1790–95 appearance. When Lane first built the house it had a gable roof and a porch across the front, but he remodeled using a gambrel roof like the one you'll see today. A great deal of the interior woodwork and flooring is original. Exterior details that match Lane's architectural touches include beaded siding, chimneys constructed of handmade brick and hand-hewn shingles. There is still one dependency on the much reduced grounds.

The period furnishings include several Lane family pieces as well as a number of items made in Wake County. In the parlor there is a slant front desk believed to have been used by Joel Lane. The walnut cupboard in the dining room is also thought to be a family piece. Looking out the side door you'll see a charming herb garden with a sundial inscribed: "I count only the sunny hours."

Guided tours of the Joel Lane House are conducted upon request by costumed hostesses. Call the Raleigh Capital Area Visitors Center at (919)733-3456.

Directions: From I-95 take Route 70 west to Route 64 (Beltline), which circles Raleigh. Then take Route 1/64 into the city. Turn right on Hillsborough Street and then right on St. Mary's Street. Take St. Mary's Street for two blocks; the Joel Lane House is on the corner of St. Mary's Street and W. Hargett Street.

Mordecai Historic Park

Five Generations Lived Here

The **Mordecai House** (pronounced Mor-da-Kee) spans Raleigh's history, predating the city's formation and stretching to the present. It is, in fact, the oldest house in Raleigh still standing on its original location. The oldest is the Joel Lane House, which was moved from its first site (see selection). Joel Lane, was a large landowner, prominent in the development of Wake County and the capital city of Raleigh.

The north portion of the Mordecai House was built in 1785 for Joel Lane's son Henry and his wife Polly, granddaughter of John Hinton, colonel in the Wake County Revolutionary militia. Henry and Polly lived in 1½ stories of what is now the rear portion of the house. Furniture in the parlor and north bedroom are regional pieces from their era.

The second owner was Moses Mordecai, who married the Lanes' daughter Margaret (Peggy). This brilliant attorney acquired a sizeable family when he married because Peggy's three sisters remained in residence at their family home. Moses's younger brother, George, also lived with them. After bearing three children, Peggy died. Moses then married Peggy's youngest sister, Ann Willis (Nancy). They had one child, born the same year that Moses died.

Through provisions of Moses's will, the house was enlarged to accommodate the extended family. William Nichols, who remodeled the North Carolina State House, added five rooms on the south wing and converted the older portion to two stories. Furniture in the dining room dates from this period.

Henry Mordecai was only four when his father died, and the house was held in trust for him until he was 21. By this time the family property was a substantial plantation cultivated by numerous slaves. Henry, whose portrait hangs in the parlor, married Martha Hinton, another descendant of the Revolutionary colonel. Through Henry's initial donation and later sale of land the Oakwood Cemetery was established.

At Henry's death in 1875 his widow and two of their daughters continued to make the Mordecai House their home. His older daughter, Patty, lived here all her life, never marrying. Her sister, Mary Willis, was married in the parlor to William A. Turk, a Southern Railway executive. The third sister, Margaret Mordecai Little, was married to Dr. William Little, a Civil War surgeon. At his death she returned to her family home with her five sons. Her youngest son, Burke Haywood Little, was the last family member to live in the Mordecai house.

Both the furnishings and architecture span the 18th and 19th centuries. The handsome antiques evoke an era of prosperity. Behind the house is the attractive **Ellen Mordecai Garden**. Ellen was the daughter of Moses and his first wife. The inspiration for this garden was *Gleanings From Long Ago*, a book Ellen wrote for her granddaughter about her childhood in the 1830s at the Mordecai House. In one of the many references she makes to the garden she writes, "A favorite place for us to play was the garden. It was a big old-fashioned garden with walks running at right angles laying off the beds. There were borders for flowers, separated by planks from the vegetable part, and on these borders grew old-fashioned flowers, white lilies, cups and saucers, butter-and-eggs, violets, poppies, fragrant white violets." The garden has been restored to look like the one Ellen so enjoyed. Two of the Mordecai House dependencies have survived; the **Double-Doored Dependency** is now used as a gift shop, and the **Smokehouse** is used for storage and garden activities. Where the out-kitchen once stood you can see the 1842 Allen Kitchen relocated from Anson County.

At **Mordecai Park** there are four historical buildings from Raleigh's first decade arranged along a village street. The oldest, the **Bager-Iredell Office**, was built around 1810 by Raleigh's, not Virginia's, John Marshall. This one room law office, heated by a brick fireplace, was sold by Marshall's heirs to Governor Hutchins G. Burton. The next owner was George E. Badger, then James Iredell Jr., who was born in Edenton and became a member of the first United States Supreme Court (see Edenton selection).

The neoclassical **Early Raleigh Office Building** recalls the early years of the city's postal service. In the early days post riders and private horsemen delivered the mail. In 1803 the stage coach began tri-weekly service, but it wasn't until the 1850s that the first post office was built on Fayetteville Street. Records indicate that the office building at Mordecai Park is that same original post office. Sorting desks, old postal equipment and other furnishings confirm its early history.

Another historic building is **St. Mark's Chapel**, built of heart pine in 1847 by slaves on a plantation in Chatham County. The last Episcopal service was held at the plantation in 1934. The chapel was subsequently deeded to the Episcopal Diocese, moved to Siler City, and used from 1957 to 1968.

The most significant building in the village is the tiny, **gambrel-roofed cabin** in which our 17th president, Andrew Johnson, was born on December 29, 1808. Johnson's parents worked at Peter Casso's inn on the corner of Raleigh's Fayetteville and Morgan Streets. This small building was a kitchen building for the inn; the Johnsons lived upstairs. The modest frame dwelling has been restored to its appearance in 1808.

There is no admission to Mordecai Park, which is open March–December on Tuesday–Friday 10:00 A.M. to 2:00 P.M. and weekends 2:00 to 4:00 P.M. Guided tours of the house are given by docents.

Directions: From I-95 take Route 64 to Raleigh then take I-40, the Beltline. Exit onto Wade Avenue. Make a right on Downtown Boulevard and a left on Peace Street, which ends at Person Street. Turn left on Person Street and proceed north about four blocks to Mimosa Street, which encompasses Mordecai Park.

North Carolina Museum of Art, Museum of History and Museum of Natural History

Spend a Day and Start a B.A.

You can do a one-day survey course of the liberal arts with an outing to Raleigh's three major museums. North Carolina has consistently been at the forefront in developing a strong museum network. Its Museum of History resembles other North Carolina state museums in having a major branch in the capital and smaller facilities elsewhere. However, its state Museum of Art, funded in 1947, is the first of its kind.

For the first 27 years the museum was housed in a renovated state office building. In 1983 it came of age when its new facility designed by Edward Durrell Stone opened. The new **Museum of Art** is bright and airy with a two-story open interior lobby providing access to the various galleries. Collections include European, American, Twentieth Century, Ancient, African, Oceanic, New World and Judaica. The last is an overview of the Jewish contributions to art in Europe, Asia and America from the 16th century to the present. The intricately crafted silver, brass and pewter objects in this collection were used in Jewish religious services and cultural life.

Four additional galleries hold 12 to 15 special exhibitions scheduled throughout each year. The museum has a film and concert series, classes and workshops for adults and young visitors, family festivals organized around a special theme, lectures and symposiums, plus guided tours. Free public tours are given at 1:30 P.M. Tuesday through Sunday. No reservations are needed.

The Museum of Art is open at no charge Tuesday–Saturday 9:00 A.M. to 5:00 P.M., Friday 9:00 A.M. to 9:00 P.M., Sunday 12:00 to 5:00 P.M. There is a museum gift shop and a café which serves lunch and afternoon tea. Friday the café is open for dinner, and on Sunday it offers a special buffet. Reservations can be made for these two meals; call (919)833-3548.

The **North Carolina Museum of History** tells the story of the state from prehistoric people to the present. Folk art, fashions, furniture, toys, weapons, sports, history, transportation, economic resources and nearly every aspect of life in the state are on display. Plans call for the museum to move into its new facility in 1992. The opportunity to enlarge the display areas means that more of the collection can be exhibited. Now 90 percent of the museum's 350,000 artifacts hide in storage.

The Museum of History is open at no charge Tuesday–Saturday 9:00 A.M. to 5:00 P.M. and Sunday 1:00 to 6:00 P.M. It is closed Mondays, Thanksgiving and Christmas holidays. There are guided tours, lectures and special programs. The Museum is at

172

109 East Jones Street. A large well-stocked gift shop is located off the lobby.

The **Museum of Natural History** displays the natural past in rooms of the past. This is appropriate because this museum is the oldest in the state, dating from 1879. One display area looks exactly as it did in 1925. In the reproduced taxidermy workshop of H.H. Brimley you'll see the old-fashioned style of exhibiting preserved specimens. The old desk and typewriter Brimley used during his tenure at the museum still sit in his re-created office. Brimley was hired in 1895, became the director in 1927 and retired in 1937.

When you enter the museum's east lobby you see suspended above your head the skeletal remains of a right whale, a harbinger of the museum's fossil hall and marine mammal hall. The right whale was so named because it was a slow swimmer that floated once it was killed, making, according to whalers, the right whale to hunt. There are fossil remains of land animals like the skull of the Tyrannosaurus rex, which roamed the swamp lands of North Carolina 75 million years ago. As you listen to the taped sounds of the humpback whales you can view the displayed skeletons of finback and sperm whales, plus other stuffed marine mammals like seals, walruses and manatees. The 50-ton sperm whale that washed up on Wrightsville Beach in 1928 is hard to miss. A children's book, *A Whale Called Trouble*, available at the gift shop, tells the story of how the whale was prepared for display. For smaller marine life there is a hall of fishes. A large collection of land mammals and birds reveals the diversity of species found in the state.

In the midst of skeletons and stuffed animals, Hapi draws extra attention. Hapi is very much alive. She is a Burmese python that replaced long-time museum resident George, who died in early 1989. George's adventures are related in the children's book, *A Snake Called George*. Hapi has her own quarters across from the hands-on Discovery Room where families can explore the mysteries of science. Other popular exhibits include the shell collection and North Carolina's precious stones.

The North Carolina State Museum of Natural History is open at no charge Monday–Saturday 9:00 A.M. to 5:00 P.M. and Sunday 1:00 to 5:00 P.M.

Directions: From I-95 take Route US 64 to Raleigh, then take the Beltline (I 40/US 1/US 64) towards Apex/Sanford. Exit on Wade Avenue, on the western edge of Raleigh. Take Wade Avenue west to Blue Ridge Boulevard and turn right. The Museum of Art is at 2110 Blue Ridge Boulevard. For the Museum of History take the Beltline to US 1 Business (Downtown Boulevard). Turn right on Wake Forest Road heading into town and then make a right on Peace Street. Go one block and turn left on North

Blount Street; travel five blocks to Edenton Street and turn right. The Museum of Natural History is on the next block of Edenton Street off the Halifax Street Plaza.

North Carolina State Capitol, State Legislative Building and Executive Mansion

Stately Triumvirate

Historians tend to lament the loss of noted buildings to the scourge of fire, but further consideration may prompt a different view. Consider the case of North Carolina's **Capitol**. When Raleigh was established as the seat of government in 1792, a simple, two-story brick State House was built, and though it was enlarged between 1820–24, state government was still small in concept and in actuality. Even if the structure had not been devastated by the fire of 1831 it is unlikely it would have proved to be a serviceable building in later decades.

The present Capitol, constructed between 1833–1840, was an enlarged and significantly improved version of the old State House. The architectural details are copies from ancient Greece. The exterior Doric columns are modeled after the Parthenon. The semi-circular plan of a Greek theater was borrowed for the House of Representatives (Commons) Chamber, which was then decorated in the Corinthian style of the Tower of the Winds. The Senate Chamber was influenced by the Ionic style of the Erechtheum. The cost of all this style was not inconsequential. By the time the Capitol was finished, the $532,682.34 price tag was more than three times the annual general income for the state. Architectural experts now agree North Carolinians got their money's worth. The Capitol is generally considered one of the finest and best preserved civic buildings of the Greek Revival style. It is also the least changed (both inside and out) of any major American civic building of its era.

When you enter the Capitol look for the information desk near the rotunda where you can pick up an informative brochure on the building and explore on your own. If you want to schedule a tour call (919)733-3456. The first thing you'll see is the impressive 97½-foot high domed rotunda with a copy of Antonio Canova's 1820 statue of George Washington. This well-known sculpture depicts a seated Washington in a Roman general's armor and tunic. The original statue was crushed during the State House fire of 1831. The Rotunda also has busts of significant North Carolina political figures.

The Capitol housed all of North Carolina's state government

Seated in the 97-foot high rotunda of the State Capitol, Raleigh, is the imposing statue of George Washington in a Roman general's armor and tunic.

until 1888 when the Supreme Court and State Library moved into a new building. In 1963 the legislative branch moved to a new legislative building. Of the original occupants only the governor and secretary of state still have working offices here. One

Capitol legend claims there was an escape tunnel for the governor's use during the Civil War. There was, in fact, a tunnel built in the 1880s, but it was for heating and electrical conduits, not for hasty exits. Do go by the Governor's Office in the Southwest Suite. When not in use the doors are opened so that visitors can see the massive 19th-century furnishings including the governor's partners' desk. When the doors are closed, detailed photographs substitute for a personal inspection. The other three office suites are closed to the public.

The former **House and Senate Chambers** are open on the second floor. The House Chamber was in use from 1840–1961. Two items you'll see were saved from the 1831 fire. One is the valuable Thomas Sully portrait of Washington, circa 1818, copied from Gilbert Stuart's *Lansdowne* portrait in the Pennsylvania Academy of Fine Arts. The *Speaker's Chair*, attributed to Thomas Constantine of New York, also predates this building. The best view of this chamber is from the third floor gallery.

Across the rotunda is the old Senate Chamber. Both chambers have star-patterned carpets, and desks and chairs made by Raleigh cabinet maker William Thompson, circa 1840. Four office rooms on the second floor, two at the north end and two anterooms, are to be furnished to the period 1840–65. Capitol legend has it that the west stairs were chipped by the rolling of whiskey barrels up and down them to the Third House, the bar set up in the Committee Room in the west stair hall on the second floor during the late 1860s Reconstruction era. No doubt there was a bar, but whether this accounts for the condition of the stairs is purely conjecture.

The third floor has two additional rooms worth seeing. Unlike the rest of the Capitol, they are finished in the Gothic style. The State Library Room looks as it did in 1856–57 with grained shelves and galleries. The State Library was located here from 1840–1888. The room has an ornate plaster ceiling. You'll discover the derivation of the expression "government red tape" when you observe the bundled documents tied with red ribbons. The realistic touches even include a twist of tobacco on one of the old wooden desks.

You'll want to see the **State Geologists Office** (Cabinet of Minerals), which was originally where the Supreme Court met from 1840 to 1843. The justices moved elsewhere because they had trouble climbing the two flights of stairs and there were no rest rooms in the Capitol. The State Geologist's Office was located here from 1852–1863.

The Capitol is open to visitors at no charge Monday–Friday 8:00 A.M. to 5:00 P.M., Saturday 9:00 A.M. to 5:00 P.M. and Sunday 1:00 to 5:00 P.M. It is closed Thanksgiving, Christmas and New Year's Day.

Bronze statue of "Three Presidents" at Capitol Square, Raleigh, honors native sons Andrew Jackson, James Knox Polk and Andrew Johnson.

At night the Capitol is floodlit. The grounds, called either Capitol or Union Square, are also worth exploring for their 12 statues and monuments commemorating individuals and events. The first, a bronze statue of Washington, cast by W.J. Hubard in Richmond and copied from a marble statue by Houdon, was placed outside the Capitol in 1857. One of the more recent statues was the *Three Presidents*, erected in 1948 and unveiled by President Harry S Truman. The three presidents are all North Carolina natives: Andrew Jackson, James Knox Polk and Andrew Johnson. Four monuments commemorate the Civil War, and others honor heroics in the Spanish-American War and World War I. There is a detailed brochure, *Heroes & Heroines on Union Square*, that you can pick up at the information desk near the Capitol rotunda.

A natural progression takes you along Halifax Street to the North Carolina **State Legislative Building**. This has the distinction of being the first building constructed exclusively to house a state legislative branch. Edward Durrell Stone, who designed the John F. Kennedy Center for the Performing Arts in Washington, chose a blend of classical and modern architecture for this building, which actually bears some resemblance to the Kennedy Center. Distinctive touches are the pyramidal roofs covering the House and Senate Chambers and the Great Seal of North Carolina in terrazzo mosaic at the entrance.

Four separate courts flanked by offices and committee rooms are inside. With their fountains and hanging gardens they bring the outdoors in. On the second floor you'll see the Senate and House Chambers. Four English tapestries hang behind the Speaker's desk in the House. They bear the coats of arms of the eight Lord Proprietors who were granted a royal charter for the Carolinas from Charles II in 1663. In addition to the working Chambers there is a display area on the third floor highlighting North Carolina's industries, scenic attractions and pageants. Leading off the third floor is a roof garden. Each of the four courts below has a garden above, and rooftop skylights provide light for the court gardens on the first floor. The State Legislative Building is open Monday–Friday 8:00 A.M. to 5:00 P.M., Saturday 9:00 A.M. to 5:00 P.M. and Sunday 1:00 to 5:00 P.M.

To round out your look at North Carolina's leading state buildings, you need to tour the **Executive Mansion**. The mansion has an interesting history, beginning with a nagging wife. After the Civil War, North Carolina's governors lived in rented houses, hotels, or if they were lucky, their own Raleigh residences. In 1883 the wife of Governor Thomas J. Jarvis vehemently stated, "It does not comport with the dignity of the State for the Governor to live at a hotel. . . ." The General Assembly agreed with Mrs. Jarvis, and work was begun on the Executive Mansion on state-owned property. The design is Eastlake Style Victorian, and it is one of the finest examples in the country.

Franklin Delano Roosevelt had ample opportunity to sample the hospitality of numerous executive mansions, and he said the interior of North Carolina's mansion was "the most beautiful in America." You will have a chance to see the Entrance Hall, five formal downstairs rooms, and the sunporch. Efforts were made both inside and out to use North Carolina building materials wherever possible. The Grand Staircase is made from North Carolina heart-of-pine. The walls are lined with portraits of former governors.

The **South Drawing Room** is also called the Gentlemen's Parlor. Decorations on a Steuben glass urn depict Blackbeard, the notorious North Carolina pirate. The central design on the mint-green carpet duplicates the ceiling's plasterwork design. Receiving lines in the drawing room move guests from here to the adjacent Ballroom. This elegant room can seat 100 dinner guests. There are matching crystal chandeliers and French mirrors at both ends of the room.

The **Library**, with its extensive collection of books on the state, is more comfortable than elegant. The large red velvet sofa in front of the fire looks inviting. Here too the woodwork is native heart-of-pine. In the formal dining room, which can easily accommodate 24 diners, you will see the state silver and china. After dinner, guests frequently retire to the North Drawing Room, the Ladies Parlor, with its early 19th-century Raleigh-made piano. You can also see the informal sunporch that was renovated in the 1980s, and from here you have an excellent view of the newly replanted gardens around the mansion.

Thirty-minute tours of the Executive Mansion are given on a seasonal basis by appointment Tuesday and Friday from 9:30 to 11:00 A.M. and 1:30 to 3:00 P.M. Reservations may be made by calling the Capital Area Visitor Center, on North Blount Street diagonally across from the Mansion, at (919)733-3456.

Directions: From the Beltline (US 64/I-40/US 70/US 401), which circles Raleigh, take the New Bern Avenue exit, west. Turn right on Person Street and go two blocks; turn left on Lane Street for the Capital Area Visitor Center and the Executive Mansion. For the State Capitol continue on New Bern Avenue (this will become Edenton Street). The State Capitol is on the left. Public parking is on the corner of Wilmington and Polk Streets.

Oakwood and Pullen Park

Going Around in Circles and Squares

If you want to sample an overview of American architectural styles from the last century take a stroll through the **Oakwood Historic District**, now listed on the National Register of Historic Places and the only intact 19th-century neighborhood in Raleigh. As you cover the district's ten streets, you'll notice that the architecture varies from house to house. The neoclassical look was favored before the Civil War, then the Second Empire style was adopted in the 1870s. The 1880s and 1890s were the heyday of Victorian design. Then, after the Chicago Exhibition of 1893, the neoclassical and colonial revivals influenced house builders.

This northeast section of Raleigh, once part of the Mordecai plantation (see Mordecai Historic Park selection), was divided into lots and sold after the Civil War. Throughout the years as styles came in and out of fashion certain southern features were nearly always included. Most of the houses have at least one porch, deep pitched roofs for insulation and lattice work incorporated in the design for ventilation.

The Capital Area Visitor's Center at the corner of Lane and North Blount Streets has a brochure for you called *A Walking Tour of Historic Oakwood*. It gives additional background on the neighborhood plus information on more than 60 sites along your route.

The walking tour map starts visitors on East Jones Street where six houses are noted. The J.Y. Joyner House, #304, is an excellent example of Second Empire with its bracketed, shingled tower crested by cast iron. The two Heck Houses, #503 and #511, are ornate Steamboat Gothic with mansard roofs, a 2½ story corner mansard towers and wrap-around porches. The Brazier-Gatling House, #504, built in 1820 is Oakwood's earliest house.

Three homes are listed on East Lane Street. The Horton-Walters House, #321, has an ornate Eastlake Gothic porch. The A.R. Love House, #323, has a wraparound back porch with a Chippendale balustrade. Elm Street is noted for the eight houses built by Richard Stanhope Pullen; in fact, this section of Oakwood was called Pullentown. Two houses are listed on Linden Avenue. The Cornelius B. Edwards House, #321, is a typical neoclassical design with Palladian motifs.

The Side Street Restaurant on the corner of North Bloodworth and Lane is a good place to enjoy lunch or dinner while exploring Oakwood. This became an historic spot for the city at the end of the Civil War. When General Sherman reached Raleigh in April 1865, the townsfolk rode out to meet him and surrendered the city. Sherman said that if no shots were fired he wouldn't burn

Raleigh. The city was not burned, but unfortunately soldiers from the Texas Cavalry looted stores and one fired on Union General Kilpatrick's cavalry troops. The Texas soldier, Lieutenant Walsh, was hanged by Union troops in an oak grove that once grew where Side Street now stands. Walsh is buried in Oakwood Cemetery.

North Bloodworth Street also has the only bed-and-breakfast in this historic district. The Oakwood Inn, #411, is in the old Strong-Stronach House built in 1871. Each of the six guest rooms (all with private baths) reflects the Victorian ambience of the house. For reservations call (919)832-9712. There are six more houses on this street on the walking tour map. Of note is one of the two houses listed on North Boundary Street, #318, which belonged to Ellen Mordecai. This house was moved to the Oakwood area in 1934. Its fluted Ionic columns are stylistically different from those of other homes in the neighborhood.

North East Street has 14 homes listed on the guide. These range from the neoclassical Samuel Glass House, #112, to the Southern Victorian J.W. Marcom House, #517. There are even two "Shotgun Houses," #407 and #409, so named because it was said the rooms were so open a shot fired at the front door could go straight out the back door.

North Person Street has the first neoclassical revival home in Oakwood, the C.J. Hunter House, #400. The Tucker Mansion, #416, with its intricate triple floor porch is now the Oakwood-Mordecai Meeting Center. Twelve more houses can be seen on Oakwood Avenue.

Many residents consider Polk Street Oakwood's main street, and 14 houses on it are described in the brochure. It is the biographies of residents that bring neighborhoods to life, such as that of North Carolina Chief Justice Walter Clark who built the house at 315 Polk Street for his mother and two spinster sisters. He gained fame as the Boy Colonel of the Confederacy. He was only 15 when he was commissioned.

If you continue down Polk Street you come to **Oakwood Cemetery** where many noted Raleigh citizens are buried. The oldest section of the cemetery is the final resting spot for Confederate dead. By order of the Federal forces occupying Raleigh the Confederate dead were moved here in 1867, before the land donated by Henry Mordecai was ready. In all 538 Confederates were moved to this cemetery from the Federal cemetery. Eventually the number of Southern dead would reach 2,800. When the women of Raleigh came to mourn their slain soldiers they carried flowers under their petticoats, hidden from the unforgiving Federal victors who wanted no tributes given to the Confederate dead. In 1869 land adjacent to the Confederate cemetery became

Oakwood Cemetery. Six North Carolina governors are buried here, several generations of the Mordecai family, along with Richard Stanhope Pullen and other prominent citizens.

Pullen donated the land for the North Carolina State University and **Pullen Park**. In this 65-acre inner–city park, you can take a walk around Lake Howell, or explore by pedal boat. You'll also find a garden, several picnic areas, two playgrounds and Raleigh's oldest swimming pool. The Huntington train travels around the park's perimeter, and there is also an amusement park with rides, the most famous of which is the original 1912 Gustav Dentzel carousel. It is the oldest carousel in the state and North Carolina's only remaining "trolley-park" carousel, qualifying it for inclusion on the National Register of Historic Places. There are 52 animal figures and two chariots. The music is played by a Wurlitzer 125 military-band organ. Great care was taken to restore the carousel as close as possible to its original appearance.

Pullen Park, 520 Ashe Avenue, is open from early June through Labor Day Monday–Thursday 10:30 A.M. to 6:30 P.M., Friday–Saturday 10:30 A.M. to 8:30 P.M. and Sundays 1:00 to 8:30 P.M. From May until early June, and September to October hours are Monday–Saturday 10:30 A.M. to 6:30 P.M. and Sunday 1:00 to 6:30 P.M. During April and October the park is open Monday–Friday 10:30 A.M. to 3:30 P.M., Saturday 10:30 A.M. to 6:30 P.M., Sundays 1:00 to 6:30 P.M. From early March to early April and from the end of October through November hours are Friday–Saturday 10:30 A.M. to 6:30 P.M. and Sundays 1:00 to 6:30 P.M. It's closed Monday–Thursday. There is a small charge for the carousel, train, pedal boats and pool.

Directions: From the Beltline (US 64/1-40/US 70/US 401) take the New Bern exit, west. Turn right on Person Street and go three blocks, turn right on Oakwood Street to Oakwood's Historic District. For the Capital Area Visitor's Center turn right on Oakwood, go one block and turn left on North Blount Street. To reach Pullen Park from 1-40 continue around to the Gorman Street exit. Take Gorman until it intersects with Avent Ferry Road and turn right. At the intersection with Western Boulevard make a right and go ¾ mile. Turn left into the park.

GOLDSBORO VICINITY

Bentonville Battleground

What Price Glory?

In the final days of the War Between the States, Union and Confederate troops met in the largest land battle ever fought in North

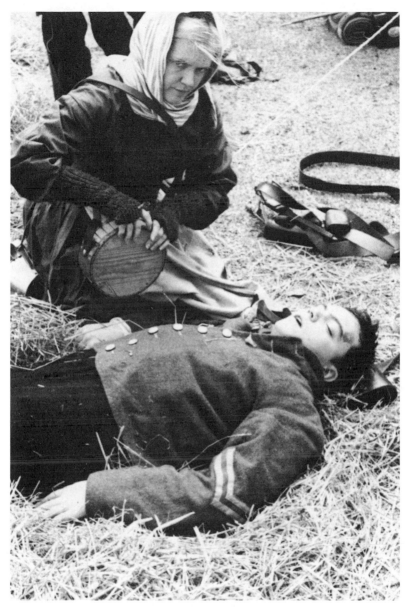

Over 4,000 men were killed, wounded or missing during the Battle of Bentonville, the Confederates last major offensive of the Civil War. Re-enactment of the battle is presented every March.

Carolina. This attempt by General Joseph E. Johnston to stop Sherman after he left Georgia was also the Confederates last major offensive. The South desperately wanted to prevent Sherman and Grant from joining forces.

General Johnston's army of 20,000 was no match for Sherman's 60,000-man force, so it became imperative to strike when, and if, Sherman divided his command. This happened on March 19, 1865, near the village of Bentonville. Johnston formed his men into a sickle-shaped trap and waited for the Federals. The left wing of Sherman's force marched into the ambush, but despite initial success the plan did not succeed in crushing the Union lines. When on the following day the other wing of Sherman's army arrived on the battlefield, the result was foreordained. Still, for two days the opposing armies fought each other over a 6,000-acre battleground. More than 4,000 men were killed, wounded or missing by the time Johnston abandoned the field. Just a little more than a month later, Johnston surrendered his army to Sherman at Bennett Place (see selection), thus ending the war in the Carolinas.

Today **Bentonville Battleground** is a North Carolina State Historic Site. A ¼-mile trail leads to still visible trenches dug by the First Michigan Engineers to keep the Confederates from circling around behind the Union lines and attacking from the rear. You can take a driving tour around the entire battlefield. There are 29 points of interest along the drive described in a brochure sold at the visitor center. The most poignant reminder of these pivotal three days is the **Harper House**, used during and after the conflict as a field hospital.

In speaking of this hospital Colonel William Hamilton of the 9th Ohio Cavalry recalled, "A dozen surgeons and attendants in their shirtsleeves stood at rude benches cutting off arms and legs and throwing them out of the windows, where they lay scattered on the grass. The legs of infantrymen could be distinguished from those of the cavalry by the size of their calves, as the march of 1,000 miles had increased the size of one and diminished the size of the other."

Men wounded in the Civil War faced amputation because bullets usually created large, ugly wounds, and the only treatment was to cut off the injured member. If a bullet entered a part of the body that could not be cut off, the surgeon would reach into the wound with his fingers to remove the lead. It is not surprising that more men died from post-operative infections than died on the battlefield.

At Harper House on the Bentonville battlefield there were at least 89 capital amputations during the battle, and 554 men were treated, including 45 Confederates. At the end of the battle the

Union wounded were sent to hospitals in nearby Goldsboro, but the Confederate wounded remained here to recuperate, some for weeks.

The Harper House is one of only two houses in the United States that have been restored to look as they did when they served as field hospitals. The other is the Old Stone House in Manassas, Virginia. These battlefield medical centers were run rather like a modern day *MASH* unit. As you'll see when you tour Harper House, the doors were removed and placed on barrels as crude operating tables. Furniture was pushed out of the way and the floor covered with straw and army blankets to absorb the blood. A triage system was employed, with those suffering mortal wounds simply left outside to perish. The surgeons worked throughout the night, never washing their hands between operations. They used chloroform, which allowed only seven minutes to operate before the patient woke up. It is hard, even now, not to hear the echoes of the men's cries as you stand in these rooms and contemplate the pain they endured.

On the weekend closest to its anniversary, the Battle of Bentonville is commemorated with tactical demonstrations and a recreation of events in the field hospital. Bentonville Battlefield is open without charge April–October on Monday–Saturday 9:00 A.M. to 5:00 P.M. and Sunday 1:00 to 5:00 P.M. From November–March hours are Tuesday–Saturday 10:00 A.M. to 4:00 P.M. and Sunday 1:00 to 4:00 P.M..

Directions: From I-95 take Exit 90, Route 701, southeast towards Clinton. At State Route 1008 turn left, and the Bentonville Battleground will be on your left.

Carolina Pottery, Southland Estate Winery and Ava Gardner Museum

Touring Trio

You can combine three very different experiences, on a one-day excursion that offers something for everyone in the family. All destinations are close to each other off I-95 near Smithfield roughly halfway between Rocky Mount and Fayetteville.

Shop-til-you-drop enthusiasts may not be able to tear themselves away from the 30 stores at the **Carolina Pottery Outlet** Center in Smithfield. In addition to the anchor store, the 80,000-square foot Carolina Pottery, which offers warehouse prices on housewares and giftware, you can try your luck at Bass Shoes, Jonathan Logan, Manhattan, American Tourister, Royal Doulton,

185

Capezio, Van Heusen, Aileen's, Le Creusest, Harvé Benard, Towle Silver and many others. The shops are open daily 9:00 A.M. to 9:00 P.M. and Sunday 1:00 to 6:00 P.M.

If the mention of a shopping mall reduces the man of the family to despair, then include a stop at the nearby **Southland Estate Winery**, where he can pick up his spirits. This is North Carolina's newest winery. Although the wine is not made on the premises, you can see an introductory film on wine-making and a wine museum, which gives the history of wine throughout the state. After that move directly to the tasting room where you can sample Southland's 11 wines. If you find a favorite, you can purchase it by the bottle or case at the Wine and Gift Shop. Southland is open daily 10:00 A.M. to 5:00 P.M., Sunday 1:00 to 5:00 P.M. It is closed Thanksgiving, Christmas and New Year's Day.

The story of Tom Banks and the movie star reads like a Hollywood script, but it's true. Tom and his friends used to tease young Ava Gardner as she commuted each day to and from her secretarial studies at Atlantic Christian College. One day she turned the tables, chased after Tom and gave him a kiss on the cheek. Shortly thereafter, in July 1941, Tom saw a story in the local paper about Ava signing a seven-year MGM contract. He cut out the story and thus began his collection of Ava memorabilia. Now almost 50 years later his museum, located in the childhood home of Ava Gardener, is considered by many the world's largest collection on a single star.

Ava Gardner moved to The Teacherage when she was two and lived there until she was 13. Her parents ran a boarding house for teachers at Brogden School right next door. When Ava returned to this area in 1978 she stopped by the museum, but it was closed. "It's OK," she remarked, "I know what's in there. I lived it." And she did. There are scripts from her movies, posters, newspaper and magazine stories about her life, costumes she wore, childhood photographs and more than 50 movies on tape. The museum is obviously a labor of love.

The museum is open 12:00 to 6:00 P.M. Thursday through Sunday during July and the first half of August. From April through October you can visit by appointment. Call the Greater Smithfield-Selma Chamber of Commerce at (919)934-9166.

Directions: For Carolina Pottery Outlet Center take I-95 Exits 95 (Highway 70A) or 97 (Highway 70) and follow Industrial Park Drive, which is parallel to I-95 and connects Highway 70 and 70A. For Southland Estate Winery take Exit 98 and the 42-acre winery will be in sight immediately. For the Ava Gardner Museum take Exit 93, turn southeast on Brogden Road for eight miles. The museum is not well marked so watch carefully the left side of the road as you approach the eight-mile spot.

Charles B. Aycock Birthplace

As the Twig is Bent

"The struggle upward is worth the cost, and without the cost would not be worth while." So said Charles Brantley Aycock who struggled upwards from his rural roots to become governor of North Carolina.

The youngest of ten children, Charles was born on this farmstead on November 1, 1859. Although bookish, the young Charles worked beside his father and siblings in the field. He attended nearby Nahunta Academy, then went to the University of North Carolina, winning an award for the best commencement oration. He completed legal studies in a year and opened a law office in Goldsboro.

Following his father's lead, Charles became involved in local politics. His gift for oratory soon made him a popular speaker. Although he had not attended public schools, he espoused the cause of public education. He felt there were three reasons to be educated: to know something, to do something and to be something. It was the issue of education that helped win him the governorship in 1900. During his term of office he raised teaching requirements, established teacher training schools, lengthened the school term and raised teacher salaries roughly 50 percent.

At the end of his four-year term, Aycock resumed his law practice and continued to speak in favor of educational reforms. It was in the midst of his 1911 campaign for the United States Senate that he died on April 2, 1912, while delivering an address on universal education.

At the **Aycock State Historic Site** visitor center you'll see a recapitulation of his career. Then before visiting the farmhouse where he was born you'll see a one-room schoolhouse that once served seven grades. Children from the ages of 8 to 21 spent 3½ months each year at this school built in 1893.

In 1847 Charles Aycock's parents built their house on their 1,040-acre farm. Now restored, the house is typical of an eastern North Carolina farmhouse. There are two small shed rooms off the front porch. The parson or travelers may have slept in these cramped quarters. However, most of the time various children probably slept there, as the Aycocks had eight sons. In the house itself there is a master bedroom and parlor filled with period pieces including a trundle bed, baby cradle, chests, chairs and spinning wheel. The curtains and rag rug suggest the economic security of Charles's parents. In addition to being a farmer, Charles's father was the county clerk of the court and a state senator during the Civil War. He also rented some of his land to a turpentine distillery.

On the farm grounds there is a kitchen dependency with the family dining room, a granary or corn barn, a large and small smokehouse and the stables. All were part of the original Aycock farm. On Wednesdays from April to the first week in June Living History Days take place at the farm. There's a celebration on November 1, Aycock's birthday. Candlelight tours begin in early December to celebrate the Christmas season.

The Charles B. Aycock Birthplace is open at no charge Monday–Saturday from 9:00 A.M. to 5:00 P.M. and Sunday 1:00 to 5:00 P.M. From November through March hours are Tuesday–Saturday 10:00 A.M. to 4:00 P.M. and Sunday 1:00 to 4:00 P.M. Visitors may picnic on the grounds.

Directions: From I-95 take Route 222 exit then turn right at Fremont on Route 117 towards Goldsboro. After two miles, turn left on State Route 1542. The Aycock Birthplace is on the right.

Country Doctor Museum

Practical Practice

This intriguing museum is way off the beaten track, but since it deals with the lifestyle of a country doctor, its rural setting is entirely appropriate. The men honored here are the doctors who served rural families; it is the only museum in the United States entirely dedicated to these inspirational practitioners.

The museum recalls an era when doctors made house calls and handled a wide range of ailments and emergencies without benefit of specialists. Housed in two authentic doctors' offices, the museum includes the former office of Dr. Howard Franklin Freeman built in 1857 and the office of Dr. Cornelius Henry Brantley built in 1890.

Dr. Freeman's office from Plantation Rosedale is now the **Apothecary Area**. Beautiful, ornate wild cherry shelves with holly inlays were made in Ohio and stored until after the Civil War. In the postwar years they graced the shelves of the first drugstore in Bailey. These glassed-in shelves contain an extensive collection of apothecary jars. The earliest bottles have painted gold-leaf labels, others made later have gold labels stuck on, while those from a still later era have recessed labels. A valuable acquisition is the museum's complete case of homeopathic remedies. On the drug counter is one of several show globes. Supposedly a colonial traveler could tell there was an epidemic in town if the apothecary shop window had a ruby-colored globe; an emerald-filled globe indicated all was well. Show globes were introduced in England during the Great Plague of the 17th century. If these jars served to inform the unlettered so did the irregularly shaped bottles that contained poison. Even in the dark the uneven surface signaled its lethal content. On the drug counter you'll see a pill tile, pill machine and balances for measuring the ingredients. Some early drug apothecary stores had two tiles, one for preparing medicine for people and another for horses. According to the early medical books and diaries that fill the museum's library, country doctors prescribed the four 'Ps' for all ailments: puke, purge, plaster and phlebotomy (bleeding). Along with these rare books is an original altarpiece painted by an unknown follower of Martin Luther. This 17th-century painting, *Christ, the Apothecary of the Soul* depicts Christ weighing the sins of mankind and dispensing virtues from labeled drug containers. There were once 70 known allegorical paintings showing Christ in a pharmacy, but now only three exist. The other two are displayed in Stockholm's Norse Museum and in the Smithsonian's Old World Pharmacy collection.

Adjoining the Apothecary Area is a **doctor's office**. There you'll see an unusual double roll-top desk in which the inside section of the second roll-top was used to store bookkeeping records. The wall-style phone was the 42nd to be installed in the Carolinas. The 1850s convertible operating table-chair used during the Civil War looks like a torture machine with its cold stirrups, instrument trays and basins.

Also from the Civil War is the medical equipment of Dr. Matthew Moore Butler, surgeon of the 37th Regiment of the Army of Northern Virginia. Moore assisted Dr. McGuire after the Battle of Chancellorsville when he amputated Stonewall Jackson's arm. The small saw and knives used for that fateful operation are on display. The general survived the surgery but died of postoperative pneumonia.

Yet another room has an eclectic selection of medical equipment and nostrums. The old wooden surgical instruments, which were never sterilized, remind visitors of the perils involved in early medical treatment. Leech jars, shock devices and blood-measuring bowls also make us realize how lucky we are to have the benefits of today's medical sophistication.

Behind the museum is a **Medicinal Herb Garden**, which is a replica of the one in Padua, Italy, the oldest existing botanic garden in the world. A listing of the healing plants grown here includes details of what ailments they help cure. For example, alum root was used for sore throats and female problems while dogwood was used for malarial fevers. Surprisingly, poison ivy was used in certain skin preparations.

The Country Doctor Museum is open at no charge Sunday through Thursday from 2:00 to 5:00 P.M. The museum is about 35 miles east of Raleigh in Bailey at 515 Vance Street.

Directions: From I-95 exit on Route 264 west, for seven miles then exit on Route 581 south to Bailey. Or from Raleigh take I-64 east to Zebulon then Route 264 to Bailey. Turn right at the sign for the Country Doctor Museum.

Richard Caswell Memorial and CSS Ram *Neuse*

Very Different Duo

A mere 100 yards separate the **Richard Caswell Memorial** and the **CSS Ram *Neuse***, although they represent periods of history separated by more than 100 years.

Richard Caswell lived through the turbulent colonial years, becoming the first governor of the independent state of North Carolina. He served six terms. The memorial stands near the family cemetery where Caswell is believed to be buried. His military and political career is presented in the memorial through a series of sound and light vignettes. Caswell became a major general in the Revolutionary army after the victory at Moore's Creek Bridge, for which he was given much of the credit (see Moore's Creek National Battlefield selection). Caswell also served in the colonial assembly for 17 years and in 1776 was the president of the Fifth Provincial Congress. He was a wealthy farmer and businessman and the Grand Master Mason of North Carolina. As the memorial proudly claims, he was a "Man for His Time."

The real draw at this State Historic Site is the CSS Ram *Neuse*, one of only three recovered Civil War ironclads (the other two are the CSS *Jackson* in Columbus, Georgia and the USS *Cairo* in Vicksburg, Mississippi). The Confederate states' navy commissioned the construction of 22 ironclad ramming vessels designed to break through the Union blockade.

Construction began on the CSS *Neuse* in the fall of 1862 at Whitehall (now Seven Springs) on the Neuse River. The *Neuse* did not have an auspicious career. Struck by Union shells before it was finished, it was poled down river to Kinston in March 1863 to be outfitted with engines, iron, ordnance and stores. Transportation problems brought about iron shortages which necessitated cutting back on the amount of plating from four to two inches. Exigencies of war dictated that she sail to New Bern on April 22, 1864, without additional iron protection. The *Neuse* covered only half a mile before running aground on a sandbar. A month later the river swelled sufficiently to release the trapped vessel, and she sailed back to Kinston. Her crew was diverted to other duties, and the ram lay idle for the next year.

After the fall of Fort Fisher (see Fort Fisher selection) in January 1865, Union troops stationed in New Bern started to advance along the Neuse River and came within five miles of Kinston. The crew of the *Neuse* placed a charge in the bow of the trapped ship and set her on fire in order to prevent capture. The exploding charge blew a hole eight feet wide in the port side and the *Neuse* sank faster than she burned.

The story of her recovery almost a hundred years later is fraught with equal measures of ill luck. In November 1961 a cofferdam was built, and three-quarters of the ship was afloat. But winter storms caused the river to rise 18 feet, the dam collapsed and the *Neuse* sank once more. It took two more years before the *Neuse* was finally raised and moved to its present site.

Enough of the hull remains for you to visualize what the *Neuse* once looked like (a model can be seen inside the visitor center). The existing hull measures 136 feet long and 37 feet wide. Since iron was such an important element of the *Neuse*'s construction there is a working blacksmith shop adjacent to the ironclad. Methods from the 1860s are demonstrated, and rope making is also featured.

The visitor center is built to resemble the top of an ironclad. Exhibits and a 12-minute audio-visual presentation provide background information on the CSS *Neuse* and its role in the Civil War. The site is open at no charge April through October on Monday–Saturday 9:00 A.M. to 5:00 P.M. and Sunday 1:00 to 5:00 P.M. From November through March hours are Tuesday–Saturday 10:00 A.M. to 4:00 P.M. and Sunday 1:00 to 4:00 P.M.

Directions: From I-95 take Route 70 Business east to Kinston. The Caswell/Neuse site is located on Vernon Avenue, which is US 70 Business.

Tarboro Historic District

Town for Tarheels

Virginians say "George Washington slept here;" North Carolinians say "the colonial government met here." Tarboro was one of many towns considered for the colonial capital. Though the colonial government did meet here, it did not retain its status as a colonial seat of government. It did, however, retain one colonial distinction: like Boston, Massachusetts, Tarboro, North Carolina retained its original Town Commons. They are the only two places in the nation to do so. The six-acre public ground in Tarboro was set aside by the founders in 1760. The fact that it still exists reflects the importance the community attaches to its history. Unlike many towns, Tarboro did not progress at the expense of the past; here past and present exist side by side.

The residential **historic district** covers 45 blocks, and you see a sizeable portion of this when you walk or drive along the Tarboro Historic District National Recreation Trail, established by the U.S. Department of the Interior. The trail starts at the **Blount-Bridgers House**, one of the town's earliest examples of Federal style architecture.

Thomas Blount built the home he called The Grove, which overlooks the Town Common, in 1808. It is a two-story house with five bays and a gable roof. Two pairs of Flemish bond chimneys are centered by fanlight windows in the attic. There are also large shuttered windows with nine-over-nine sash (the nines refer to the number of panes).

Thomas Blount and his immediate family lived for 36 years in their home in Tarboro and played a significant role in North Carolina history in politics, the military, commerce and religion. Thomas not only served in the North Carolina House and Senate but was in the U.S. House of Representatives from 1793–99, 1805–09 and from 1811 until his death the following year.

The next owner and 20-year resident, Louis Dicken Wilson, was also a state senator and held numerous other political offices. A few years after he died in the Mexican War, The Grove was purchased by John L. Bridgers whose wife was a Wilson cousin. During their 32-year tenure, 1849–1881, the picturesque Italianate porch was added to the house. There have been six long-term owners and 17 owners in all, the last being the city of Tarboro, which used the house as a community house for many years.

The portraits of a number of owners hang in the elevator foyer where the tour starts. The house is not fully furnished, but there are family pieces belonging to various owners. Upstairs is the studio of Hobson Pittman where his art, personal belongings and furnishings are displayed. Pittman, a native of Edgecombe County, was a noted American regionalist painter. His work is included in major collections nationwide, and he served on the faculty of the Pennsylvania Academy of Fine Art. Pittman was known as the Poet-Painter because of his haunting landscapes and interior studies of Victorian houses. The Blount-Bridgers House is open at no charge Monday–Friday 8:30 A.M. to 5:00 P.M. Sunday 2:00 to 5:00 P.M. and on Saturday by appointment (919)823-8121.

The other Federal house in Tarboro, the Irwin House (601 Saint Andrew Street), is not open to the public. It is noteworthy for its delicate ornamentation in the fanlight, the beaded weatherboard, detailed dentils and the exterior chimneys. If you are trying to spot examples of successive architectural periods, the only true Greek Revival home is the Pender-Lanier House (1002 Main Street). The bilateral symmetry, Doric columns, and low-pitched roof are all characteristic of the period. The final significant antebellum style was the Italian Villa design. Two houses on the National Register of Historic Places reflect this period: The Barracks (1100 Albemarle Avenue) and the Coats-Walston House (1503 Saint Andrew Street). Neither is open for tours.

Another house built before the Civil War is the **Silas Everett House**, circa 1810, which is now the Pender Museum (1018 Saint Andrew Street). This restored small farmhouse originally stood in the country, but was moved into town in 1969. The restoration duplicated the beaded weatherboard, marbleizing and unusual period colors. The house is filled with period furniture and historical artifacts. Tours are available through the Blount-Bridgers House: call (919)823-4159.

Agriculture supported many of Tarboro's citizens; those with extensive rural holdings frequently had a town house in this thriving community. At the time of the Civil War Edgecombe County had roughly 68,000 acres of cotton under cultivation, making it one of the biggest cotton producing areas in North Carolina. A reminder of "King Cotton" is the newly restored **cotton press**, moved to the Tarboro Common from Norfleet Plantation. The press is now on the National Register of Historic Places. This is thought to be the last remaining great wooden cotton press in the state, dating back to about 1830. It could press about eight bales of cotton in a day. One distinctive feature is the large topknot, or roof, made of hand hewn cypress shingles. Beside the press stands a small dependency of pre-Civil War vintage from the Philips plantation. It contains artifacts from the cultivation and harvesting of cotton.

One final stop you may want to make along the Recreation Trail is at the fine old brick **Calvary Episcopal Church**, circa 1859, and its adjoining churchyard. Although the original plans called for the bricks to be covered with stucco they never were, and the mellow bricks lend a beauty to the towered structure. The interior oak chancel carvings were done from huge blocks left over from the construction of the Confederate Ram *Albemarle*. The church boasts a number of attractive stained-glass windows. The churchyard is noted for its eclectic collection of trees grown from seeds and roots gathered from around the world, including a Spanish cork tree, Japanese magnolia, English yews and silver firs as well as such local favorites as osage orange, buckeye and incense cedar.

On your walking tour you will see the various architectural styles that followed the Civil War. Of particular note are the Queen Anne homes and those from the neoclassic period. In recent times there has been a Main Street Renaissance, a National Trust for Historic Preservation and renovation project that has given Tarboro's business district attractive store fronts.

If you want to spend the night in Tarboro, one of the historic Edwardian-styled homes, formerly the Pennington House but now known as the Little Warren, is a bed-and-breakfast inn. The rooms in this charming home on Tarboro's Common are filled with antiques from around the world. For information call (919)823-1314.

Directions: From I-95 take US 64 Bypass Rocky Mount. Continue on Route 64 to Tarboro.

Tobacco Farm Life Museum

Curing Curiosity

There are well over six thousand museums in the United States. From simple exhibits to state-of-the-arts glitz these attractions explain, present and preserve various aspects of our lives and our past. A particularly valuable museum provides the visitor with background then presents the modern context with an on-going activity. That is just what the **Tobacco Farm Life Museum** does.

Half of America's annual harvest of nearly a billion pounds of flue-cured tobacco is grown within 50 miles of Kenly. Tobacco has been a significant economic reality in eastern North Carolina since the early 1900s. The influence of tobacco on the farm community is presented in this museum and in the on-site farm tours the museum arranges.

Actually tobacco was being grown in this region long before the 20th century. The Indians were the first tobacco farmers and the exhibits begin with a collection of their artifacts. Tobacco was native to the western hemisphere and was first introduced to Europeans after Columbus's landing in the Caribbean in 1492. The early colonial economy used tobacco as a form of currency— houses, horses and slaves were offered for so many pounds of tobacco. It was also America's first exported crop.

As North Carolina is the birthplace of soil conservation, it is appropriate that the museum's story of tobacco starts with an explanation of the role of soil conservation in good crop production. Next comes a step-by-step explanation of how tobacco is grown, cured and marketed. One exhibit lets you touch the looping horse on which the tobacco was strung on sticks for curing. You'll also see the grading bench, "sticking up horse" and tobacco presses which were used in the packhouse to prepare tobacco for market.

Model rooms—kitchen, bedroom and wash house—furnished to represent farm life in the 1900s reveal all kinds of details. An old medical bill shows that the doctor charged $2 for an office visit and $20 for a pregnancy (nine months of care plus delivery). If you're visiting with children, be sure to point out the letter from Santa Claus written in 1886 explaining that the candy and good things to eat were all locked up in the community store.

The entire museum looks like a tobacco barn, but the collection of farm tools, tractors and buggies especially suggests a working barn. The equipment here was used for many other crops in addition to tobacco. One unusual piece is the cotton mop poisoner. Farmers mixed poison and molasses, then coated the cotton plants to kill the boll weevil.

One of the most fascinating aspects of the tobacco industry is the auction. A video lets you see and hear an auctioneer selling tobacco at 500 words a minute. If you'd like to see a live auction, plan a visit sometime between August and the middle of October. There are auctions in nearby Smithfield and Wilson. If you visit in August you can combine a visit to the museum with a tour of a nearby farm and a tobacco auction. Guided farm tours are given Monday–Friday in July through mid-August at 10:00 A.M. and 2:00 P.M.

The Tobacco Farm Life Museum is open Monday–Saturday 9:30 A.M. to 5:00 P.M. and Sunday 2:00 to 5:00 P.M.. A nominal admission is charged. Be sure to watch the 15-minute movie on the history of the tobacco industry. The museum has a Country Store which sells hand-crafted items; honey, homemade jellies and jams, as well as blended smoking tobacco. The museum is planning to expand to include a reconstruction of the Iredell Brown Farm, a typical depression era farm.

Directions: From I-95 take Exit 107, US 301 north towards Wilson for 1.5 miles, and the museum will be on your left in Kenly.

FAYETTEVILLE AND PINEHURST VICINITY

Fort Bragg and Pope Air Force Base

Attention!

Fayetteville's past is heavily intertwined with America's military history. Wherever you go in the area you hear war stories. Even the city's name derives from an American Revolutionary hero, the Marquis de LaFayette. After the war many new American cities were named in LaFayette's honor, but Fayetteville, N.C. was the only one of these the Marquis visited when he returned to America in 1825. His carriage is still displayed in the headquarters of the Fayetteville Independent Light Infantry.

Fayetteville's military significance dates from 1918 when Congress established Camp Bragg, an army field artillery site named for Confederate General Braxton Bragg. Added the following year was a landing field named after First Lieutenant Harley H. Pope, a flier whose plane crashed in the Cape Fear River. Within five years the camp became a permanent army post, upgraded to **Fort Bragg**.

During World War II Fort Bragg was the training ground for all five airborne divisions, and now many of the most prestigious units in the military are based here: the XVII Airborne Corps, 82nd Airborne Division, First Special Operations Command, John F. Kennedy Special Warfare Center and the First Corps Support Command. Pope is home base for the 317th Tactical Airlift Wing and the Military Airlift Command. Even visitors without knowledge of the military can get a clear picture of Fort Bragg's importance from a tour of its two museums, and at certain times they have a chance to witness world-class parachute jumping.

The **82nd Airborne Division War Memorial Museum** has the largest collection in the army museum system. In World War I, the 82nd won the distinction of being the army's first airborne division. Later it won even greater honor during World War II. In July 1943, the 82nd made the first airborne assault ever launched by the U.S. when they attacked Sicily. In September of that year they distinguished themselves during the invasion of Italy at Salerno. In June 1944, the 82nd performed an important role in the D-Day invasion by parachuting behind the lines in Normandy. In September 1944, the 82nd invaded Holland by air in the last official airborne assault until the recent December 1989 assault on Panama. So outstanding was the 82nd's contribution to the war effort, they were the lead unit in the January 1946 stateside victory parade in New York. The museum has films, uniforms, weapons, supplies and more than 3,000 artifacts ranging from photographs to outdoor exhibits of planes and weapons.

Be sure to see the dioramas with costumed mannequins and background sounds of battle. The weapons collection not only covers the ordnance development for American forces, but includes captured enemy weapons, such as Soviet and Czech weapons captured in the Grenada conflict in 1983. A uniform, a rifle and selected photographs recall the heroism of Corporal Alvin York who single-handedly killed 20 Nazi soldiers, destroyed 35 machine guns, and captured 135 men armed only with his regulation rifle and a pistol. The indoor exhibits are open at no charge Tuesday–Saturday 10:00 A.M. to 4:30 P.M. and Sunday 11:30 A.M. to 4:00 P.M.

Outside there is a Curtis C-46 Command, the first aircraft to have a jump door. The Douglass C-47 was known as the Skytrain and was the workhorse of the Army Air Corps Transport Unit, carrying the 82nd into Sicily, Salerno, Normandy and Holland.

The Fairchild C-119, known as the Flying Boxcar, was the first aircraft to handle large parachute loads. It was used from the 1940s through the 1960s. The Provider, a Fairchild C-123K, with its full-section rear ramp door was an ideal support aircraft for airborne operations from the 1950s to the 1970s. The C-7 Caribou provided support in Vietnam. Another craft used in Vietnam was the UH 1A Iroquois, or "Huey". Among the weapons displayed are a 15cm medium-field howitzer captured in Normandy in June 1944 and an antitank gun, the M-156. A small statue commemorates the Golden Knights, Fort Bragg's team of precision parachutists whose flying aerobatics and free-falls mesmerize onlookers. The team has won more national and international parachuting awards than any other team, military or civilian. They perform approximately 300 times a year; for training jumps and performance schedule call (919)396-2036. You can also watch the 82nd do training jumps; a daily recorded tape gives the schedule, call (919)396-MEMO. Directions to drop zones are posted at the museums.

The second museum on the base is the **John F. Kennedy Special Warfare Museum** where you see the stuff of real cloak and dagger operations. Fort Bragg is home base for the army's 1st Special Operations Command, which includes the Special Forces, Rangers, Psychological Operations, Civil Affairs and Special Operations Aviation. Guerrilla warfare is not new as you'll discover at this museum. The Revolutionary War and the Civil War had irregular forces such as those led by Francis Marion, the "Swamp Fox," and John S. Mosby, the "Gray Ghost."

Psychological warfare was widely used in World War II. The museum covers Tokyo Rose and Axis Sally as well as the Office of Strategic Services. You can see a genuine survival kit, not the James Bond variety, as well as trick cameras and other items not devised by "Q," Bond's weapon supplier. Another major exhibit displays memorabilia from John Wayne and his movie *The Green Berets*. Near the museum at the JFK Chapel grounds is a statue John Wayne commissioned in appreciation for the cooperation and assistance he received from the 82nd Airborne during the making of his film.

The Special Warfare Museum has a fascinating collection of espionage weapons, including a lethal sleeve dagger, an assassin's glove, a "little fire-fly" demolition device and Viet Cong booby-trapped punji stakes, poisoned-tipped cane stakes hidden in the ground or among the vegetation. The display on terrorism is alarming because it demonstrates the danger to the civilian population. The banner confiscated from the airport in Grenada during the October 1983 operation is as timely as yesterday's headlines. The museum is open Tuesday- Sunday 11:30 A.M. to 4:00 P.M.

Across the street from this museum, at the First Special Operations Command (SOCOM), is the **Hall of Heroes**. Here are portraits of 17 Special Forces Medal of Honor recipients. The Hall of Heroes is open Monday–Sunday 8:00 A.M. to 4:30 P.M.

Two special events at these bases are the April Open House and the July CAPEX. Pope Air Force Base has an annual spring Open House featuring state-of-the-art as well as vintage equipment, demonstrations by precision flying teams, plus the Golden Knights parachute team. CAPEX stands for the Capabilities Exercise held at Fort Bragg in July when mass personnel and heavy equipment drops are made from C-130 aircraft. The army on parade makes you proud to watch it. For dates of special events call (919)396-5620 or 2920. Before leaving Fort Bragg be sure to see the statue *Iron Mike*, a World War II paratrooper in full combat gear.

While in the Fayetteville area you may also want to include a stop at **Heritage Square**, where three historic properties on the National Register have been restored. The two-story Federal style Sandford House was once the home of noted North Carolina artist Elliot Daingerfield. Next door is the Oval Ballroom, built in 1818 by architect Robert Halliday, reputedly for the wedding reception of his daughter Margaret and John Sandford. The interior is noted for its attractive plaster cornices and pilasters. The last of the trio, the Baker-Haigh-Nimocks House, was built in 1804. This white frame house has colonial dormer windows, an interior free-standing staircase and moldings carved with nautical details. The properties are open Monday–Friday 9:00 A.M. to 3:00 P.M. by appointment; call 483-6009. Several other historic spots in town are also open by appointment, including the 1789 Cool Spring Tavern (323-4111) and the Market House (483-2073). For more information about these and other Fayetteville attractions, stop at the 1790 Barge's Tavern building at 515 Ramsey Street. This National Register property is now the Fayetteville Area Convention and Visitors' Bureau (CVB), open Monday–Friday 8:30 A.M. to 5:30 P.M.; call (919)483-5311.

Directions: Fayetteville and all its attractions are directly off I-95. Take I-95 Business US 301 to Grove Street, turn right on Grove Street and right again on Route 401, Ramsey Street, for Fayetteville's CVB. For the Fort Bragg Visitors Center continue on Grove Street, which will become Fort Bragg Blvd., Route 24. The Fort Bragg Visitors Center is ten miles west of Fayetteville off Route 24 on Randolph Street. Follow the signs on Route 24.

House in the Horseshoe

Not a Good Luck Charm

The **House in the Horseshoe** did not bring its builder, Philip Alston, the good fortune its name would suggest. Alston, who built the riverfront plantation house in 1772, moved here reputedly to escape a counterfeiting charge. In time he would be indicted twice for murder, removed from public office, suspended from the general assembly and worse.

In 1776, Alston devised a peculiar scheme for obtaining real estate. In the wake of the battle at Moore's Creek (see selection), defeated Scottish troops, having fought for Britain, were required to pledge their allegiance to the colonial cause in order to retain their land. As clerk of the court, Alston refused to permit Scots to sign the pledge, forcing them to relocate in Pennsylvania. After they were gone, he confiscated their property.

A colonel in the British army, David Fanning, was sent to the area to protect Scottish property owners, and on the morning of August 5, 1781, Colonel Fanning and his Tory troops attacked a band of Alston's revolutionists who were camped at the House in the Horseshoe. The Tories riddled the house with bullets (numerous holes are still there to see). After four hours, Fanning, who had only about 50 men, became concerned that Alston might be reinforced, so he attempted to burn the house. Alston's wife saved the house, however, by talking with Fanning and arranging a surrender. Local lore has it that Mrs. Alston not only talked with the British colonel but also disappeared with him for several hours.

Alston signed a parole stating that he would not "have any intercourse or hold correspondence with the enemies of his Majesty," and that he would remain peacefully at home. But peace keeping was not his forte. In a few years he was admonished by the Lord Proprietor Governor for cold bloodedly killing one of the men in his command with his gun butt for suspected treason. Later, Alston made his head slave kill a political opponent. It was this act that forced him to flee North Carolina in 1790. One year later he was killed in his sleep by a bullet fired through a window, perhaps by the very slave he had co-opted for his own nefarious scheme.

In 1798 the 2,500-acre plantation was acquired by four-term Governor Benjamin Williams. The first board house built in this area, the two-storied plantation house was considered a showpiece in its day. It has a gable roof and large double-shouldered Flemish bond chimneys. The interior woodwork is elaborate and well designed. The furniture dates from 1720 to 1840. A reconstructed loom house may once have been the summer kitchen.

The visitor center also houses a gift shop. The House in the Horseshoe is open at no charge April–October, Monday–Saturday 9:00 A.M. to 5:00 P.M. and Sunday 1:00 to 5:00 P.M. From November–March hours are Tuesday–Saturday 10:00 A.M. to 4:00 P.M. and Sunday 1:00 to 4:00 P.M. Each year on the weekend nearest August 5 a re-enactment of the skirmish fought here is staged.

Directions: From I-95 in the Fayetteville area take North Carolina 24 to Carthage. At the intersection of North Carolina 24/27 and US 15-501, you'll see a brown and white State Historic Site sign; turn right and go ten miles on Country Road 1006. If you are travelling south on I-95 take US 421 north from Dunn to Sanford. In downtown Sanford pick up NC Route 42 west and go about 12 miles. Follow the brown and white State Historic Sites signs.

Malcolm Blue Historical Farm

Down on the Farm Fun

You'll discover the real meaning of the term "horse power" at the **Malcolm Blue Historical Farm** museum. Farmers long ago would put a horse on a truck bed, like the one displayed at the farm, and lead the horse in a circle to generate power to run machines like threshers. The museum not only instructs about farm machinery but also tobacco processing and turpentine making.

Malcolm McMillan Blue, son of Scottish immigrants who settled in the Sandhills region, prospered in the turpentine and lumber industry and acquired 6,885 acres of land. In 1825 he built a farmhouse on the Old Pee Dee Road (now Route 5) between Aberdeen and Southern Pines. The house, called Bethesda Farm today, is one of the few surviving examples of an early 19th-century Scottish homestead. The house is furnished with period pieces. During the Civil War General Kilpatrick, in command of the Second and Third Cavalry Division of General Sherman's Union army, spent a night here. Malcolm Blue's youngest daughter, Belle, had a pet deer, that narrowly escaped being the main course for the hungry men in blue. The family did lose every cow, hog and chicken on the farm as well as their grain, flour and other foodstuff.

The farm still has a working gristmill, stable, water tower, horse barns, tobacco packhouse and herb garden. The last weekend in September is the time for the annual Malcolm Blue Historic Crafts and Skills Festival. The barns are filled with animals, corn is ground at the mill, and a barbecue and square dance are held for guests. On the second Sunday in December the Malcolm

Blue Holiday Open House takes place. The house is also open for tours on weekends in the spring and fall; call (918)944-3840 or 944-1115. You are welcome to picnic on the grounds.

The Malcolm Blue Farm has the oldest structures in Aberdeen, but this historic town, once called Blue's Crossing, has other prominent homes. A walk around Aberdeen will take you past the 1879 home of Malcolm James Blue, who followed in his father's footsteps in the turpentine business. The John Blue House, built by Malcolm's nephew, dates from 1880 and the Allison Francis Page Home, from 1879. Also worth a visit is the Bethesda Presbyterian Church, located ¼ mile from the Malcolm Blue Farm on the outskirts of Aberdeen. The first church was built here in 1793 and the present church in 1861.

Directions: From I-95 at Fayetteville pick up Route 401W to Raeford. At Raeford take Route 211W to Aberdeen. Just before entering Aberdeen take a right on Pee Dee Road. Go one block and take another right. Pass Old Bethesda Church on the right, and the Malcolm Blue Farm is ⅛ mile on the left.

Museum of the Cape Fear

Fear Not!

If you've ever peeked at the end of a mystery novel, eaten your dessert before your vegetables, or seen the end of a movie first— then you'll want to start exploring the **Museum of the Cape Fear** on the second floor because that is where you'll find the fun exhibits.

You can run a model train around a mock-up of a toy shop or climb aboard a steamboat model and hear about the days when this was a common mode of transportation from Fayetteville to Wilmington. The ship appears to be pulling along the dock ready to unload wares and pick up rifles from the Fayetteville Arsenal. The engineer (an appropriately attired mannequin) is in the engine room, and at the rear of the boat there is a paddle wheel.

Here, too, you'll learn all about the Fayetteville Arsenal, the reason this city was one of Sherman's main targets on his march through the Carolinas. From out the museum's window you can see where the arsenal once stood, and a model will help you imagine the size and scope of its operations. You'll also see Civil War weapons, including Fayetteville rifles, and an exhibit on North Carolina's role in the war. Moving even farther back in time you'll learn about the 1825 visit of the Marquis de Lafayette, for whom the town was named.

Returning to the first floor, you can begin with the artifacts from prehistoric Indians, the Woodland Indians and the Mississippi culture. There are exhibits on the daily life of the North

Carolina Indian tribes and of the tragic Trail of Tears that took the Cherokees west. Then the story of European settlement is told beginning with the arrival of Verrazzano in 1524. The inevitable clash of the two cultures is also covered—the introduction of European diseases among the native population, the tragically different concept of land ownership, the betrayals and the battles.

Two exhibits that appeal to the adventurous are the tales of the pirate Stede Bonnet, who hounded the British around the Carolina shores, and the story of fiery Flora MacDonald, who hid Bonny Prince Charles after his defeat by the British in 1745. When she and her family sailed for the New World she signed an oath not to oppose the British in America. She was just one of many Scots who settled in the Cape Fear area. It was Scottish soldiers who lost to the colonials at the Battle of Moore's Creek (see selection). Before the battle Flora MacDonald rallied Loyalist troops near Cool Spring. Reminders of the battle and battle dress are displayed.

You'll also see an old gristmill from Cumberland County, plus a display on textiles, the cooperage trade and an apothecary chest. The Museum of the Cape Fear is open Tuesday–Saturday from 10:00 A.M. to 5:00 P.M. and Sunday 1:00 to 5:00 P.M.

Directions: From I-95 take Exit 49. Take Highway 210-53 west towards Fayetteville. Go straight through the intersection of Route 301-I-95 Business; you will be on Grove Street. Travel approximately 1.3 miles to the fifth stoplight, turn left on Bragg Boulevard and go 2/10 of a mile. Then turn right on Cashwell Street, which merges into Hay Street at yield sign. Continue on Hay Street to first stoplight on Woodside, make a left at stoplight, and the museum will be on your right one block down. Turn right on Arsenal Avenue for parking.

PGA World Golf Hall of Fame

Golfers' Heaven

If you're traveling with an avid golfer, you must visit the **PGA World Golf Hall of Fame** in Pinehurst. Even for those indifferent to the sport, this shrine provides a fascinating look at the game.

The World Golf Hall of Fame opened in 1974, but it wasn't until 1984 that it was taken over by the Professional Golfers Association of America (PGA). Of the 9,000 members in the PGA, only 56 have been inducted into the PGA World Golf Hall of Fame. Among these are men even the uninitiated will recognize: Ben Hogan, Gene Sarazen, Jack Nicklaus and Gary Player (the only four players to win the Grand Slam), plus such renowned golfers as Bobby Jones, Arnold Palmer, Sam Snead and Babe

With more than 30 championship courses in the area and the site of the PGA World Golf Hall of Fame, Pinehurst is a golfer's mecca.

Zaharias. Two show biz golfers, Bing Crosby and Bob Hope, have also made the cut. A bronze plaque honors each inductee.

Many aspects of the game are covered at this newly updated mecca. The origins of golf are traced along the History Wall. You can see the tools of the clubmakers trade in a facsimile of a shop in St. Andrews, Scotland. The sign listing a cost of seven shillings and six pence, or less than seven dollars, for custom-made clubs, will make golfers weep, but that price was back in 1850. The Auchterlonie Collection has one of the most complete arrays of antique clubs in the world. Laurie Auchterlonie was a clubmaker from St. Andrews who started as an apprentice in his father's shop in 1920. In fact, some of the clubs in the collection were gathered by Laurie's father including two of the oldest clubs in existence, the 1690 Play Club and a 1690 putter. There are 25 wooden putters in the rare collection of more than a hundred antique clubs, some made by Laurie Auchterlonie.

Other special exhibits include a tribute to the Ryder Cup matches, an extensive golf library and displays on Bobby Jones and Arnold Palmer. If you've ever made and reported a hole in one your name is stored in the Hall of Fame computers, and you can get a printout verifying your skillful, or lucky, shot.

There are ambitious plans to add a Play Room with hands-on displays evaluating and advising golfers on their swings and putts. An indoor practice area and putting green plus the advice of traveling pros will help improve your game. You'll be able to learn what's new in equipment and training techniques.

Situated between Pinehurst Country Club's famed No. 2 course and the new No. 7 course, the PGA World Golf Hall of Fame couldn't have a more auspicious location. According to *Golf Reporter Magazine* for the eight years they have been selecting favorite courses, Pinehurst's No. 2 course has been chosen No. 1 in the Carolinas. No matter who does the voting—golf professionals, golf writers, top amateurs, magazine subscribers—the decision is the same. The Hall of Fame is attractively designed with newly landscaped gardens in the foreground and the golf courses in the background. The new Shrine Gardens have as their focal point the PGA logo planted in flowers. For those who want a reminder of their visit, the Hall of Fame's Out of Bounds Gift Shop has a wide assortment of golf clothes and memorabilia.

The PGA World Golf Hall of Fame is open 9:00 A.M. to 5:00 P.M. daily March through November. Admission is charged.

Once you are inspired by the Hall of Fame, it's time to test your own skill against **Pinehurst**'s famed courses. Pinehurst Hotel and Country Club now has seven courses, five of which start and end at the Pinehurst Golf Resort Club where the 19th hole watering spot is called the 91st hole. Pinehurst also has one of the top 50 tennis clubs in the country. There are golf and tennis schools as well as package rates. For information from inside NC call (800)672-4644. If calling outside NC the number is (800)334-9560.

There are about 30 championship golf courses in the Pinehurst area. It is said golfers don't want to go to heaven when they die, they want to go to Pinehurst. Some consider the two synonymous. Few areas in the world are identified with a sport to the degree that Pinehurst and the surrounding Sandhills area are linked with golf.

Directions: From I-95 at Fayetteville take Route 211 to Aberdeen. Route 211 will intersect Route 15/501 (in fact there is a short stretch that is a combination of Route 211, US 1 and US 15/501). Take Route 15/501 north until you reach the Pinehurst traffic circle where you will take the well-marked Hall of Fame turnoff.

Shaw House

Something Old, Something Borrowed. . .

Three historic buildings—the Shaw, Loom and Garner Houses—stand together where two Revolutionary roads crossed, the Pee Dee and the Morganton Road. In 1820 Charles C. Shaw acquired 2,500-acres at the crossroads of an Indian trail and the road to the market in Fayetteville. Although the date 1840 is still visible on the chimney, historical architects believe the **Shaw House** was built even earlier.

Squire Shaw built a comfortable house, not as grand as those of seacoast plantation owners but still more stylish than the early settlers' cabins built in the Sandhills. The Squire's son, Charles Washington Shaw, who inherited the house was elected the first mayor of Southern Pines in 1887.

When you tour the Shaw House you'll see Moore County furniture dating from 1820 to 1880 (although there is one piece that dates back to 1790). Most of the furniture is simple in design, but more decorative touches can be seen in the beautifully carved cypress mantles.

The Shaw House is open for tours from February through April. Afternoon tea is served beginning at 2:30 P.M. Monday through Saturday. Before leaving be sure to visit the herb garden and the two additional houses on the grounds.

The more than 200-year-old **Britt-Sanders cabin** now serves as a Loom House. When you look at the intricately placed stones forming the mortarless chimney you can appreciate the painstaking work required to make this a "perfect restoration," to quote the North Carolina Division of History and Archives. This rustic pioneer cabin is furnished with simple pieces including a 125-year-old loom. Members of the Sandhill Weavers Guild demonstrate weaving at the Loom House.

The **Garner House**, built around 1793, has also been moved to the Shaw grounds. The background on this house is hazy, and it may have been built later. It stands today as an excellent example of rural Moore County architecture. Original hand-forged hinges and posts can be seen on the doors, and the blue-painted pegged mantle is an example of early folk art. The walls are paneled with wide heart pine except in the upstairs loft area. Much of the furniture is original.

Directions: From I-95 Bypass to exit 49, Route 210/53, this will become Highway 210/53/24/87. Follow Route 24 west, Bragg Boulevard, six miles to Route 401 Bypass south toward Raeford. After three miles make a right at the intersection of 401 south. When you intersect Route 211 (about 20 miles) take Route 211 to Aberdeen. Route 1/211 will take you to the Southern Pines/Pinehurst area. Stay on Route 1 until you reach the intersection with Morganton Road (in about a block), turn right and the Shaw House will be on your left at the corner of South West Broad Street.

Weymouth Woods Sandhills Nature Preserve and Weymouth Center

Beauty—Natural and Manmade

Every once in awhile you come across a museum that challenges your imagination. This is the case with the Natural History Museum at the **Weymouth Woods Sandhills Nature Preserve**. One exhibit children love is the darkened "sounds of night" exhibit where you can listen to crickets, bats, owls, katydid and a red fox. To view another exhibit on the subterranean life of the preserve, you have to get down on your hands and knees and crawl into a cave-like space. Through a glass wall you see a fascinating cross-section of life around the tree roots. Specimens here include snakes, moles, salamanders, weasels and an assortment of bugs.

The museum also traces the evolution of pine forests and sandhills, good background for helping visitors appreciate the natural world they'll see while hiking the preserve's nature trails. The names of the trails help identify the terrain. The longest walking time is the hour it takes to hike Holly Road Trail. Both the Pine Barrens and Bower's Bog Trail can be covered in a half hour, and it takes only 15 minutes to explore the Gum Swamp Trail.

This protected area represents only a small portion of the Sandhills region, which covers one million acres in south central North Carolina. It is noted for the flat-topped sandy ridges separated by broad level valleys. The headwaters of James Creek cut through Weymouth Woods. This creek widens into a small hardwood swamp common to the valleys of the Sandhills. The predominant vegetation is longleaf pine, the last known stand of virgin longleaf pine in the state. Springtime is particularly lovely here because of the many wildflowers, wild azalea, dogwood and dwarf iris. Wildlife includes the ubiquitous gray squirrel and the fox squirrel, plus red and gray foxes, deer, raccoons, opossums and rabbits. You may even spot the more elusive mink and otter. Birdlife is abundant with quail, morning dove and owls year-round. Migrating songbirds often winter at Weymouth. The red cockaded woodpecker, an endangered species, lives in the hollow of old pine trees at this preserve. The Natural History Museum is open at no charge daily 9:00 A.M. to 6:00 P.M. and Sunday 12:00 to 5:00 P.M.

Adjoining this preserve is the **Weymouth Center**, a cultural arts facility housed in the Georgian home of the Boyd family. Novelist James Boyd and his wife turned this house into a gathering place for writers and musicians, and the tradition continues. James Boyd wrote *Drums, Marching On, Long Hunt, Roll River* and *Bitter Creek*. Among the authors who have stayed here to write are F. Scott Fitzgerald, Thomas Wolfe, Sherwood Anderson, Paul Green and Ernest Hemingway. The house is now on the National Register of Historic Places. The estate once covered 2,000 acres and even included a 9-hole golf course.

James Boyd loved to ride and was the first Master of the Southern Pines Hunt. In the entrance hall of Weymouth Center you can see a collection of hunting pictures. His portrait hangs in the reception, or fireplace, hall. This is a copy of the painting in the Southern Pines Library. The Center still has some Boyd family furniture. The room where James Boyd once did his writing is now an art gallery. There are changing art exhibits as well as monthly lectures and concerts given at 3:30 P.M. on selected Sundays from September through May. The Center also sponsors a writers-in-residence program for North Carolina writers.

Directions: From I-95 pick up Route 401 in the Fayetteville area and travel westward to Route 211. Take Route 211 to the Southern Pines area and then turn onto US 1 north (also Route 15/501). Take downtown exit to Broad Street. (You will first be on Southwest Broad Street, which has two-way traffic. When it becomes one-way you will be on Northeast Broad Street). From Northeast Broad Street make a right on East Vermont Avenue to the entrance for Weymouth Center. When you leave the Center, exit via Connecticut Avenue (this is not the same way you entered Weymouth Center). Turn right on Connecticut Avenue, then take another right on Fort Bragg Road. The entrance to the Weymouth Preserve will be on your right.

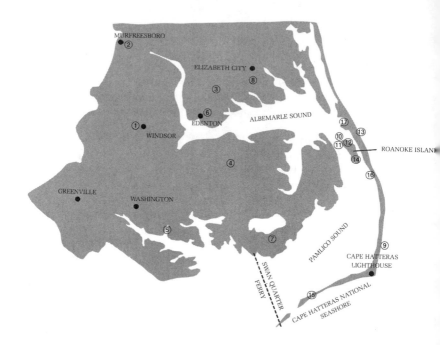

NORTHERN COAST

Mainland
1. Hope Plantation
2. Murfreesboro
3. Newbold-White House
4. Somerset Place and Pettigrew State Park

Along Rivers and Sounds
5. Bath
6. Edenton
7. Mattamuskeet National Wildlife Refuge
8. Museum of the Albemarle

Outer Banks and Roanoke Island
9. Cape Hattaras National Seashore
10. Elizabethan Gardens
11. *Elizabeth II*
12. Forth Raleigh and the Lost Colony
13. Jockey's Ridge State Park and Kitty Hawk Kites
14. North Carolina Aquarium   Roanoke Island
15. Ocracoke Island
16. Pea Island National Wildlife Refuge and Bodie Lighthouse
17. Wright Brothers National Memorial

Truth is stranger than fiction, so don't be surprised to learn Sir Walter Raleigh's intrepid band of explorers sailed to the New World on ships called the *Lion*, the *Tiger* and *Dorothy* (in addition to the *Elizabeth*). This is just one example of little-known facts from the past that can awaken interest in our nation's history. To visit the homes where our leaders were born, the taverns where they relaxed, the businesses that supported them and, not to forget, the battlefields where they died brings our forebears and their times vividly to mind.

English-speaking America began in North Carolina with the Lost Colony. Roanoke Island's outdoor drama of the same name re-creates that tragic saga every summer. Visitors wander around the site of Fort Raleigh nearby and climb aboard the *Elizabeth II*, a re-creation of one of the ships used by Raleigh's expeditions, docked in Manteo.

In Edenton, Bath, Murfreesboro and Ocracoke you find historic districts that span many decades. Not just a few old houses but entire blocks have survived. A stop at the Museum of the Albemarle puts the history of the entire region in perspective for you.

The major draw of the Northern Coast region is the unspoiled beauty of the Atlantic beaches, protected under multiple government auspices such as the Cape Hatteras National Seashore, the Pea Island National Wildlife Refuge and Jockey's Ridge State Park. These great expanses of protected land give you a great feel for what the country was like before it was settled. Walk along an unpopulated shore, listen to the gulls screech, watch the waves crash and the crabs scurry along the beach, and leave your footprints in the sand.

MAINLAND

Hope Plantation

Don't Give Up Hope

David Stone might well be considered North Carolina's Jefferson, for he also was a Renaissance man, interested in a wide range of intellectual pursuits. Stone entered Princeton (then called the College of New Jersey) when he was 14 and graduated at the top of his class four years later. At 19 he was chosen to attend the state convention to ratify the federal Constitution, and a year later he was elected to the North Carolina legislature. He became the second youngest superior court judge in the state, and his 1,400-volume library was one of the most extensive in all of North Carolina. This toast raised to him in 1809 might just as easily have described Jefferson, "a friend of man and a patron of the arts and sciences." Both of these early leaders took great pride in their efforts to establish a strong educational system in their states. Jefferson founded the University of Virginia, and Stone was on the board of trustees for the University of North Carolina and helped select Chapel Hill as the site of the new university.

The land on which **Hope Plantation** was built was a wedding gift to David Stone from his father, who had acquired it through his marriage to Elizabeth Shriver Hobson (the Hobson family was granted the land in the 1720s by the colony's Lord Proprietors). David married in 1793 and began building his home several years later. Acting as his own architect, he used an 18th-century architectural manual, *The British Architect*, to design Hope Plantation. That is why, even though it was built during the Federal period, it follows a Georgian design. Essentially it's a double house with a center hall downstairs and upstairs. The Chinese Chippendale balustrade on the double portico creates a pleasing exterior. This design is repeated on the rooftop widow's walk. Federal touches you'll see in addition to this fretwork balustrade include the enclosed staircase, the enlarged window panes with candles in the transoms over the doorway, and the smaller size of the bedrooms.

By 1803 the house was virtually complete, which was fortunate because David Stone's political career demanded a great deal of his time. He was elected seven times to the North Carolina House of Commons and served two terms as United States representative and two as senator. In 1808 he began the first of his two terms as governor.

David and his wife had ten daughters and a son, although six of the girls died in childhood. In 1816 his wife and youngest daughter succumbed to a fever epidemic. A poignant reminder of this loss can still be seen on the inside of Stone's library bookcase. He had been accustomed to making notes on the wall when he loaned books, but after his wife's death he wrote, "O for the past gone days when I could gaze at my wife." A year later he married Sarah Dashiell in the ballroom at Hope. David Stone died suddenly the following year on October 17, 1818. His son and heir sold Hope Plantation in 1836.

An eight-minute film about Hope that you can see before you

tour the mansion provides additional details about David Stone. A new museum and education center is to be built in the adjacent Hope Forest; a nature trail through the woods is also planned. The mansion is furnished with items similar to those listed on an 1818 inventory, plus a few original pieces. The 1798 tall caseclock in the family parlor duplicates the one purchased in 1836 for $75 at the Stone estate sale, the highest priced item in the lot. Efforts are now underway to reconstitute David Stone's comprehensive library. About one-fourth of the volumes were legal items. In the hall just outside the library there is a rare mourning handkerchief, called The Tears of America. The printed fabric was made in Philadelphia in 1800 to commemorate the death of George Washington.

The second, more modest, house you can tour was moved to the plantation grounds. Known as the **King-Bazemore House**, it was built in 1763, and its hall and parlor design combines elements of medieval English, Georgian and Federal styles. This was originally the home of William King, a Bertie County planter and cooper. His initials and that of his wife, Elizabeth, can still be seen in the exterior brick end of the house. Mr. King's cooperage skills can also be discerned in the design of the attractive barrel-back cupboards on either side of the fireplace. Although none of the furniture is original it does duplicate items listed on the 1778 inventory. This house is unusual in that it has closets, made possible by the spaces on either side on the interior chimneys. The closets even have small windows.

A kitchen dependency and additional period outbuildings will be added to the plantation. A perennial flower and vegetable garden suggests one that might have been planted in 1800.

The Hope Mansion and King-Basemore House are open March through December 23 on Monday–Saturday 10:00 A.M. to 4:00 P.M. and Sunday 2:00 to 5:00 P.M.; closed on Thanksgiving. The admission is comparable to a first-run movie.

Directions: From I-95 take Route 64 east to Williamston, then Route 13 north to Route 308 at Windsor. Take Route 308 west for four miles to Hope Plantation on the left.

Murfreesboro

Quietly Appealing

Visiting **Murfreesboro**, you may find yourself agreeing with a letter that appeared in a Raleigh newspaper. The writer asks, "Do you know . . . anything of Murfreesboro? . . . it is one of the prettiest places in North Carolina . . . the country villages throughout our good old State are far from presenting that thriving, cultivated appearance seen in most of the New England villages; but the citizens of this borough may well challenge any section of the country to produce a place of the same size containing more handsome private residences . . ." This letter was written April 30, 1860.

The first visitors to this area arrived in the 1500s on an expedition from the Roanoke Island settlement; then in the 1600s the Meherrin River was explored by settlers from Jamestown. During this era the territory was inhabited by Nottoway, Meherrin and Chowanoke Indians. In the 1700s the settlement of Murfree's Landing grew at the head of the river; by the 1740s it was a King's Landing, a port where imports and exports to England were inspected by representatives of the crown. In the 18th and early 19th century the town developed into a thriving port on the triangular trade route with New England, England and the West Indies.

Most of the houses on the Murfreesboro tour guide were built in the 1800s. There are 62 points of interest on the map, but these must be sought out like truffles; this is not a town with an obvious main street. The houses are scattered on back streets over a broad expanse. Those who prefer to walk will find a large concentration of houses over a five-block area in the center of town. Paved paths link these sites. Five listed spots are open to the public, beginning with **The Roberts-Vaughan Village Center**. This is the headquarters for the Murfreesboro Historical Association and the Chamber of Commerce. It also serves as the town library and the visitor center.

The visitor center is open Monday–Friday from 8:30 A.M. to 5:00 P.M. except Wednesday when it closes in the afternoon. On Saturday tourist information can be obtained at the library from 10:00 A.M. to 12:00 P.M. and 2:00 to 5:00 P.M. The other houses in town are open for guided tours at a nominal fee. Tour arrangements can be made at the center, or by calling (919)398-5922.

While at the center take the time to explore the **Roberts House**. It was built in the 1790s and enlarged and given a Greek Revival facade in the 1850s by Uriah Vaughan. Despite years of neglect and deterioration all the wooden doors, mantels, wainscoting and floors are original. Although several rooms are offices, others are decorated with period pieces. Romantics should enjoy the story of Mary Ann Roberts who in 1818, although promised in marriage to an elderly general, ran away to Murfreesboro, Tennessee with Matt Brickel Murfree. The record is unclear whether they lived happily ever after, but it is known that they had eleven children. The **Winborne House**, a Murfreesboro bed-and-breakfast, is a small version of the Roberts House (for information on accommodations call (919)398-5224).

Another Murfreesboro house open to the public is the **Wheeler House**. When you visit, try to image 19 children living in this four-room brick home. Of course, the children were born over a long span, and many were half-siblings as John Wheeler was married three times. Wheeler, a successful shipper from New Jersey, purchased the building in 1814. Previously it had been used as both an ordinary, or inn, and a community store. Additional space was available in the brick dependency, which was used as both dining room and office. This is one of the few, if not the only, brick dependencies to survive in the state. Several of Wheeler's offspring distinguished themselves; one son taught at West Point and wrote books about warfare, and another wrote the first history of the state and became the first U.S. minister to Nicaragua.

Across the street from the Wheeler House and past the town garden is the **Winborne Law Office and Store**. The downstairs portion houses the Parker Country Store Collection. Shelves are filled with a wide assortment of useful items from teapots to oil lamps, from bonnets to bromides. Upstairs the front room has been furnished with the desk and law books from Judge B.B. Winborne's office. In the back room there is an exhibit on sewing and weaving.

In the same block you can also tour the 1790 **William Rea Museum**, situated in the oldest commercial brick structure in North Carolina. Rea was a wealthy Boston merchant and shipper who traded between Murfreesboro and New England. In 1803 he added a law office for his good friend Thomas Maney. When Lafayette came to town on February 25, 1825, Maney, who was fluent in French, gave the official welcome. Lafayette stayed at the Indian Queen Inn, but bad weather delayed his arrival and he missed the ball planned in his honor. The museum highlights other local figures of interest. You'll discover the background for the song the *Yellow Rose of Texas*. When James Morgan moved from Murfreesboro to Texas, he took his slaves with him, although he listed them as indentured servants. The Mexican revolutionist Santa Anna became infatuated with Emily, one of Morgan's slaves. Supposedly she distracted Santa Anna before the Battle of San Jacinto in 1836, giving the Texans time to prepare and ultimately defeat the Mexican army. Emily is the heroine of the song.

One museum room is paneled with woodwork salvaged from the Gatling Plantation, five miles outside of town, where Richard Jordan Gatling was raised. Gatling developed the rapid-fire gun in hopes that it would deter people from fighting, but it had the opposite effect. The museum also has architectural displays to help you recognize points of interest while touring Murfreesboro, as well as exhibits on local Indians, agriculture, religion and the river trade.

Just a short detour off Route 158 on the way to Murfreesboro,

213

is **Historic Halifax**. This community is noted for the Halifax Resolves, the April 12, 1776, resolution in favor of independence. The passage of this measure by the Fourth Provincial Congress made North Carolina the first colony to vote for freedom from Great Britain. This colonial river port figured prominently in the history of the area. For more background see the audiovisual presentation at the Historic Halifax Visitor Center. Guided tours of the town's old houses and public buildings begin here. The visitor center is open Monday–Saturday 9:00 A.M. to 5:00 P.M. and Sunday 1:00 to 5:00 P.M. Tours are given of the town's oldest building, the 1760 Owens House, and also of the 1808 Sally-Billy House and the Clerk's Office, which was built between 1832–33.

Directions: From I-95 take Route 158 east into Murfreesboro. If you want to detour to include Halifax, then turn right on Route 301 and go roughly seven miles south to Historic Halifax on the left.

Newbold-White House

State's Oldest House

In 1663 King Charles II granted a charter for land, including what is now North Carolina, to eight loyal supporters, called Lords Proprietors. Not many years later, in 1684, Joseph Scott, a wealthy planter, magistrate and legislator, settled on a 640-acre tract on the west bank of the Perquimans River. Historical, architectural and archaeological resources suggest that Scott completed construction of his small brick home by 1685.

Joseph Scott was one of the first Quakers in North Carolina. In 1672 Quaker founders, William Edmundson and George Fox, were holding meetings in the Albemarle region. Fox recorded visiting "Joseph Scot's", probably at his old farm on the opposite side of the river from his 1684 property.

Due to the lack of public buildings, private homes were often used for public meetings during the proprietorial era. Between 1689 and 1704 Scott's house was for a time the seat of local government, virtually the capital of the colony. Now called the **Newbold-White** house (after the last private owners), it was the scene of the General Assembly meetings, the meeting place for the Governor's Council and the site of court sessions. This is the oldest surviving seat of local government in the state.

The Newbold-White house is a medieval hall-and-parlor design. Constructed of bricks made on the property, the 1½-story dwelling uses a Flemish bond pattern and has leaded casement windows and a handsplit cypress shingle roof. Nearly 90 percent

Of medieval design and built from bricks made on the property, the Newbold-White House (1685) in Hertford is the only house in the state to depict life in 17th-century North Carolina.

of the house's brickwork survives intact, and much of the interior woodwork is original.

This is the only house in the state to depict life in 17th-century North Carolina. In the downstairs portion of the house there is a great hall, which was used as a kitchen and work area, and a more formal parlor. Upstairs are two bed chambers with heart pine paneling and ceilings. Note the closets; later in the colonial period closets were taxed as rooms and hence omitted from most homes.

For more background you can watch a ten-minute video on the history of the house and early agricultural methods in the area. You can also have a look at the ongoing archaeological digs uncovering the foundations of various dependencies. Visitors are encouraged to assist on these digs.

Tours are given for a nominal fee March 1 to Thanksgiving on Monday–Saturday 10:00 A.M. to 4:30 P.M. If time permits take a walking tour of nearby Hertford, incorporated in 1758. The bridge leading into Hertford (Route 17 Business) was once a float bridge and is now an S-shaped bridge, reputedly the only such design in the country. Pick up a walking-tour map while you are visiting Newbold-White House for the background on the 25 in-town sites. Hertford's English roots are apparent in such street names as Hyde Park and Covent Garden.

Directions: From I-95 take Route 158 east. After you cross the Chowan River turn right on Route 37 and head south to Hertford. The Newbold-White House is on secondary road 1336, 1½ miles southeast of Route 17 Bypass at Hertford.

Somerset Place and Pettigrew State Park

A Carolina Tara

It is a common error to believe that all of the antebellum south consisted of large plantations worked by slave labor. Most North Carolinians never owned slaves, and just prior to the Civil War only one percent of slave owners had more than 50 slaves. In the entire state only four planters owned more than 300 slaves; the Collins of Somerset Place were among this small group (for another of this wealthy quartet see the Stagville Preservation Center selection).

Josiah Collins arrived in Edenton from England in 1777, after spending a brief time in Providence, Rhode Island and Halifax, North Carolina. By 1784, he had established himself as one of Edenton's leading merchants and with two other businessmen formed the Lake Company, which purchased more than 100,000 acres on the shores of Lake Phelps. This land was once called the Great Alegator (sic) Dismal, and the swampy terrain had to be cleared for cultivation. Collins took the unusual step of sending his brig the *Camden* to Africa to bring back 80 slaves from the Ivory Coast. In addition to preparing the land for the growing of rice, the slaves were also given the task of digging a six-mile canal from Lake Phelps to the Scuppernong River.

By 1816 Josiah Collins had bought out his partners and he named his holding **Somerset Place** in remembrance of his English birthplace. Neither he nor his son, who inherited it in 1819, ever lived on the property. It was Josiah Collins III who built the elegant plantation house that visitors now tour. The house, built in 1830, was originally 11 rooms and three more were added later. A report on the lifestyle of this North Carolina aristocrat appears in Edward Warren's *A Doctor's Experiences in Three Continents*. He writes, "Mr. Collins was pre-eminently a social man, and it was the delight of his heart to have his house filled with guests. . . . Such a host of servants, horses, carriages, games, boats, guns, accoutrements, musical instruments, and appliances generally for interesting and entertaining people, I ever saw collected together. His table was a most sumptuous one. It groaned . . , beneath the load of every delicacy that taste could suggest . . ."

It was Josiah Collins III who expanded Somerset Place into one of the largest plantations in North Carolina. At his death in 1863, 282 slaves worked the 1,400 acres under cultivation. By this time there were also more than 130 miles of canals and secondary ditches. Slaves had built a chapel and hospital, and an inventory made just a few years after his death lists 23 one-room slave cabins and three larger two story structures. As you walk the grounds of Somerset Place you will see where these buildings once stood. You'll also see a number of outbuildings including the dairy, bath house, laundry, ice house, kitchen, smokehouse and the storehouse plus the replanted formal garden. Neither the sawmill or gristmill that once stood on the Somerset canal still stands.

Guided tours are given of the furnished plantation house. Some of the pieces that fill the rooms belonged to the Collins family; all represent the antebellum south. In the Victorian parlor a portrait of Josiah Collins I hangs over the mantle. By contemporary standards it seems a pity that the builders used wood graining over the lovely natural interior woodwork. They also applied faux marbling on the steps. On the second floor there are bedrooms for all but the younger members of the family, who slept in the low-ceilinged attic rooms. Once the children reached a teachable age they moved to the Colony House, which now serves as the visitors center.

Somerset Place is open at no charge from April–October 9:00 A.M. to 5:00 P.M. Monday–Saturday and 1:00 to 5:00 P.M. on Sun-

217

days. November–March hours are Tuesday–Saturday 10:00 A.M. to 4:00 P.M. and Sunday 1:00 to 4:00 P.M..

Just up the road is the **Pettigrew State Park Visitor Center** on Lake Phelps. This spot, popular with boaters and fishermen, has a collection of Indian dugout canoes. Thirty canoes have been located in the lake, some have been recovered. Twenty-two canoes have been radiocarbon dated. The oldest of the collection is 4,380 years old, the second oldest canoe recovered in the United States. Two canoes are between 3,000 and 4,000 years old, three are between 2,000 and 3,000, and 16 are over 1,500 years old. One of the canoes is 37 feet long, which makes it the longest dugout canoe recovered in the south. This park on North Carolina's second largest natural lake also offers camping, a hiking trail to Bee Tree Overlook, and a boardwalk at the north edge of the lake to Moccasin Overlook. Pettigrew State Park is open 8:00 A.M. to 8:00 P.M. daily.

Directions: From I-95 take Route 64 east to Creswell. Signs just before the downtown district will direct you to turn right at the sign for Somerset Place and Pettigrew State Park about seven miles south of Creswell.

ALONG RIVERS AND SOUNDS

Bath

Under A Spell

Legend tells us that back in the 1740s, fiery minister George Whitfield put a curse on **Bath**. This charismatic English revivalist made Bath his headquarters while preaching the gospel in the wilds of North Carolina. After reputed mistreatment by the villagers, he left in a huff, dooming Bath to remain forever just a small town. There are those who consider that a blessing not a curse, but it is prophetic because Bath has remained unspoiled.

As North Carolina's oldest incorporated town, Bath was established on March 8, 1705, but the region had been inhabited for hundreds of years prior to European settlement. The Secotan tribe was centered in the Bath area in the 16th century. When smallpox decimated the Indian population in the late 17th century, settlers moved into the region to take advantage of the rich soil.

After a time the settlers realized they needed a port to promote trade and commerce and chose the present site of Bath. The original town was laid out by John Lawson, noted explorer and surveyor general to the crown. The 12 original inhabitants had to follow Lawson's guidelines. Livestock had to be fenced, underbrush cut and public lands clearly marked. Lots were set aside for a church, courthouse and marketplace. All this was planned for a space only a mile long and less than a quarter mile wide.

Even today the town of Bath is almost entirely contained by the boundaries of the original. The ideal way to explore its Old World charm is to take the walking tour, which covers roughly two blocks and encompasses nine points of interest. Whether you walk or drive, the place to start is the visitor center where a 23-minute introductory film will supply additional background on the town. Visitor center hours are Monday–Saturday 9:00 A.M. to 5:00 P.M. and Sunday 1:00 to 5:00 P.M. from April through October. From November through March hours are Tuesday–Saturday 10:00 A.M. to 4:00 P.M. and Sunday 1:00 to 4:00 P.M. The nominal admission charge includes the movie and a guided tour through two historic houses: the Van der Veer House and the Palmer-Marsh House. When you leave the center take the path to the left for the 1790 **Van der Veer House**. This frame gambrel-roofed house is now a museum you can explore on your own.

The museum has an exhibit on the town's most notorious resident, the pirate Edward Teach. When George I became king, he offered pirates pardon for their misconduct if they surrendered to the throne. Teach turned himself in to Governor Charles Eden, who already had a reputation for leniency towards pirates. Teach, pretending to abandon his former practices, made Bath his base of operations and from his home at Plum Point monitored shipping activity. While living there he married his 13th or 14th wife, the daughter of a Bath County planter. Teach's overt attacks on North Carolina vessels soon were detected, and again he became a hunted outcast. (See Ocracoke selection.) On a lighter note the museum has audio tapes of Edmund Harding, a North Carolina humorist, plus exhibits about Thomas R. Draper, another humorist and a Bath resident.

From the museum, follow the oyster-shell path to the 1744 **Palmer-Marsh House**. This National Historic Landmark is noted for its large double chimney; its appearance has fostered the nickname "pants chimney." Once a two-room cabin built by a French merchant, Michael Countanch, this is one of the oldest surviving houses in the state. When the leading citizen of Bath, Colonel Robert Palmer, acquired the property in 1764 he enlarged the house and added a formal garden, turning his home into a showplace. The elegant English furnishings you'll see reflect this more affluent era. One of the most unusual pieces in the house, found in the basement kitchen, is a chair with springs on the front legs, a variation on a rocking chair.

As you walk down Main Street you'll pass the Glebe House, which is not open for tours. It is part of the Episcopal Diocese of East Carolina. Behind this house is the oldest church in the state, **St. Thomas Church**. Built in 1734, this living landmark is still used for services. It has not survived the years unscathed as a storm in the 1840s destroyed the roof, bell tower and much of the interior furnishings. Repairs were not completed until after the Civil War. In the late 19th century the church interior was given a Victorian appearance; restoration included replacing these Victorian fixtures.

Retracing your steps to Main Street, head towards Bath Creek for the last historic house open for tours, the 1830 **Bonner House**. It probably is the most picturesque spot in town. Certainly surveyor John Lawson thought so since this is where he built his cabin while laying out the town. In 1830 the land was purchased by Captain Joseph Bonner, a prosperous farmer who owned 3,000 acres in the Bath area. He built and lived in this comfortable country home with his wife and six children. This is the type of historic old home many visitors long to own. It retains its Old World charm yet seems to offer modern comfort and style. The furnishings reflect 19th-century tastes and the out-kitchen is completely functional. When you learn how effectively gourds can be used to scrub dishes you may be tempted to plant them in your yard and harvest a supply of scrubbies.

Across the street from the Bonner House overlooking Bath Creek there is a picnic area; from this vantage point you will see Plum Point where Blackbeard had his home. Another spot to consider is Goose Creek State Park just outside of town. In addition to picnic areas, the park also has nature trails, campgrounds and during the summer months a guarded swimming beach. Take Route 92 west out of Bath, then turn left on State Route 1334. The park entrance will be on the right.

If you have time you can catch the ferry across the Pamlico River to Aurora and visit the **Aurora Fossil Museum**. Open Tuesday through Saturday from 10:00 A.M. to 5:00 P.M. June through August and by appointment the rest of the year (919)322-4238, this museum has exhibits and an audio-visual program on the natural forces that created the Carolina Coastal Plain. You will learn how to identify fossils and have a chance to look for them in the fossil dump outside the museum. You may even get lucky and find sharks teeth if you look carefully. Children enjoy having their picture taken looking through the giant jaws of a shark.

There are still other historic communities worth exploring near Bath. To the west is **Historic Washington**. A walking-tour map is available Monday–Friday 9:00 A.M. to 5:00 P.M. at the Beaufort County Arts Council, located in an old depot at the corner of

Main and Gladden Streets. This map will acquaint you with the many charming old houses in the roughly ten-block historic district. There are 23 sites of architectural or historic significance on the walking tour route, which is 1.9 miles and takes just slightly more than an hour. Like Bath, this area was explored as early as 1585 and settled in the 1690s. It wasn't until 1790 that the town was established. Originally called Forks of the Tar, it changed its name in 1776 to honor General George Washington. This Washington is the first town, but far from the last, to be named for America's first president. The town thrived during the Revolutionary War when it served as a major supply port. But during the War Between the States it was devastated. On April 30, 1864, much of the town burned when Federal forces set fire to the naval stores. A second fire on September 3, 1900, destroyed much of the rebuilt community. Despite these twin disasters several of the old houses date back to the late 1700s. The 1786 **Old Beaufort County Courthouse** is the second oldest courthouse in the state. An original courtroom may be seen on the second floor, but the building is now a regional library. Many of the houses date from the early 1800s. One house, Elmwood, was described in an 1857 edition of *Harper's Weekly* as one of the most distinguished homes in the South. Havens Gardens, the town park on E. Third Street, overlooks the Pamlico River. There is a picnic area and a playground.

The **Belhaven Memorial Museum** to the east of Bath houses an amazing collection of oddities. Belhaven resident, Eva Blount Way, spent a lifetime gathering many diverse items, starting in 1940 with a button collection that grew to 30,000. But she didn't stop there. She collected everything: clothes, preserved snakes, medical specimens, perfume bottles, dolls, Indian artifacts, shells, kitchen utensils, farm equipment and such oddities as the money in her husband's pockets the day they were married in 1887 and the shingles off the roof. This is a great place to play "do you remember?" More than one visitor has remarked that this is a collection that P.T. Barnum would have amassed if he turned his talents to museums rather than carnivals. Barnum would have loved the fleas dressed as bride and groom. It takes a keen eye and a magnifying glass to appreciate this feat. The Belhaven Memorial Museum, on the second floor of City Hall on Main Street (which is Business Route 264), is open daily 1:00 to 5:00 P.M. Donations are encouraged.

Directions: From I-95 take Route 64 east to the intersection with Route 17. Take Route 17 south to Washington, then turn east again on Route 264. You will make a right turn on Route 92 for Bath. For Belhaven Memorial Museum return to Route 264 and continue east, or you can take Route 99 from Bath to Belhaven.

Edenton

Called the South's Prettiest Town

North Carolina's first colonial capital is remarkably preserved, wonderfully serene and full of interesting stories about the people that lived in the attractive houses lining the tree-shaded streets.

The area was settled in 1685, and the town of **Edenton** was planned in 1712. It became the first capital of the province of North Carolina when it was incorporated in 1722. By 1743 a good bit of the population had shifted south, and New Bern was chosen as the first capital of the state of North Carolina. But Edenton continued to thrive as a port. Between 1771 and 1776 more than 800 ships sailed out of this harbor bound for northern ports, Europe and the West Indies. Legend has it that incoming captains would leave a jug of liquor on the protruding knees of the Dram Tree, a gnarled cypress. Captains leaving Edenton harbor would take a pull to bring them luck on their voyage.

An excellent place to view the Dram Tree is from the porch of the **Barker House**. This 1782 house, now serving as the visitor center, is on the National Register of Historic Places. Thomas Barker was a pre-Revolutionary colonial agent in London. His wife, Penelope, is credited with helping to organize the Edenton Tea Party on October 25, 1774. This was not the typical ladies social event. A group of 51 Edenton women gathered, signed and mailed a resolution to support the 1774 action of the First Provincial Congress that banned the import and consumption of British tea. Their protest, published in a London paper, was considered one of the first political actions by American women. It caused a great stir, and the ladies were caricatured in a cartoon in the **London Adviser**. This old newspaper cartoon is now a postcard, on sale at the Barker House gift shop.

The story of the events that took place in the Barker House is just part of the free 14-minute slide show at the visitor center. The center has maps for self-guided walking tours with details on 28 points of interest. Guided walking tours (roughly the price of a first run movie) can also be arranged. Tours include two historic homes, the courthouse and St. Paul's Episcopal Church. The Barker House is open Monday–Saturday 10:00 A.M. to 4:30 P.M. November–May; 9:00 A.M. to 4:30 P.M. June–October and 2:00 to 5:00 P.M. on Sunday. It is closed on major holidays.

As you leave the Barker House and head towards the **Courthouse Green** you will see cannons pointing towards Albemarle Sound. These are only part of the shipment of 45 cannons that Benjamin Franklin purchased in France to aid the Revolutionary cause. When the cannons arrived the colony was not able to pay

Historic houses like the Barker House above (now the visitor center) grace the restored port town of Edenton, North Carolina's first colonial capital, settled in 1685.

the captain, so they were anchored on a barge in Edenton harbor until payment could be made. Fully half of the war was fought with the cannons sitting dead in the water. Even worse, when the British headed towards the Carolina coast the colonists sank the barge to keep the cannons out of enemy hands. Salvaged in 1786, they were never fired. During the Civil War, Union officers broke the cannon's trunnions because they determined that the weapons would be more of a threat to those who fired them than to the enemy. Three of the seven recovered cannons now guard the harbor, unfired and unthreatening. Adjacent to the Courthouse Green sits a Revolutionary cannon with a bronze teapot perched on top, commemorating the Edenton Tea Party.

At the end of the green is **Chowan County Courthouse**, a National Historic Landmark. This is lauded for both its design and age. Built in 1767 it is the oldest continuously used courthouse in North Carolina. It is also considered the finest Georgian style courthouse in the South. The sandstone steps were ballast stones used to stabilize ships on sails to America. When the steps were turned a hundred years after being laid, it was found they had already been turned once before during the intervening years. While the exterior is felicitous the interior is somewhat spartan. The floors are of unpolished marble, and though the seats now have backs they were originally backless benches. The paneled meeting room upstairs looks more inviting. It was used for banquets and balls, and President Monroe was entertained here in 1819.

Four blocks up Broad Street is **St. Paul's Episcopal Church**, which is listed on the National Register of Historic Places. Like the courthouse, the church dates from the earliest days of Edenton. It was chartered under the Vestry Act of 1701, and its building was begun in 1736 making it the second oldest surviving church in North Carolina. St. Thomas in Bath is the oldest. Three colonial governors are buried in the churchyard. There are nine graves beneath the floor of the church, and the first pastor rests beneath the altar.

Just down Church Street is the **James Iredell House**, one of the sites included on the guided tour. In 1768 at age 16, James Iredell was appointed deputy collector of customs at Port Roanoke. He arrived in North Carolina on Christmas Day and quickly made a name for himself. He studied law under Samuel Johnston, an Edenton judge, U.S. senator and governor and then married Johnston's sister. In 1778 Iredell and his wife Hannah bought this Georgian house built in 1773. A Federal wing was added in 1816, 16 years after Iredell's death. After serving as attorney general of North Carolina, Iredell capped his legal career with his appointment by George Washington as an associate judge to the first Supreme Court. Iredell's only son, James Iredell, Jr., became governor of North Carolina 1827–1828 and United States senator.

Heading back along Broad Street towards the waterfront you'll find the remaining historic house that is open for tours, the 1725 **Cupola House**. This National Historic Landmark is considered by experts to be the best example of wooden Jacobean design in the country. Period touches include the second-story overhang (the only extant house in the South with that feature), circular stairs up to the cupola and elaborate woodwork. You would think with Edenton's importance as a port that the cupola was planned as an enclosed widow's walk, but that is not the case. It was actually designed for ventilation purposes. The Dickinsons were the third family to own the house, but they retained it for 140 years. One descendant literally made her mark on the house. Sarah Penelope Bond carved a message on her bedroom window pane: "When this you see, remember me. SPB, April 15, 1835."

Historic preservation in Edenton actually began with efforts to rescue this house. Locals became concerned when they learned that the last owner was selling the very walls of her old home. When representatives of the Brooklyn Museum of Fine Arts heard about the interior woodwork of this house they became so enthusiastic they purchased it for the museum. Speedy action saved the staircase and woodwork upstairs, but the downstairs woodwork had to be duplicated. Restoration has succeeded in filling the rooms once more with handsome period furniture, circa 1725–1775. Equally appealing is the lovely fenced formal garden that has been restored according to details provided by the valuable Sauthier map of 1769.

Directions: From I-95 take Route 64 east to the intersection with Route 17. Head north on Route 17 across the Chowan River to Edenton; follow signs for the Barker House Visitor Center.

Mattamuskeet National Wildlife Refuge

The Wisdom of Wildness

Wildlife refuges offer sanctuary to more than the numerous birds and aquatic life that find protection there; they also offer man a sense of serenity—a world where the pace is natural, changing with the sun not the clock.

This is certainly true at **Lake Mattamuskeet**, North Carolina's largest natural lake, stretching 18 miles in length and six in width. The refuge includes the lake's 40,000 acres plus some 10,000 acres of surrounding marsh and forest. The lake's name means dry dust, reflecting the days when the lake was dry and the Algonquin Indians hunted in this area. Legend says that the lake dried up as a result of a ceremonial fire lit here to end a long drought. One scientific explanation is that the site was a natural depression, once part of the sea. Another theory postulates that a shower of meteors struck this part of the Carolina coastal plain. The lake was dry yet again in 1914 when it was drained to provide farm lands for the community of New Holland. Surviving from this period are a series of canals used to drain the lake.

In 1934 a waterfowl sanctuary was established here. The Civilian Conservation Corp converted the pumping station into a lodge with a 120-foot observation tower; this historic building may soon be under renovation.

Mattamuskeet is on the Atlantic Flyway, and thousands of Canada geese, snow geese, tundra swans, ducks and coots spend the winter at this refuge. November through February is the best time to observe them. The great blue heron lives year-round at Mattamuskeet, and the osprey population has increased dramatically since 1963 when the first nest was built; in 1988 there were 71 osprey nests in use. In addition to a variety of waterfowl, bird enthusiasts are apt to spot the bald eagle, pileated wood-pecker, king rail, glossy ibis and prothonotary warbler. The best vantage point for bird watching is from the water. The refuge is ideal for canoeing and there are many spots to launch a boat. Unfortunately no rentals are available. It's strictly BYOB (bring your own boat). Another place from which to see the birds is on the six miles of wildlife drive and entrance roads. Various hiking paths can also be explored. Photography blinds are available; it's best to call a few days before you visit for information on blind locations and birding hot spots.

Even though Mattamuskeet is a wildlife refuge fishing is per-mitted. The catch includes black bass, striped bass, crappie, white perch, catfish and bream. Herring-dipping and crabbing are also popular. A carefully managed waterfowl hunt is con-ducted for approximately 16 days in December and January. Wa-terfowl hunted here include tundra swans, ducks and coots. There are 16 hunting blinds. Ask the refuge manager about cur-rent regulations and seasons.

Mattamuskeet is open daily during daylight hours. This is not the only wildlife refuge in the area. Down the road ten miles is the 15,500-acre Swanquarter National Wildlife Refuge in the Pamlico Sound. Most of this refuge is flat salt marsh islands largely inaccessible to visitors. The main recreational feature is an 1,100-foot fishing pier located at the terminus of the refuge entrance road. This refuge, too, was established to provide a winter home for migratory waterfowl.

Approximately 35 miles northwest near Plymouth is **Pungo National Wildlife Refuge**. A 12-mile wildlife drive around Pungo Refuge takes you through the marsh, brush and croplands of this 12,350-acre refuge. Visitors in the fall and winter are sure to see the plentiful Canada and snow geese, ducks and tundra swans that winter here. An observation tower provides an overview of the lake. The animal population of the refuge includes black bear, most often seen in the early morning and late afternoon, white-tailed deer, rabbits and raccoons.

Directions: From I-95 take Route 264 east to the village of Swan Quarter. You will see the sign for the Swan Quarter National Wildlife Refuge on your left about three miles west of Swan Quarter. For Mattamuskeet National Wildlife Refuge continue to New Holland and turn left on Route 94. Turn right on the refuge entrance road and follow it for two miles to refuge headquarters and the wildlife drive. For Pungo, take Route 64 east to Plymouth and then Highway 45 south for about 17 miles. All three refuges are administered from the Mattamuskeet NWR office, (919)926-4021, Route 1, Box N-2, Swan Quarter, NC 27885.

Museum of the Albemarle

The Rose and the Crown

North Carolinians believe in diversification, rather than centralization. The state's aquariums and many of its museums have regional branches. The **Museum of the Albemarle** in Elizabeth City is the northeastern branch of the North Carolina Museum of History (see selection).

The Albemarle is made up of three distinct sections: the Albemarle Sound, the Great Dismal Swamp and the Barrier Islands. The entire region, comprising 10 counties, is called the Cradle of America because so many significant events occurred here, dating back to the Lost Colony at Fort Raleigh. The first representative assembly in the colony met in the Albemarle region in 1665. At Hertford you can tour the Newbold-White House (see selection), virtually the seat of colonial government because of the range of public meetings held there. Culpeper's Rebellion, the first organized resistance to British rule, occurred in the Albemarle region. These and other events like the Halifax Resolves and Edenton tea party are the focus of museum exhibits.

The heritage of native Americans is the first exhibit you will see. Throughout North Carolina place names recall the Indians who once lived here. The Museum of the Albemarle is itself in Pasquotank County, named for the local Indian tribe. The Mattamuskeet and Pungo National Wildlife Refuges (see selection) both take their names from Indian words. Indian artifacts exhibited here date back to the Paleo-Indian era, 15,000–8,000 B.C.

Second only to their interest in Indians, young boys seem to enjoy the information on the pirates of the region. Girls find piracy was not solely a masculine pursuit when they learn about Anne Bonny, who sailed on Captain "Calico Jack" Rackham's ship. Anne gained fame as a bloodthirsty pirate, and when captured she was tried and convicted of piracy.

The effect of the American Revolution and Civil War on this region is presented. Other exhibits focus on the economic pursuits of the Albemarle area including lumbering, agriculture and hunting. A fiber-to-fabric display shows raw wool, flax and cotton being processed. To sum up the frugality of the times a rule of thumb was to "Use it up, wear it out, make it do, or do without."

Large agricultural tools, a printing press, a 1888 fire engine pumper, a 1917 hook and ladder, a fire call box and regional furniture round out the museum's exhibits. Ambitious plans are afoot to relocate the museum on the waterfront in Elizabeth City. The Museum of the Albemarle is open at no charge 9:00 A.M. to 5:00 P.M. Tuesday–Saturday and 2:00 to 5:00 P.M. Sundays.

227

While in **Elizabeth City** take the time for a leisurely stroll through its two National Register Historic Districts, the West Main Street District and the Downtown District. Elizabeth City was incorporated in 1793. During the antebellum period it was a busy West Indian trade center. Economic reverses occurred when the town was occupied, then partially burnt by Union troops during the Civil War. A walking-tour map highlights 32 National Register historic structures and sites.

Elizabeth City's reputation among those who travel the Inter-coastal Waterway is not for its old houses but rather its older residents, a number of whom are known as Rose Buddies. These retirees established a tradition of impromptu parties at the dock welcoming boaters to their city. The tradition began in 1983 with Joe Kramer and Fred Fearing. The name comes from their practice of presenting visitors with a rose from Joe's garden. When Joe Kramer died in 1987 his rose bushes were planted at the town dock where boaters can anchor for 48 hours at no charge. The Rose Buddies were given a golf cart by Willard Scott when NBC televised a news segment from Elizabeth City.

Directions: From I-95 take Route 158 east. Just before Elizabeth City it will merge with Route 17. The Museum of the Albemarle is on Highway 17, approximately two miles south of town.

OUTER BANKS AND ROANOKE ISLAND

Cape Hatteras National Seashore

By Yourself, By the Sea!

When travelers think of North Carolina's popular Outer Banks, they often recall the miles and miles of unspoiled beach within **Cape Hatteras National Seashore**. Spread out across three barrier islands—Bodie, Hatteras, and Ocracoke—the seashore extends for 77 miles along Highway 12 with the sound on one side and the ocean on the other. The eight villages along the coast, which predate the national seashore, add a quaint charm to the drive. You won't see any high-rise condominiums in these small communities. The beach houses are primarily weathered wood on stilts, and the rental properties remind travelers of the days when one went to the beach to swim and fish, not to visit boardwalks, carnivals and casinos. Although there are a few night spots, night life on the Outer Banks, still means night fishing.

Cape Hatteras National Seashore, and the entire Outer Banks region, is a sports fisherman's paradise with more than 100 miles of accessible beach. The area offers some of the nation's best angling waters. Fishing is the number one participant sport with enthusiasts having the option of surf and pier fishing, sound and freshwater fishing, and in-shore and off-shore charter fishing. The catch changes with the seasons, but includes channel bass, flounder, sea mullet, spot, bluefish, trout and croaker. Another group of sportsmen, windsurfers, have started to gather at Cape Hatteras National Seashore. They come from as far away as Canada to experience the thrill of surfing on Pamlico Sound. Even non-surfers park between Avon and Buxton to watch hundreds of young people sailing colorful butterfly-like boards.

A good place to start your tour is at **Bodie Island** at the northern end of Cape Hatteras National Seashore. Here you'll see a 156-foot white lighthouse with eye-catching black bands. Across Highway 12 from the lighthouse is the National Park Service's **Whalebone Junction Information Center** where you can obtain brochures on the national seashore. There is also a nature trail accessible from the center's parking lot. After you cross the Oregon Inlet bridge you will enter the Pea Island National Wildlife Refuge (see selection), which is just south of Bodie Island. This refuge is not part of Cape Hatteras National Seashore.

After Pea Island, you'll re-enter the Cape Hatteras National Seashore and continue south on Hatteras Island to the nation's tallest brick lighthouse, erected to protect ships from the deadly Diamond Shoals, otherwise known as the Graveyard of the Atlantic. Ships are forced to negotiate these treacherous shifting sand shoals about ten miles off Cape Hatteras because of the way the Gulf Stream (used by north and eastbound vessels) and the Virginia Coastal Drift (used by southbound ships), converge and pinch in towards shore.

Although the danger of the shallow shoals was acknowledged as early as the 16th century, a lighthouse was not authorized at Hatteras until 1794 and not built until 1803. Even then it was not built adequately; complaints were frequent and vociferous. The tower was too short, the light too dim and the whole result not dependable. During storms, when the lighthouse was most needed, the wind often shattered the windows, broke the lamp and extinguished the light sometimes for days at a time. In 1837 a captain reported, "As usual no light is to be seen from the lighthouse."

A Lighthouse Board was created in 1852, and changes were made. After the Civil War a new lighthouse, 600 feet north of the original, was built. This dramatic black and white spiral-striped lighthouse is now in jeopardy, threatened by beach erosion and structural weaknesses. Two solutions have been offered; the first is to relocate the lighthouse and adjacent buildings and the second, to build a sea wall around the tower. The sea wall would eventually create an island under the lighthouse. If the lighthouse is moved, plans call for repairs to make it safe for visitors to climb the 257 steps to the balcony where the observation area is located. For the record, there are 268 steps to the light at the top. The view from the balcony is splendid, and those who have enjoyed the experience would like to see the lighthouse once more accessible.

The **Hatteras Island Visitor Center** in the lighthouse keeper's quarters adjacent to the tower has an exhibit on the early Life Saving Service (the forerunner of the U.S. Coast Guard), the operational details of the lighthouse and its functioning, and the shipwrecks off Hatteras. During World War II when U-boats patrolled the coast the Germans called this passage the "American Turkey Shoot" and the Outer Banks area, "Torpedo Alley."

Down the park road from the lighthouse, along a well-marked route, you'll find the **Buxton Woods Nature Trail**, a ¾-mile trail that takes 30 to 45 minutes to explore. If you visit in late spring or summer, be sure to use an insect repellent.

The park has campgrounds at Oregon Inlet (see Pea Island National Wildlife Refuge selection), Cape Point, Ocracoke (see Ocracoke Island selection), Salvo and Frisco. The first three are open mid-April to mid-October, while the last two open in mid-June and close in mid-August. The last two also have convenient nearby fishing piers. All campgrounds except Salvo are on the ocean side; Salvo is on the sound. Frisco is located among the sand dunes, and the other four campsites are on level ground. The fee for camping is nominal. During the summer reservations can be made for the Ocracoke campground through Ticketron, (804)456-CAMP, or write Ticketron, Dept. R, 401 Hackensack Avenue, Hackensack, New Jersey 07601.

Directions: From I-95 take US 64 or US 264 east to the coast. At Whalebone Junction just south of the town of Nags Head you will find a National Park Information Center at the entrance to Cape Hatteras National Seashore. Head south on NC Route 12.

Elizabethan Gardens

Lost But Not Forgotten

"From this hallowed ground on Roanoke Island, they walked away through the dark forest and into history," reads the marker at the **Elizabethan Gardens**. After establishing a colony on the shores of Roanoke Sound, the first English settlers vanished without a trace. The Elizabethan Gardens were created by the Garden Club of North Carolina on what is likely the very spot where Sir Richard Grenville, Walter Raleigh's cousin, first set foot in 1585 after leading the second English expedition—a flotilla of seven ships and 500 men—across the Atlantic.

The concept for these gardens began modestly with the objective of planting a two-acre garden like one a successful colonist might have planted had the early colony succeeded. The unexpected opportunity to acquire the statuary and garden fountains of the honorable John Hay Whitney, ambassador to England, required a more elaborate design. Whitney had been considering giving his collection to the Metropolitan Museum in New York, but instead these valuable garden statuary were given to this historic garden site. Some of these ancient statues date from the time before Queen Elizabeth's reign. These formal pieces inspired the designers, Umberto Innocenti and Richard Webel, to plan a 16th-century English pleasure garden. Visitors are the beneficiaries, as every bend in the path offers a charming vista.

The Gate House Reception Center is modeled after a 16th-century orangerie and furnished with early English pieces. There is a portrait of the aging Queen Elizabeth I painted in 1592 when she was 59, as well as a portrait of Sir Walter Raleigh. A wall panel lists the men, women and children who in 1587 settled what became the Lost Colony.

Work on the Elizabethan Gardens began on Queen Elizabeth II's coronation day, June 2, 1953, and the gardens formally opened on August 18, 1960, on the 373rd anniversary of the birth of Virginia Dare, the first English child born in America.

To help you find your way around the garden, there is a walking tour map which pinpoints 22 focal spots. As you leave the Gate House, you enter the **Shakespearean Herb Garden**. There are approximately 45 varieties found here, most of which are identified. To understand their uses you can purchase a booklet called *Shakespeare's Herbs* in the Gate House Gift Shop.

The most striking area is the **Sunken Garden** with 32 identical parterres outlined in clipped helleri holly. The flowers change seasonally beginning with spring pansies, then summer ageratum and begonias, and fall chrysanthemums. The garden radiates out from a 16th-century Italian fountain and pool. One of the spokes leading from this garden leads you to the **Mount**, the highest elevation in the garden. Here too is a piece from the Whitney collection, a carved marble wellhead. One path from the Mount leads to a water gate on the shores of Roanoke Sound and an octagonal thatched-roof gazebo, designed and constructed in the 16th-century manner. Another path from the Mount leads to the statue of Virginia Dare. This full-sized idealized impression of what Virginia Dare would look like as a young woman, carved by American artist Maria Louise Lander in the mid-1800s, has a dramatic history. The ship on which the statue was being brought to America from Rome sunk, and the statue nearly had a watery grave. But after two years it was salvaged, only to narrowly escape being destroyed by fire. When exhibited in Raleigh's Hall of

History, the statue draped only in fishnet was lambasted as obscene. Almost a hundred years after its creation the statue found a perfect home at Virginia Dare's birthplace, now the area of the Elizabethan Gardens.

Garden collections of note include a rose garden with a rose bush from Queen Elizabeth II's garden, one of the finest assortments of camellias in the south, hybrid lilies and daylilies, and thousands of annuals. One of the most popular areas in the spring is the natural wildflower garden. While the center portion of the Elizabethan Gardens is formal the surrounding area looks much as it might have when the English first came to North Carolina.

The Elizabethan Gardens are open at a nominal charge daily from 9:00 A.M. to 5:00 P.M. In December and January they are closed on weekends. During the Lost Colony season the gardens stay open until 8:00 P.M.

Directions: From I-95 take Route 64 east towards Manteo. When you cross Croatan Sound the Elizabethan Gardens and the adjacent Fort Raleigh National Historic Site (see selection) will be on your left off Route 64, before you reach Manteo.

Elizabeth II

Off to See the Wizard?

The lion, the tiger and Dorothy conjure up images of the yellow brick road and the Emerald City, but on Roanoke Island the trio is known for being the names of three of the seven ships that sailed with the *Elizabeth* on the second of three voyages that Sir Walter Raleigh sponsored to the New World. The first voyage in 1584 was to explore the area, the second in 1585 was to establish a military colony, and the final trip in 1587 established a settlement. This settlement on Roanoke Island became known as the Lost Colony (see selection).

During the summer you will feel transported to the 16th century as you tour the *Elizabeth II*. Staff dressed as mariners and colonists express the manners, attitudes and speech of the Elizabethan era. Year-round an excellent 20-minute multi-media program at the visitor center puts you aboard the *Elizabeth II*. You'll hear the views of Captain Thomas Cavendish (he later became the third captain to sail around the world), as well as a common sailor and a soldier who were forced to endure the 2½-month voyage below deck (six weeks to cross the Atlantic, two weeks in the West Indies, and two more to reach North America). When you watch the movie depiction of a storm at sea, the very walls of the theater seem to shudder at the lightening and thunder.

Cavendish both owned and commanded the original three-masted barque. *Elizabeth II*, the current representative, is a com-

A composite of 16th century ships, Elizabeth II represents the original on which British soldiers arrived in 1585 to establish a garrison in support of England's claim to the New World.

posite design of 16th-century ships as no records survived to give the exact dimensions of the first *Elizabeth*. The ship you will explore is 69 feet long and 17 feet wide with a 65-foot main topmast. Rated by 16th-century standards as a 50-tunne ship (a tunne is a 252 gallon barrel), this ship was small even for its time, as the average merchant ship was 125 tunnes.

Guides are available year-round to escort you around the ship. In summer they add a living-history flavor to the tours. As you pace the deck of this comparatively small vessel, you will be surprised to learn that it carried a crew of 25, under the command of seven officers, plus 30 soldiers. The soldiers were needed to establish a military garrison in support of England's claim to the New World. The crew slept on deck exposed to the elements, but even this uncomfortable berthing was preferable to the fate of the soldiers who spent the entire time at sea below deck. They were considered living cargo. The six officers shared a cabin on the main deck, and the captain had his own quarters, the only private space aboard ship.

After you tour you will understand such nautical terms as forecastle, bowsprit, beakhead, hold, capstan, bittacle, whipstaff, mizzen and billage. You will also discover that small as the *Elizabeth II* was, she still needed a ship's boat to navigate the shallow waters along the shore. This small craft, the *Silver Chalice*, was used to transport passengers and cargo to shore.

For more information on the *Elizabeth II* and early North Carolina settlements, see the exhibits in the visitor center. If you are doing research on the era you can use the adjacent Outer Banks History Center.

The *Elizabeth II* is directly across the Shallowbag Bay from Manteo. There is a passenger walkway across the bridge to the Manteo waterfront where you will find a collection of shops, restaurants and the charming Tranquil House Inn with individually furnished rooms, wide verandas overlooking the bay, and breakfast in bed or on the porch (919)473-1404.

The *Elizabeth II* is open November–March, 10:00 A.M. to 4:00 P.M. Tuesday–Sunday, with the last tour given at 3:00 P.M., April–October hours are 10:00 A.M. to 6:00 P.M. daily with the last tour at 5:00 P.M. Admission is charged.

Directions: From I-95 take Route 64 east to Manteo. Turn left on Budleigh Street and follow it to the end. Take a left on Queen Elizabeth Avenue, and travel one block, then take a right on Highway 400, which will take you over the bridge and into the *Elizabeth II* State Historic Site parking lot.

Fort Raleigh and The Lost Colony

Mystery Enshrouded Fate

It has all the ingredients of operatic tragedy. The man, the vision, the followers—all came to a violent end. Sir Walter Raleigh, favorite of Queen Elizabeth, had the imagination to envision English outposts in the New World. Winning the support of his queen, he sponsored voyages to America, only to see his followers lost forever. Ultimately because of suspected treason against James I, Raleigh lost his head on the executioner's block.

It was Sir Walter Raleigh's half-brother, Sir Humphrey Gilbert, who in 1578 first considered establishing an English colony in North America. Gilbert's mission from Queen Elizabeth was "to inhabit and possess . . . all remote and heathen lands not in actual possession of any Christian prince." On his second voyage to the New World, Sir Gilbert died, but his quest was continued by his brother, Sir Walter.

Raleigh sponsored three voyages to America, although he never sailed on any of these. His first sponsored voyage in 1584 was a scouting mission to the New World, and the word sent back was that North America was "a most pleasant and fertile ground." The following year seven ships commanded by Raleigh's cousin, Sir Richard Grenville, sought to establish a military settlement on Roanoke Island. (See Elizabethan Gardens selection.) Of the 500 men who sailed with this expedition, 108 were colonists. Under the direction of Ralph Lane, governor of the colony, they built **Fort Raleigh**. Today you'll see a reconstruction of this earthenworks fort built on the original site by the same methods of construction. A moat was dug and the dirt from the ditch thrown inward to form a 50-square-foot enclosure. The colonists built their thatched-roof houses just outside the fort.

The settlement in 1584 was essentially a military garrison dependent on England for supplies and survival. But instead of being supplied by England, the colonists came to depend on the Indians. Throughout the spring and summer of 1585 this arrangement succeeded, but during the cold harsh winter it did not. The Indians had little food to spare, and what they had they would not sacrifice for trinkets. To make matters worse the Indians fell victim to measles and smallpox brought to their land by the English.

Several factors—hostility with the Indians and the hope of finding either gold or the Northwest Passage—prompted Lane and the colonists to seek a new location for their settlement. Their bad reputation preceded them, unfortunately, and the Indians in their path deserted the settlements. Discouraged, the colonists returned to Roanoke Island. By late spring of 1586, hostilities broke out between Indians and English. When Sir Francis Drake's fleet sailed into Roanoke Sound and offered a chance to abandon the settlement the colonists set sail for England. Within two days, the long-awaited supply ship arrived, and two weeks later Grenville returned to Roanoke, only to find the colony deserted. He left 15 men to guard the settlement and set sail for England to recruit new settlers.

Raleigh's third expedition sailed in 1587 with the objective of establishing a permanent colony, "The City of Ralegh" (sic). To achieve this goal women and children were included: 84 men, 17 women and 9 children sailed to America. These pioneers, seeking a new life, not gold or riches, were each deeded 500 acres. Their destination was to be a spot on the lower end of the Chesapeake Bay, but ill luck brought them back to Roanoke Island. The pilot felt it was too late in the season to travel farther. Under the leadership of Governor John White, the artists who had traveled on the first voyage, the new settlers attempted to parlay with the Indians, who had in the interim massacred the fifteen Englishmen left to safeguard the fort. These new attempts to reach an accord with the Indians failed.

If the colonists had to grapple with misfortune, they also had occasion to rejoice. Governor White was particularly heartened by the birth of his granddaughter, Virginia Dare, on August 18, 1587. She was the first English child born in the New World. A week after her birth, White sailed back to England to obtain supplies for his colony. But along with all maritime England his ship was pressed into service against the Spanish Armada, and he did not return to Roanoke until 1590. When White arrived he found the colony uninhabited. The only clues to the colonists' departure were the letters CRO carved on a tree and the word CROATOAN carved on a palisade post. It had been agreed that if the colonists were threatened they would carve a message and add a Maltese cross, but the cross did not appear. Despite White's fervent desire to discover what had happened to his daughter and her family, as well as the others, it was not possible to sail for the nearby island of Croatoan. Attempts to locate the colonists failed, and no trace has ever been found of the Lost Colony. It is thought that they were massacred. If any did survive they were probably assimilated into an Indian tribe.

The story of the Roanoke Island settlement was dramatically captured by Pulitzer Prize winner, Paul Green, in his commemorative drama, The Lost Colony. Since 1937 this outstanding outdoor drama has been presented every summer at the Waterside Theatre, overlooking Roanoke Sound. America's oldest outdoor drama has had famous cast members and distinguished guests in the audience. Franklin Roosevelt watched the performance from his car parked at the top of the amphitheater on Virginia Dare's 350th birthday. The most well-known of the cast alumni is Andy Griffith, who played Sir Walter Raleigh in 1952–53.

The Lost Colony is presented at Waterside Theatre in Fort Raleigh National Historic Site from early June through August, Monday–Saturday at 8:30 P.M. Admission is charged. For more information or reservations call (919)473-3414 from 10:00 A.M. to 6:00 P.M.. Backstage tours depart from the theater box office Monday–Saturday at 1:30, 2:30 and 3:30 P.M. There is a nominal charge for this 45-minute tour.

When you visit Fort Raleigh, open daily 9:00 A.M. to 5:00 P.M., be sure to see the orientation film at the visitor center. Displays at the center include artifacts recovered when the fort was reconstructed as well as a 16th-century Elizabethan room that suggests the homes of wealthy British investors who financed the Roanoke explorations. If time permits take a walk along the .5-mile **Thomas Hariot Nature Trail** and see the native plants the settlers used. Hariot was the chronicler of the 1585 voyage, and his descriptions of the native animals, plants and Indians did much to encourage future ventures.

Directions: From I-95 take Route 64 east towards Manteo. Three miles before you reach Manteo you will see Fort Raleigh on your left. The Elizabethan Gardens are adjacent to Fort Raleigh.

Jockey's Ridge State Park and Kitty Hawk Kites

A Natural High!

Visiting **Jockey's Ridge** makes you appreciate Anne W. Simon's remark, "Sand . . . Hold it in your hands and you are in touch with the planet's essence." The dunes at Jockey's Ridge State Park are the highest live dunes in the United States. A dune is said to be alive when it does not have vegetation holding the sand in place. In fact, planting grass to stabilize the dune on which the Wright Memorial was erected was a frustrating and time-consuming project, though eventually successful.

There once were numerous dunes in the Nags Head area; now only the two at Jockey's Ridge remain. These dunes, or medanos as they are geologically termed, shift in height from 110 to 140 feet depending on changes in wind velocity and direction. Adventurous visitors have been climbing the dunes since the mid-19th century. Now there are two designated routes to the ridge. The view at sunset is spectacular and romantic. Locals recall the old adage that if a woman climbed to the summit with you, she would become your wife. Today, she's likely at least to be your classmate, as more and more visitors sign up for hang gliding lessons at Kitty Hawk Kites just across the highway (Route 158).

Jockey's Ridge's preeminent position among hang gliders is not new. It enjoys a rich heritage that goes back to the Wright brothers who tested gliders on the dunes just a few miles to the north at Kill Devil Hills in 1900, three years before they flew the first powered airplane. If these gentlemen are the fathers of aviation, the father of modern hang gliding is Francis Rogallo. He lives just a few miles north of the dunes and can often be found at Kitty Hawk Kites. A NASA engineer, he designed a flexible flying wing in 1948. It attracted little interest so he scaled it down to the Rogallo Flexikite, which was sold in toy stores. His idea came of age with the space program, and his flexible wing was used for rocket booster recovery. In the 1970s his design caught on with sports enthusiasts, first in Australia then in the United States.

It doesn't take long to experience the first thrill of hang gliding. Beginner's lessons last three hours and offer a guarantee of five

Hang gliding at Jockey's Ridge from the highest live sand dunes in the U.S. continues the conquest of flight that the Wright brothers started at nearby Kitty Hawk in 1903.

---

flights off Jockey's Ridge. John Harris, part owner of Kitty Hawk Kites, insists that this is primarily a mental sport, and as such is easy for older novices. It is often easier for women, he says. Men try to exert too much muscle when flying.

The injury rate is roughly one in every thousand participants and usually involves wrists or arms. The sand is very forgiving. The only restrictions are that you must weigh between 85 and 220 pounds, and if you are under 18 you will need a signed parental permission slip. Since opening in 1974 Kitty Hawk Kites has taught more than 140,000 visitors to hang glide. Even timid visitors often attempt this exciting sport after watching the action. If you are here in June you can attend the Rogallo Kite Festival.

It's worth a stop at Kitty Hawk Kites and their adjacent sports supply outlet, Kitty Hawk Connection, even if you do not want to try hang gliding. In addition to offering instruction Kitty Hawk Kites has a large, colorful kite collection plus more than 700 types of toys. The sports shop outfits enthusiasts for a broad range of athletic activities in addition to hang gliding. The cost to purchase new hang gliding equipment (that's the sail and harness) is about $3,000. The equipment for windsurfing (essentially a surfboard with sail) is about half that. Windsurfing and sailing lessons are also available year-round weather permitting. For current prices call Kitty Hawk Kites at (919)441-4124 or write them at P.O. Box 340, Nags Head, N.C. 27959.

Hours at Jockey's Ridge State Park are 8:00 A.M. to 6:00 P.M. November through February; 8:00 A.M. to 7:00 P.M. March and October; 8:00 A.M. to 8:00 P.M. April, May and September; and 8:00 A.M. to 9:00 P.M. June through August.

Directions: From I-95 take Route 64 east to the coast and turn north on Route 158. Jockey's Ridge State Park's entrance is at milepost 12 on Route 158 Bypass, South Croatan Highway, in Nags Head. Kitty Hawk Kites is directly across Route 158 from Jockey's Ridge just past the park entrance. There are picnic tables at the park.

North Carolina Aquarium—Roanoke Island

Eau de Estuary

More than 30 American cities have plans to become part of the "Age of Aquariums," but for North Carolina that age has already arrived. The state's three aquariums (see Pine Knolls and Fort Fisher selections) are the most visited state facilities. Educational programs, informative exhibits and entertaining aquatic specimens like the sharks at Roanoke Island attract more than a million visitors each year.

The **Roanoke Island Aquarium** places its emphasis on the Albemarle Pamlico Sound system, the second largest estuarine system in the country. Only the Chesapeake Bay system is more extensive. This region where fresh river water meets the salt water of the ocean is a nursery and breeding ground for many ocean-going species. In 1988 the Roanoke Island facility opened a prize-winning exhibit, Secrets of the Salt Marsh, to increase visitors' understanding and knowledge of the marshes and broad sounds so prevalent along the Outer Banks.

Children enjoy the estuarine touch tank. Colorful photographs help you identify the specimens within the glass-sided tank. You can pick out and pick up oysters, scallops, clams, sea urchins, pinfish, whelks, sea stars and a variety of crabs including horseshoe, blue, hermit and spider. Larger freshwater specimens like long nose gar, channel catfish, bowfin, carp, yellow perch and largemouth bass swim in enclosed tanks—these you can see, but not touch.

Fishermen may be envious when they behold the 94-pound world record channel bass caught on November 7, 1984. This was not pulled in by a commercial fisherman but by a sportfisherman on his first try at channel bass. Coincidentally this catch replaced a record catch made on the very same day a few years earlier. The aquarium has an exhibit that details the life story of the striped bass and how it is affected by the environmental problems plaguing this area. As the water quality of the sounds has dropped, the striped bass population has declined sharply.

The Salt Marsh exhibit also has interactive computers, a video on the problems of the estuary, a discovery room with projection microscopes and computers, and a built-in teaching center where live animal presentations are given.

A tank-filled corridor has a wide assortment of fish including the unusual sharksucker with a sucking disc on its back that allows it to cling upside down to its host, and a menacing-looking reticulated moray eel. Beyond this is the shark exhibit where three lemon sharks have become so aggressive they may be replaced by younger specimens. They now are eating the sponges used by the aquarium staff to clean the inside of their 3,000-gallon tank. When you see the hanging devilfish you will probably think the iridescent purple color is not the original shade of this ray, but it is indeed.

The aquarium has a display on the Pea Island Life Saving Station, the only station manned entirely by a black crew. One former crewman, Richard Etheridge, is buried on the grounds of the aquarium. Before leaving take the short path along the Croatan Sound and see the area of natural plantings; these salt tolerant plants are hardy specimens. There is no charge to visit the aquarium open Monday–Saturday 9:00 A.M. to 5:00 P.M. and Sunday 1:00 to 5:00 P.M.

While in the area you might want to visit the popular **Christmas Shop**, where the air is redolent of the holidays and trees are alight all year round. Room after room is filled with all manner of decorations and delights. It is a treasure trove of holiday items as well as other bibelots.

Directions: From I-95 take Route 64 east to Manteo. After crossing the Croatan Sound bridge and just before you reach Manteo you will see a sign for the North Carolina Aquarium—Roanoke Island. It is on the right adjacent to the small Dare County airport. The Christmas Shop and the Island Gallery (an adjacent boutique filled with handcrafted items) are roughly 4½ miles farther east on Route 64 on the left.

Ocracoke Island

Undiscovered Treasure

Ocracoke is the least accessible of the three barrier islands that make up Cape Hatteras National Seashore. This small remote island can only be reached by ferry. A free 40-minute crossing takes you from Hatteras to Ocracoke, or you can make the 2½-hour trip from Swan Quarter or Cedar Island.

On Sir Richard Grenville's 1585 expedition to Roanoke Island (see Fort Raleigh and *Elizabeth II* selections) his ship the *Tiger* stopped for repairs at Ocracoke. Even today the English influence is discernible. In fact, a part of the island is British. During World War II, while patrolling allied shipping lines, the HMS *Bedfordshire* was sunk by enemy torpedo fire. Four British sailors washed ashore at Ocracoke and were buried there. As part of the 1976 bicentennial, the state purchased the property on which the sailors were buried and leased it back to Great Britain as an official piece of English soil. A British flag flies here, and a marker on the fence surrounding their graves is inscribed with the words of Rubert Brooke, "If I should die, think only this of me: that there's some corner of a foreign field, That is for ever England."

The **British cemetery** is one of seven stops on the island walking tour. The complete tour circuit is 2½ miles. It is ¾ of a mile from the visitor center to the lighthouse, so you can take a mile walk and then drive past the lighthouse if time is limited. The tour starts at the visitor center where you'll see exhibits on the history of the island and obtain free maps and literature. The maps unfortunately do not purport to be treasure maps. Edward Teach, commonly called Blackbeard because of his bushy beard and with the real name of Captain Edward Drummond, is believed by many to have secreted his ill-gotten gain here. Blackbeard, along with other pirates, found protection in the waters around Ocracoke in the early 1700s. Here the pirates performed needed repairs and made forays against unsuspecting ships that had the misfortune to sail these waters. It was while Teach was in home port, so to speak, that he was engaged in battle on November 1718. Lieutenant Robert Maynard was sent after Blackbeard by Royal Governor Spotswood of Virginia. After defeating the pirate, Maynard cut off his head and sailed to Bath with it hanging from the bowsprit of his ship. A popular legend that has amused all ages for years claims that after decapitation Blackbeard's body swam around the boat seven times looking for its head.

The **walking tour** of the island covers the Post Office, Methodist Church, Ocracoke School and Wahab-Howard Cemetery. You'll see sandy lanes and old homes with detached kitchens, cisterns and several widow's walks. The school serves kindergarten through twelfth grade and is the smallest public high school in the state.

The last stop on the tour is the **Ocracoke Lighthouse**, the oldest operating lighthouse on the Carolina coast and the second oldest in the country. This 75-foot solid white tower was built in 1823. Interestingly with all the changes experienced by the opening and closing of inlets along the Outer Banks, the Ocracoke Inlet is the only one continuously open since the Portuguese first reported it in 1532.

Ocracoke has one other reminder of her colonial history. When Sir Walter Raleigh's colonists came to the Carolina coast over 400 years ago they brought with them much they thought they would need in the New World, including horses. Descendants of the horses still survive on Ocracoke. There are conflicting explanations about the origins of these Banker ponies, as another theory states they were brought to America by Ponce de Leon. The small, wild Spanish ponies roamed freely on the island until 1959 when the main highway was constructed; at that time they were penned in a pasture on the sound side of the island. Only a few horses remain of the thousands that once lived here, and these can be seen at the Ocracoke Horse Pen about seven miles north of town.

Ocracoke is popular with sports fishermen and swimmers who enjoy the 16 miles of deserted beach. For a small island it offers a surprising number of excellent restaurants and picturesque spots to stay. Along the harbor are the Anchorage Inn, Harborside Motel and the Island Inn to name just a few. Perhaps the most picturesque is Berkley Center, a completely remodeled wooden country inn. Locals boast of the crabs you can enjoy at Captain Ben's and the fresh seafood served at Pony Island, while the menu at the Back Porch has delicious gourmet cuisine.

If Ocracoke isn't remote enough for you, then take the ferry from there to Portsmouth Village, part of Cape Lookout National Seashore. This pilot town was established in 1753, when a main shipping lane to the Carolina colony ran through shifting Ocracoke Inlet and residents were called on to lead ships through the tricky waters. At Portsmouth Village heavily laden ships could be lightened to allow them to cross the bar, or their cargoes could be lightered ashore for shipment to the mainland. Although the village is no longer inhabited, the church and a house, which now serve as a visitor center, are open during the summer months. There is a self-guided walking tour of the village. Portsmouth mosquitoes, it should be noted, have a well-deserved reputation. It's said that bug repellents just attract them, so visitors are advised to cover up. (See Cape Lookout National Seashore selection.) The island is known for its secluded beaches and excellent shelling.

Directions: From I-95 take Route 158 east to the coast. At Whalebone Junction take Route 12 south to Hatteras. From the village of Hatteras there is a free ferry to Ocracoke. But during the summer the lines can be long, and on some crossings priority is given to commercial vehicles. You can also take the Cedar Island or Swan Quarter Toll ferries to Ocracoke. Reservations are required. For information call North Carolina State Ferries (919)225-3551 at Cedar Island, or (919)926-1111 at Swan Quarter.

Pea Island National Wildlife Refuge and Bodie Lighthouse

Double Protection

Flanked on either side by Cape Hatteras National Seashore, the 5,915-acre **Pea Island National Wildlife Refuge** is a sprawling 12-mile coastal barrier-island wildlife sanctuary. The adjacent 25,700 acres of Pamlico Sound are also protected—from man's incursions, but not the vicissitudes of nature.

Pea Island was established in 1938 to offer a safe wintering habitat for migratory waterfowl. Thousands of snow and Canada geese, whistling swans and 25 species of ducks take advantage of it each year. The refuge's bird list contains 265 species sighted regularly and 50 additional species sighted occasionally.

One of the best ways to observe the seasonally changing bird population is by taking the four-mile trail around the North Pond impoundment. On the dikes of this impoundment, quite near the parking area, there is an observation platform. During the mosquito season, which may begin in late spring, be sure to apply an insect repellent before venturing along a refuge path.

In the spring, portions of the impoundment may be closed to protect the nesting shore and wading birds. Least terns, willets, black skimmers and oystercatchers are among the birds that raise their young here. In the marshy areas of Pamlico Sound ibis, herons and egrets make their nests. Several endangered species make this a stop on their north/south migration. You are apt to see brown pelicans congregating in the sound in March, and their young, although hatched elsewhere, are brought to Oregon Inlet in August to learn how to fish. Peregrine falcons are often sighted in November and may be seen as early as September. Other raptors seen in the fall are kestrels, merlins and sharp-shinned hawks. During the warm summer months it is not uncommon to spot bald eagles.

Birds are not the only endangered species to be seen. Loggerhead sea turtles begin nesting here in June, coming ashore at night to lay their eggs in the sand. Year-round residents include otters, muskrats and nutria.

Bird watching and nature photography are popular pastimes at Pea Island Refuge. It is also a noted fishing spot; the 12.2 miles of undeveloped beach provide fishermen with ideal surf conditions. The catch often includes speckled and gray trout, spot, flounder, blue fish and red drum. The shore along Oregon Inlet is excellent for crabbing. If you are in the area in late afternoon, around 4:30, leave the refuge, cross the inlet bridge, and stop at the Oregon Inlet Fishing Center to watch the catch unloaded from the charter and commercial fishing boats.

Watching the rough water in the inlet and along the coast you can understand why this has been called the Graveyard of the Atlantic. Several shipwrecks can be seen in this area. Across from the Pea Island Refuge headquarters the remains of an unidentified barge are visible at low tide. If you drive north to the first turnout on the left, three miles north of the Pea Island Headquarters, you'll find the remains of the 1862 Civil War transport *Oriental*. Part of the boiler of this Union ship shows in the breaking surf. Three miles north of Oregon Inlet at Coquina Beach you can see the remains of the four-masted schooner, *Laura A. Barnes*. The wooden hull of this old ship is beached alongside the parking lot. These remains represent only a fraction of the more than 600 ships of 50 tons or more that have sunk off the Outer Banks. In the first six months of 1942 more than 80 ships were sunk off these shores by German U-boats.

A series of operational lighthouses along the Outer Banks help ships through this dangerous stretch. One you can visit while in this area is **Bodie Lighthouse**, just across from Coquina Beach. The present lighthouse is the third Bodie Lighthouse. The first, constructed in 1847, was the first on this part of the Carolina coast. Unfortunately it was built out of line, or plum, and this lack of balance resulted in its being replaced. The second one, erected in 1859, was blown up during the Civil War. The third was started in June 1871 and cost five times more to build than the previous lighthouse. It was first lit on October 1, 1872. Less than a month after it began operation, on October 29, a flock of geese smashed into the tower, breaking three panes of the glass lantern and damaging the lens.

During an inspection of the lighthouse in 1877, cracks were discovered on all landings from the second to the seventh. The metal stairway up the tower became highly charged during electrical storms causing the landings to crack. After another major lightning strike in 1884 the grounding of the tower stairs was finally improved.

The Bodie Lighthouse is painted alternate belts of black and white. It is not open to the public but is a frequently photographed Outer Banks landmark. For those interested in details, there are 214 steps to the top, 54 fewer than the Cape Hatteras Lighthouse, the country's tallest lighthouse. The former lightkeepers' quarters is now a Park Service visitor center. It is open during the summer months. At the **Chicamacomico United States Life Saving Service Station** in Rodanthe at the south end of Pea Island (actually on Hatteras Island) National Park Service personnel re-enact early rescue drills on Thursdays at 2:00 P.M. from mid-June until Labor Day.

Directions: From I-95 take US 64 or US 264 east to the coast. At Whalebone Junction just south of Nags Head you will find a National Park Information Center with information on all the attractions in the area. Proceed south on NC Route 12 to Bodie Island and the lighthouse then cross Oregon Inlet to the Pea Island National Wildlife Refuge.

Wright Brothers National Memorial

The Wright Stuff

The Wright brothers literally took a crash course in flying in December 1903. Wilbur won the toss of the coin and was the first to try to fly their custom-made plane on December 14. The brothers had been at Kitty Hawk since September and were eager to fly their engine-powered airplane. With only an eight mile-per-hour wind, Wilbur stalled the plane. Repairing the damage took several days, but on December 17 they were ready to try again. At 10:35 A.M. Orville became the first man to successfully fly—a 12-second ride that took him 120 feet. The brothers were able to make three more flights with ever greater distances—175 feet, 200 feet, 852 feet—before a wind gust resulted in a landing that destroyed the plane. But they had achieved their objective; they had proved that man could fly.

Orville lived long enough to realize the magnitude of their accomplishments and its impact on the future. He died in 1948, a year after Chuck Yeager broke the sound barrier. When you visit this national monument you can trace the development of aviation from an idea to a reality.

In 1900 Wilbur Wright wrote, "I am intending to start in a few days for a trip to the coast of North Carolina . . . for the purpose of making some experiments with a flying machine. It is my belief that flight is possible . . ." The Wright brothers had written the National Weather Bureau requesting a list of locations where the winds were constant, and Kitty Hawk most closely met the required conditions. They had begun experimenting with gliders around their home and bicycle shop in Dayton, Ohio, but wind conditions there were not suitable. In September and October of 1900 they experimented with a glider from the dunes of Kitty Hawk. They returned the next year in July and spent about a month flying an even larger glider with disappointing results. So downcast were they that Wilbur said he did not believe men would fly in a 1,000 years.

Disheartened but not defeated, Wilbur and Orville returned to Dayton and built a wind tunnel to compile their own aeronautical data. They tested over 200 air scale wings in their jerry-built tunnel. Since then sophisticated computers have checked a chart the brothers compiled of wind pressure data and found only a one percent error ratio. Pilots still use it. From this data they built an even larger glider which they tested more than 1,000 times from August 28 to October 28, 1902. That was the most successful glider testing in history and convinced them that the next step was to add a small engine and propellers to power the craft.

The Wright brothers had to rely on their own ingenuity to build the aluminum block gasoline engine and to combine the wing warping and rudder control that became the key to successful controlled flight. That accomplished, they were ready to return to Kitty Hawk on September 25, 1903, and the stage was set for their historic December flight.

What took the Wright brothers six months and $1,000 to construct entailed far more effort and money to reproduce. To build the reproduction of the 1903 Wright Flyer you'll see at the visitor center it took 50 craftsmen three years and a half million dollars. And they already had the plans!

With this prodigious accomplishment you might think neither brother would have time for a hobby, but fortunately for history Orville's hobby was photography. The visitor center features prints made from Orville Wright's glass negatives. Exhibits also include a reproduction of the 1902 glider. Just outside is a faithful reproduction of the Wright brothers' camp, filled with furniture and even canned food. Wilbur called it a five-room house, all, however, as he said, in one room. Just outside the camp are markers indicating the takeoff point and landing for the first four flights.

On December 17, 1928, Orville Wright was on hand along with his guest Amelia Earhart for the laying of the cornerstone of the Wright Memorial. He returned for the 1932 dedication. Wilbur had died of typhoid fever in 1912 at age 45.

During the summer months you can climb to the top of the Wright Memorial Monument Shaft, a 60-foot tall pylon atop Kill Devil Hill, the takeoff point for many of the Wrights' glider flights. This 90-foot dune was once one of four high hills, but a 1912 hurricane blew two hills away. The inscription at the base of the monument reads: "In commemoration of the conquest of the air by the brothers Wilbur and Orville. Conceived by genius. Achieved by dauntless resolution and unconquerable faith"—a sentiment visitors heartily endorse.

The Wright Brothers National Monument is open daily 9:00 A.M. to 5:00 P.M. Programs are given on the hour from 10:00 A.M. to 4:00 P.M.

Directions: From I-95 take Route 158 east to the coast. The Wright Brothers National Monument is at milepost 8 on Route 158, South Croatan Highway, in Kill Devil Hills. An alternate route is to take Route 64 east to Route 158, then go north to Kill Devil Hills.

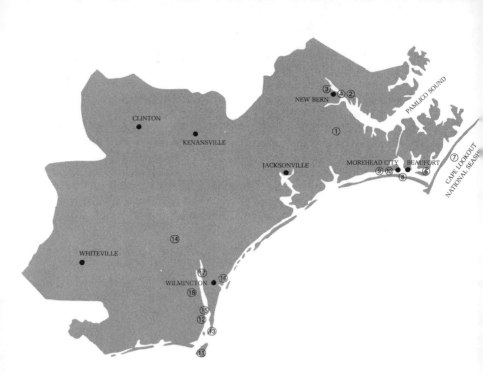

SOUTHERN COAST

New Bern and Vicinity
1. Croatan National Forest
2. John Wright Stanly House and Dixon-Stevenson House
3. New Bern Historic District
4. Tryon Palace and Gardens

Beaufort, Morehead City and Vicinity

5. Beaufort By the Sea
6. Beaufort's Old Burying Ground
7. Cape Lookout National Seashore
8. Fort Macon State Park
9. North Carolina Aquarium-Pine Knoll Shores
10. North Carolina Maritime Museum

Wilmington and Vicinity
11. Bald Head Island
12. Brunswick Town and Southport
13. Fort Fisher and North Carolina Aquarium
14. Moores Creek National Battlefield
15. Orton Plantation
16. Poplar Grove Plantation, Airlie Gardens and Greenfield Gardens
17. USS North Carolina Battleship Memorial
18. Wilmington Historic Homes

Southern Coast

Even within small family groups there will be different interests and travel preferences. You can design one-day trips to accommodate a breadth of enthusiasms. In the Southern Coast region, beginning at the Virginia border and extending halfway down North Carolina's coast, the options for satisfying diverse interests are numerous.

Anyone who owns a boat or enjoys being on board will be intrigued by the North Carolina Maritime Museum where you see how boats are built and how commercial fishermen worked the Carolina coast. Another nautical attraction in this region, the USS *North Carolina* Battleship Memorial, is one of the most frequently visited attractions in the state. The nightly summer sound-and-light extravaganza about the ship's action in World War II vividly recalls those tumultuous days.

Garden lovers have only to follow the calendar, catching the spring shrubs and bulbs at Airlie and Greenfield Gardens in the Wilmington area, the summer annuals at Orton Plantation or anytime of the year, the Tryon Palace Gardens. Nature lovers take to the trails at Croatan National Forest to find its unique insect-eating plants. Anyone who wants total escape from the tensions of daily life can head off the mainland to the tranquil deserted beaches of Cape Lookout National Seashore or Bald Head Island.

Antique and architectural enthusiasts mustn't miss the Hope Plantation or the private homes in the Tryon Palace Complex and on the walking tours of Beaufort, New Bern and Wilmington.

As if that weren't variety enough, the Southern Coast region also harbors three aquariums where you have a chance to get up close to the aquatic wonders of its waters. No wet suits needed here, only appreciation for the raptures of the deep.

NEW BERN AND VICINITY

Croatan National Forest

Floundering Around

North Carolina has four national forests totaling 1.2 million acres—the Pisgah, Nantahala, Uwharrie and **Croatan**. These recreational meccas offer a wide disparity of terrain from rugged mountain and rolling piedmont hills to the coastal plains' sandy pine forest.

Croatan, an Algonquin word meaning council town, is the most coastal national forest in the eastern United States. Its 158,000 acres run close to the Atlantic Ocean on both the southern and northeastern sides. The water provides a moderating influence on the climate, and visitors can enjoy year-round recreational options.

There are three nature trails within Croatan—Cedar Point Tideland Trail, Island Creek Forest Walk and Neusiok Trail—covering many different types of terrain. Two loops on the Cedar Point Tideland Trail offer a one or two-hour hike. This trail provides a close look at the ecological balance of an estuary, that part of a river where fresh water meets sea water. Wildlife is abundant, as 95 percent of all ocean life either begins in or is dependent upon estuaries. Interpretative signs explain the flora and fauna as you traverse through hardwood and pine forests. Then follow the raised boardwalk over the tidal-marsh area. The Island Creek Forest Walk takes you through an upland area with piedmont hardwoods and associated plants. The .5-mile hiking trail along Island Creek is popular with naturalists because of the diversity of plant life.

If you take the Neusiok Trail you can see pocosins, areas unique to this forest. Pocosin, another Indian word, means swamp-on-a-hill, an apt description for this wet upland bog. Croatan National Forest is noted for its unique insect-eating plants, most of which thrive in the pocosin. This coastal forest is home to five kinds of insectivorous plants. If you look closely you can spot the Venus's-flytrap, a low-growing plant whose hinged leaves close on its prey. More visually striking is the round-leafed sundew, named for the dew-like drops which secrete a sticky substance to trap and anesthetize victims. The pitcher-plant drowns unwary insects that intrude into its vase-shaped flower. The rosette-like butterworts trap insects by secreting a waxy, sticky substance then curling around the insect. Finally, there are aquatic bladderworts that float across the lake surface and catch insects and small marine animals through unique valves in trailing stolons.

To learn the best places to spot these unique species stop at the Ranger's Office off Route 70, a short distance past New Bern. Hours are 8:00 A.M. to 4:30 P.M., Monday through Friday.

The 20-mile Neusiok Trail is intersected by forest roads to provide access and egress to the trail as few hikers attempt the entire length. Check at the Ranger's Office for information on the different sections of the trail. Hikers may spot endangered species like the southern bald eagle, red-cockaded woodpecker and in the deep swamp areas perhaps an alligator. Several species of poisonous snakes are also found in this forest including cottonmouth moccasin, canebrake rattler, eastern diamondback rattler, pygmy rattler and copperhead.

Croatan is also a favorite with fishermen. Within the forest there are 40 miles of streams and 5,500 acres of lakes. Both freshwater and saltwater fishing are popular. You can also go oystering, crabbing and floundering. The latter is done on summer nights. Fishermen shine lights in the shallow water along the shore, and when they spot the bottom-hugging flounder they gig them with spears. Hunting, camping and boating are other recreational options.

Directions: From I-95 take Route 70 about 8 miles east past New Bern. Turn left on Fisher Avenue. Look for sign to Ranger's Office right before this turn. For more information call the Ranger's Office (919)638-5628.

John Wright Stanly House and Dixon-Stevenson House

Complex Pleasures

When William Tryon, the designated Royal Governor, sailed for the North Carolina colony in 1764 he brought with him an architect, John Hawks. Young Hawks had studied with one of the noted London architects and was familiar with design books, which were often the sole guides for 18th-century contractors, or undertakers as they were then called.

Hawks didn't get right to work when he arrived. It was several years before he began the Governor's Palace, the project he had traveled so far to do (see Tryon Palace and Gardens selection, the linchpin of the Tryon Palace Complex). Perhaps it was just as well he had ample time to plan this remarkable edifice, for it was to be the crowning accomplishment of his career. Although there is no documentation to prove it, historians believe that Hawks was also responsible for another of the Tryon Palace Complex buildings, the **John Wright Stanly House**.

Hawks built this elegant Georgian residence between 1779–1783 for a New Bern merchant and shipowner. John Stanly, reported to be the wealthiest man in the colony, wanted the most lavish home in North Carolina. As one of New Bern's leading shipowners, Stanly sent privateers after British ships to obtain their cargoes for the Revolutionary cause. Winter clothes were only one of the spoils of war sent to the soldiers at Valley Forge. Stanly's privateers even succeeded in capturing a major British warship, the *Lady Blessington*.

In 1791, several years after Stanly died of yellow fever, George Washington spent two nights at the Stanly house. The townspeople reportedly brought in furniture for Washington's visit as the house was empty. Washington described the mansion in his diary as "exceeding good lodging", while also noting that the palace where he was entertained by the citizens of New Bern was "a good brick building . . . now hastening to ruin."

Yet another military leader, General Ambrose E. Burnside, also stayed at the Stanly House. After capturing New Bern in 1862, Burnside chose this august residence as his headquarters. Visitors today can see the stately mansion as it would have looked when Stanly first decorated it. Although it isn't furnished with family pieces, the house contains 18th-century items that match the Stanly inventory. You may be surprised at the informality of the red-and-white-check chair coverings in the stylish central hall. But this style was often employed in the 18th century. The halls were frequently used for entertaining. There is a mirror halfway up the hall stairs. Local lore has it that Mrs. Stanly positioned the mirror so that she could see who was calling without being seen. There is a Peale portrait of two of the Stanly children over the gold brocade parlor sofa. The master bedroom's furniture made in Philadelphia reflect Stanly's flourishing trade with that northern port. The dining room has a portrait of their son, John. The Stanly silver is proudly displayed.

The gardens have been restored and have as their focal point two matching gazebos that appeared in a drawing made when Burnside was in residence at the Stanly home.

A second house in the Tryon Palace Complex, the **Dixon-Stevenson House**, was built between 1826–1833 by New Bern Mayor George W. Dixon on one of the original 12 palace lots. This sprawling Federal style house has a captain's walk between the chimneys. Although romantics like to imagine anxious women watching for their loved ones from these rooftop walks, the more likely use was to provide a platform for the chimney sweeps. It's interesting to note how decorating styles changed from the 18th to the 19th century because, like Stanly, Dixon was a prosperous New Bern merchant. Decorative touches in the front parlor feature symbols popular during the Federal period: a sunburst on the mantle, pineapples on the mantle mirror, a Federal eagle in another mirror design and lyres on the table base. This house does not represent a family inventory; it's furnished in the popular 19th-century neoclassical style. The upstairs green bedroom is done in the Empire style with an exquisite needlepoint carpet and a handsome sleigh bed. The Dixon-Stevenson House also has a restored garden, this one featuring all white flowers that change with the seasons. In winter there are white pansies, in the spring white azaleas and tulips. Summer brings white impatiens and fall white chrysanthemums. The Stanly House and the Dixon-Stevenson House may be visited individually or they can be included on a combination ticket that includes Tryon Palace and Gardens, giving a comprehensive look at the Tryon Palace Complex. Guided tours are available every 30 minutes Monday–Saturday 9:30 A.M. to 4:00 P.M. and Sunday 1:30 to 4:00 P.M. The Tryon Palace Complex is closed Thanksgiving, December 24–26, and January 1. A 15-minute audio-visual program is given at the visitors center from 9:30 A.M. to 3:30 P.M. on the hour and the half hour. For ticket information call (919)638-1560.

Directions: From I-95 at Smithfield take Route 70 east for 82 miles to New Bern. Highway signs on Route 70 outside New Bern will direct you to the Palace Complex. The Complex is at the intersection of George and Pollock Streets, one block off Route 17 (Broad Street) in the heart of New Bern.

New Bern Historic District

New Bern's Old Look

New Bern, North Carolina's second oldest town, is a treasure trove of architectural points of interest. There are over 90 listings on the walking tour map of the tree-lined streets in the **historic district.**

The town was established in 1710 by Swiss and German Palatine colonists under the leadership of Baron Christopher von Graffenried of Bern, Switzerland. He called the settlement on the banks of the Neuse and Trent Rivers, New Bern. The location de Graffenried picked for the new government house is now Union Point Park. He bought the land from the Chatauqua Indian, Chief King Taylor. But harmonious relations between Indians and settlers lasted only briefly. The colonists had a rough start facing a bitter war with the Indians, crop failures, arson and a raft of other problems. The settlement survived and joined in the triangle trade routes, shipping tar, pitch and turpentine to New England, England and the West Indies.

Prosperity came to New Bern with the colonial government. Royal Governor William Tryon selected the town as the first permanent capital. His palatial residence, Tryon Palace, is the hub of an outstanding architectural complex (see selection). There are 14 additional buildings in town that pre-date the Revolution.

Behind the Samuel Smallwood House (#57 on the walking tour map) there's an old cypress tree. Beneath its hanging boughs the settlers signed a peace treaty with the Indians. George Washington wanted to see this imposing specimen when he visited in 1791. Today it is one of 20 trees on the Hall of Fame of American Trees.

In addition to pre-Revolutionary cottages, Georgian town houses and gambrel-roofed homes there are excellent examples of Federal style architecture such as the Rebecca Delastatius House at 206 Change Street and the Anderson-Sprenger House at 214 Johnson Street. The Victorian era also left its mark on New Bern as evident in the Foy-Munger-Smith House at 516 Middle Street and the remodeled Alonzo T. Jerkins House at 611 East Front Street. Many of the private homes in the historic district are open for special occasions. In April there is the New Bern Spring Historic Home and Gardens Tour, and in November a candlelight New Bern at Night progressive tour is conducted. One home, the Attmore-Oliver House at 511 Broad Street, is open April through December, Tuesday through Saturday afternoons from 1:00 to 4:30 P.M. The house was built in 1790 by Samuel Chapman, one of George Washington's first lieutenant's, and later enlarged in 1834. Furnishings in the six restored rooms include 18th and 19th-century antiques. Upstairs there is a Civil War exhibit and a doll collection.

If few homes are open for tours, several have turned into bed-and-breakfast spots. These include the New Berne House, the Harmony House Inn, the King's Arm, the Aerie and the Bradbury Manor.

Two other points of interest are open to visitors: the **Fireman's Museum** and the Bank of the Arts. The obvious pride of North Carolina's earliest fire company is evident in their collection of early fire fighting equipment. They've also stuffed Fred, well, at least his head. Fred was a stalwart fire horse who died in the line of duty, answering what proved to be a false alarm. The Fireman's Museum at 411 Hancock Street is open at a nominal charge Tuesday–Saturday 9:30 A.M. to 12:00 NOON and 1:00 to 5:00 P.M., and Sundays 1:00 to 5:00 P.M.

The Bank of the Arts, 317 Middle Street, is open at no charge weekdays 10:00 A.M. to 4:00 P.M. and Saturdays 10:00 A.M. to 1:00 P.M. The 1915 neoclassical bank is now a one-room art gallery with constantly changing exhibits. If you want a knowledgeable resident's-eye tour contact New Bern Guided Tours. Two affable locals have set up a company to conduct visitors around their town. These 1½-hour walking tours are enhanced by lively anecdotes and legends associated with the ageless charm of New Bern. Call (919)638-2914 for information and prices for escorted tours.

Directions: From I-95 Smithfield exit, take Route 70 east to New Bern. From US 70 Bypass, exit at Front Street. Turn left after the bridge onto Tryon Palace Drive and left again at the second light. The visitor information center is on the right at 101 Middle Street.

Tryon Palace and Gardens

Flamboyant Phoenix

Tryon Palace is only one of the buildings, though the grandest, that make up the Tryon Palace Complex. Also part of this 13-acre, 18th-century world are the John Wright Stanly House and the Dixon-Stevenson House (see selection).

Tryon Palace was deemed the most beautiful building in the colonies, outshining even the Governor's Palace in Williamsburg. The North Carolina Capitol and Royal Governor's residence proved that it was not only a pretty edifice, it was also a sturdy one. Several years after construction had begun, but a year before the December 5, 1770 dedication, the Carolina coast was hit by a strong hurricane that nearly destroyed New Bern. The palace, however, with its 3-foot-thick walls escaped with only slight flooding in the cellar.

It is ironic that William Tryon planned for every eventuality in the building of the palace except his early departure from New Bern. Before he left England to take up his duties in the North Carolina colony, he arranged for John Hawks, a noted architect, to accompany him and build an appropriate residence in the new capital. Yet not 13 months after the palace he had dreamed of and planned for was finished, King George appointed him Royal Governor of New York.

The Georgian mansion Tryon commissioned served two royal governors, Tryon and Josiah Martin. Four state governors were inaugurated in the palace although only two, Richard Caswell and Abner Nash lived there. In 1798 the palace burned to the ground, only the stable wing survived. Today you see it as it looked in all its glory when Royal Governor Tryon was in residence.

Tryon Palace was rebuilt on its original foundations using John Hawks's drawings. Once it was completed, Governor Tryon's inventory was used to purchase antique furnishings such as once filled these rooms. The best way to experience Tryon Palace is to take one of the living-history tours given six times a day during the summer months. Actors impersonating Governor and Mrs. Tryon, household servants, and John Hawks recreate a typical day in June 1771. Hawks will tell you that the most important room in the palace is the council chamber. The stern visage of King George the III, as well as a portrait of his wife Queen Charlotte, looked down upon the colonial delegates meeting here. The council chamber, where the council met in sessions shaping

Restored to its original grandeur, Tryon Palace, New Bern, is part of the elegant Georgian complex built in 1770 for colonial officials. The formal gardens are in bloom most of the year.

laws of the day, contributes to Tryon Palace's unique place in American history. This is the only building in the country where both royal and state governors lived, began their administrative terms, met with legislatures and conducted the business of the colony and later of the state.

It is, however, the living quarters that interest most visitors. Mrs. Tryon delighted in playing the spinet for her guests in the elegant parlor. President George Washington was entertained in this room while attending a ball in his honor. The ornate dining room has a cut-glass chandelier hanging above the Adam-Chippendale mahogany table. The tour takes you both upstairs and down. The deep, rich mahogany central staircase, lit by a skylight, seems to glow. The informal living quarters are upstairs, family drawing and supper rooms plus the bedrooms. Nine-year-old Margaret Tryon's pink bedroom is appropriately girlish, although letters indicate she was always expected to be well behaved and mature. One letter recalls the time she accompanied her parents to Williamsburg; she sat all day in a chair and didn't even dare accept tea and cakes. As you would expect the largest upstairs suite was Governor Tryon's bedroom. It has a canopy bed and an English-made carpet of Turkish design. A portrait of

William Tryon's father hangs on the wall. The adjoining alcove bedroom, designed for a lady, is far more feminine in soft pink and Wedgewood blue.

Taking the lesser stairs to the lower levels does not mean the end of elegance. The marble-floored entrance hall has raised recessed alcoves with life-size marble statues depicting the four known continents. You'll also see the coachman's room and preparation room. The kitchen, however, is in the east wing, which you will also tour. The brick floor and solid tables in the old kitchen provide the necessary work space for dinner preparation. It wasn't uncommon for the governor to entertain 50 or more guests for dinner. The governor's hard-working secretary had his office in this wing, removing him from the bustle in the palace. Upstairs in this wing are servants bedrooms and a sewing room. The west wing, or stable wing, was the only area to escape the fire and is 85 percent original. It is not open for tours.

If William Tryon consulted with John Hawks about the design of the palace his successor, Josiah Martin, took an interest in the grounds. He commissioned a dovecote, smokehouse and poultry house. But it is the **garden** that delights visitors. The colorful parterres of the Maude Moore Latham Memorial Garden are in bloom throughout the year with colorful spring tulips, bright summer annuals and autumn chrysanthemums. The design of the Green Garden and the walled Privy Garden can best be appreciated from the upper-story palace windows. It's hard to see the complete patterns unless you have a birds-eye view. The tranquility and beauty of both gardens should also be enjoyed up close. There is also a kitchen garden with vegetables and herbs. At the garden shop you can purchase plants grown at Tryon as well as hand-crafted items.

Begin your visit at the reception center where you will see an orientation film. Tours of the Tryon Palace Complex are given daily every 30 minutes. Hours are Monday–Saturday 9:30 A.M. to 4:00 P.M. and Sunday 1:30 to 4:00 P.M. (the last tours of the day are at 4:00). The Tryon Palace shops including the garden shop and museum shop stay open until 5:00 P.M. each day. You can purchase tickets to tour the entire complex or any of the individual attractions.

Directions: From I-95 at Smithfield take Route 70 east to New Bern. Highway signs on Route 70 outside New Bern will direct you to the Palace Complex, at the intersection of George and Pollock Streets, one block off Route 17 (Broad Street) in the heart of New Bern.

BEAUFORT, MOREHEAD CITY AND VICINITY

Beaufort By The Sea

A Peak at the Past

North Carolina's third oldest town, **Beaufort**, was settled by French Huguenots and English sailors in the early 1700s. The village, named in honor of the Duke of Beaufort, Henry Somerset, retains much of its historic charm. More than 100 homes still stand where they were built during the colonial to pre-Civil War period, and all have plaques noting their construction dates. You can explore on foot or by bicycle, a particularly enjoyable way to make your way around this flat well-laid-out community. Green and white bike-route signs lead you on a six-mile loop around Beaufort.

The best place to start any tour of Beaufort's historical sites is at the town's welcome center in the **Josiah Bell House** on Turner Street. Docents give tours of this and five other historical properties. (For the Old Burying Grounds, see selection. You have to make special arrangements or take a self-guided tour). If you prefer to be driven around Beaufort, you can take a tour on an old English bus. It operates April through October at a nominal charge.

The Josiah Bell House is a Victorian country home. Two of the downstairs rooms were built in 1790; the rest of the house was added in 1825. The furnishings span the years from 1825 to 1860. Unlike some Victorian rooms, the two front parlors are light and airy. There is a 19th-century Regina music box and a record cabinet for the 27-inch discs. Upstairs is a children's bedroom filled with toys and dolls and two additional bedrooms.

The next house you'll tour is the **Joseph Bell House**, grandfather of Josiah. This restored 1767 home built by Colonel Bell, plantation owner, is on its original site. The woodwork up to the chair rail is original, as are the floor boards and mantle. The conch-red exterior with white shutters duplicates the colors Bell selected. The 18th-century furnishings reflect the period. There are no family pieces. Downstairs you'll see Colonel Bell's office, where he conducted business related to his two inns in town and his fleet of ships. One of the upstairs bedrooms has a Virginia pineapple bed and the other has a hand-turned bed that is covered by an appliqued quilt. Just outside the house is a formal English boxwood garden.

A few steps away is another house from about the same time but representing a different economic level. The 1778 **Samuel**

Leffer's Cottage represents the home of an 18th-century school-master. Built in a fisherman's cottage design with a typical early Beaufort roofline, this modest dwelling is furnished with primitive antiques. The half-story upstairs area was constructed in that way to avoid paying the tax on a second floor.

The next building on the grounds, the 1796 **Cateret County Courthouse**, is the oldest public building in the county. Before 1796 it served as the meeting place for Beaufort's Church of England congregation. The cabinets and other furnishings are original to the courthouse. In addition, because Masonic meetings were held here as well, you'll see an old Masonic ballot box. Otway Burns, military leader in the War of 1812, attended the first Masonic meeting.

Prisoners awaiting trial or serving sentences may well have languished in the 1829 **Cateret County Jail**, your next stop. This is a 500-ton structure with walls 28-inches thick. Two large cells held up to 30 prisoners who had only the warmth of their bodies to keep them from freezing; the jailer's quarters was the only heated part of the building. Within this old jail is a gallows where at least one prisoner lost his life. Outside are the stocks, pillory and whipping post, used for less severe sentences.

The last building you'll tour is the 1859 **Apothecary Shop and Doctor's Office**. The shelves of the Apothecary Shop are filled with old medicines that seem to come out of *Alice in Wonderland*. You could buy Dr. William's Pink Pills for Pale People or Oil of Youth, which was 60 percent alcohol, or an Egyptian Herb Tonic for Women, advertised as "pleasant to take." In addition to the old nostrums there are doctor's tools, medical equipment and an examination table. One of the doctor's devices is a Renu-life machine that theoretically passed ozones over the body to cure ailments. Outside the shop is an herb garden, like one the doctor had for various curatives he prepared.

It's not part of the tour, but before you explore the rest of Beaufort you might want to see the art at the gallery located in the 1732 R. Rustell House, which is the last building at the site.

These historic structures are open year-round Monday thru Saturday 9:30 A.M. to 4:30 P.M.

Directions: From I-95 take Route 70 east through Goldsboro, Kinston, New Bern and Morehead City. Just past Morehead City you will cross a high bridge and then a drawbridge. Make a right turn at the first traffic light after the drawbridge onto Turner Street. Go three blocks to the Old Town Beaufort Historic Site on your right. Just past this, turn right or left onto Front Street for Beaufort's waterfront.

Beaufort's Old Burying Ground

Restful Resting Place

Ordinarily cemeteries are not high on the list of attractions one must see, but it's worth taking a walking tour of **Beaufort's Old Burying Ground** just to hear the intriguing tales associated with those interred here.

On Thursday afternoons at one o'clock members of the Beaufort Historical Association give guided tours. At other times the brochure available just inside the cemetery gates gives ample information. The cemetery, now listed on the National Register of Historic Places, was deeded to Beaufort in 1731, but historians surmise that victims of the 1716 Indian wars were already buried here. The oldest legible marker, grave #13, is dated 1756.

The graves in the north corner, some of the oldest in the cemetery, face east because 18th-century custom held that when those buried there arose from the dead on Judgment Morn they would face the sun. A number of these early graves are bricked over to protect them from storm-swept flood water.

Many fallen military men are buried here. Grave #14 is that of Beaufort's highest ranking Revolutionary officer, Colonel William Thompson. The marker over Captain Josiah Pender is an official Confederate government marker. But probably the most interesting military grave is that of a British naval officer who didn't want to lie on foreign soil; he's buried standing up, saluting King George. The marker reads:

> Resting 'neath a foreign ground,
> Here stands a sailor of Mad George's crown
> Name unknown, and all alone,
> Standing in the Revel's (Rebel's) Ground.

Then there's the story associated with grave #16. When the temperature drops below 20 degrees around Beaufort, natives remark, "It's gonna get cold as the night the *Crissie Wright* went ashore." The sailors who died together are buried together. These seamen froze to the death, lashed to the riggings of the three-masted *Crissie Wright* on the night of January 11, 1886. The ship was dashed onto North Carolina's Outer Banks in a screaming gale. Though the ship was in sight of a roaring fire on Beaufort's shore, the raging surf prevented rescue efforts. This tragedy resulted in the establishment of the Cape Lookout lifesaving station in 1887.

Two markers negate a "happily-ever-after" love. Poor James W. Hunt had the unusual fate of remarrying, drawing up a will and dying all on the same day. For the suspicious reader let it be said that there was not even a hint of foul play. Another story without a happy ending is that of Nancy Manney French, grave #24. Young Nancy fell in love with her tutor, Charles French, an unsatisfactory suitor in her family's view. The pair were separated, and French went off to seek his fortune, vowing to return and claim his love. He succeeded at the former, becoming Associate Chief Justice of the Arizona Territory, but not the latter due to the interference of the Beaufort postmaster, a friend of the Manney family who intercepted French's letter to Nancy. His deathbed confession to Nancy at least let her know that French had not forgotten her. When both were old, French returned only to find Nancy dying of consumption. They married a few short weeks before her death.

One final story should be told. Marker #26 is the plot of Mary and Robert Chadwick, who took in a young Chinese boy discovered hiding aboard a ship that came to port in Beaufort. The bright lad went on to attend Trinity College (now Duke University) and then returned to China as a Methodist minister. He fathered two of China's most influential women, the legendary Soong sisters—Madame Chiang Kai-shek and Madame Sun-Yat sen.

Many other stories fascinate visitors as they trod the cemetery's narrow footpath. The entrance to the Old Burying Ground is on Ann Street beside the Methodist church.

Directions: From I-95 take Route 70 east through Goldsboro, Kinston and New Bern. Just past Morehead City you'll cross the Grayden Paul Bridge into Beaufort. At the first traffic light turn right on Turner Street. After two blocks there will be a blinking light, turn left on Ann Street. The Old Burying Ground is a half block up Ann Street on your left.

Cape Lookout National Seashore

Lookout—Outlook!

When you take the ferry to **Cape Lookout National Seashore** (the only way to get to this park is by boat) you not only get away from it all, you have to bring it all with you, at least all you need. Nature reigns supreme on this 55-mile shifting barrier-island chain. On the map it looks like nature has put a giant check mark beside the Carolina coast, or perhaps a fish hook, a fitting symbol for this fishermen's paradise.

Standing on the high dunes at Cape Lookout you'll feel like a pioneer; the beach stretches unmarred by human encroachment from horizon to horizon. The natural world of Cape Lookout offers its own challenge to visitors. There is no air-conditioned relief from the beating sun. There are no snack bars or any other kind of bars. You need to bring your own water, food, sun and insect protection. Then create your own fun. Remember whatever you bring you have to carry, whether it is picnic hamper, fishing gear or surf board. Some ferries do transport four-wheel vehicles as well as passengers.

A sand-worthy vehicle is the ideal way to explore Cape Lookout. The miles and miles of glistening white sand are home to a wide variety of water birds, particularly during the migratory season. There are three main visitor areas along this beach wilderness—Shackleford Banks, Core Banks and Portsmouth Island (see selection). Within these areas the Outer Banks constantly shift, and the topography of the 324 miles of barrier islands along the North Carolina coast has undergone numerous changes. Today there are 16 open inlets, but within the last 150 years there have been as many as 88 inlets. Some islands, like Shackleford Banks, which was once connected to Cape Lookout, link and disengage as the sand shifts. The ever-moving sand creates a domino effect on the natural environment. Ghost forests like those you see on Shackleford occurred because the sand dunes moved over and covered the maritime forest and then moved on, exposing the trunks of the former forest. The Core Banks, on the other hand, seem little more than an overgrown sandbar with marsh grass and ground-hugging bushes.

Man too has felt the shifts, as is evident at **Portsmouth Village**, a ghost town, except for its well-kept appearance. The only way to visit what was once the largest settlement on the Outer Banks is by private boats or by the ferry that leaves from Ocracoke (see selection). For the schedule call (919)928-4361 or (919)928-4281.

Ferries leave from **Harkers Island** for half or full-day outings to the **Cape Lookout Lighthouse** (919)728-3866. These are passenger-only ferries, but a jitney will take you to the beach or to the lighthouse. As early as 1590, maps indicated the dangerous shoals of what was called the "Promontorium tremendum" or "horrible headland." This danger was ignored until 1804 when Congress finally authorized a lighthouse "at or near the pitch (tip) of Cape Lookout." Finished in 1812 it met with mixed reception. Many mariners questioned the visibility of this much-needed beacon; it wasn't until 1856 when the Fresnel lens, which looked like a giant glass beehive, was installed that the efficacy of the lighthouse was insured. The Cape Lookout Lighthouse is still operational, though unmanned, and is off limits to visitors. However, rangers offer summertime beach walks and programs highlighting the history of the lighthouse.

Two other ferries transport visitors to the Core Banks. One leaves from Davis to Shingle Point (919)729-2791 and the other from the Atlantic to Portsmouth Island roughly 3 miles north of Drum Inlet (919)225-4261. To get information on ferry schedules contact these private ferry services directly. For general information on Cape Lookout National Seashore stop at the Cape Lookout Seashore Station on Front Street in Beaufort, about a 30-minute drive from Harkers Island. Currently there is no ferry service to Shackleford Banks, but it may resume in the near future. If it does it will probably dock at the west end, not the east end where it formerly docked. Private boats now offer the only access.

Before visiting any of the points of interest in Cape Lookout National Seashore you should stock up on insect repellent, although the Portsmouth mosquito is in no way daunted by even the heaviest applications. A wide-brim hat and long-sleeve shirt are also advisable as the sun is intense on the shadeless beach. Be sure to take plenty of water as well. If you have any trash bring it back to the mainland when you return. Camping is permitted in the park, but again you have to transport all your gear. Insect season is from May to October, so mosquito netting is a must. Getting to this beach takes effort. It is more rugged than most vacationers are accustomed to, but if you want your natural world unspoiled this is the place for you.

Directions: From I-95 take Route 70 to Beaufort where the park headquarters is temporarily located on Front Street. For Harkers Island continue on Route 70 east. Just past Otway turn right on the unnumbered county road known locally as Harkers Island road for Harkers Island ferry. There will be a sign.

Fort Macon State Park

Makin' It

Over one million visitors explore **Fort Macon State Park** each year, making it North Carolina's most visited park. It has a dual appeal—a wide beach beckons, while on a bluff above the shore the parapets of Fort Macon offer a scenic vista and a historical perspective.

This is the third fort to stand on this vulnerable spit of land. Over the years coastal North Carolina was threatened by Spanish, British, Union and German forces. The first fortification, Fort Dobbs, was begun during the French and Indian War. This unfinished battery was supplanted in 1808–09 by Fort Hampton, which protected Beaufort during the War of 1812. The final fort was begun in 1826 as part of a network of coastal forts. At the beginning of the Civil War only one unarmed caretaker manned the fort. The Confederates sent him home, then armed and staffed Fort Macon. Nine hundred men were stationed here at the fort's busiest period, 40 to a room.

By 1862 when the Union troops penetrated this southern bastion, the fort held a complement of 441 men under Colonel Moses

J. White. Following victories at Roanoke Island and New Bern, a splinter force of Major General Burnside's army attacked Fort Macon. Federal mortars fired at the fort from protected dune bunkers ¾ mile from the fort's walls. Since the Confederates had no mortars they could not disable the land batteries; consequently they sustained heavy damage. The 11-hour battle for Fort Macon was only the second time that modern rifled cannons were used against the old-style brick-masonry forts. These guns were so powerful they could shoot through the walls. The Confederates surrendered when it became obvious that the powder magazine would be detonated with untold loss of life. Battles like the one for Fort Macon made all forts of this type obsolete.

Federal troops occupied Fort Macon for the remainder of the war and subsequently used it as a federal penitentiary from 1865 to 1877. The fort was briefly resuscitated during the Spanish-American War in 1898. But after two years it was again abandoned until 1924 when it was acquired by the state as a park. It quickly became a popular recreational park, but such frivolity ended with World War II. Coastal America was vulnerable to U-boat attacks, and the army artillery occupied this fort after December 1941. It was headquarters for the defense of Beaufort Harbor.

It wasn't until 1946 that the state regained its park. The fort was restored and continues to be developed as a tourist attraction. A tape can be activated in the restored casemate quarters of Colonel White. The simulated voice of the Colonel explains his duties at Fort Macon. In the restored soldier's barracks, you'll learn that the men slept two to a bed. At some posts the medical officer had the men lie head to toe, believing that this reduced the spread of communicable diseases. This fact along with the knowledge that the soldiers bathed infrequently gives you a good idea of life in these barracks. The audio in this casemate includes excerpts from letters the soldiers stationed here wrote their loved ones.

For more details about life at Fort Macon you can visit the Museum Bookstore open 9:00 A.M. to 5:00 P.M. on weekends in the fall, winter and spring and daily during the summer months. It is closed in January and February. If time permits you can also hike the ¼-mile Elliot Coue Trail. Coue was a physician stationed here in 1869–70. He studied the flora and fauna of the shrub thicket that surrounded the fort. Herons and egrets often nest in the park's cedars while painted buntings populate the thickets. You can swim at the guarded beaches during the summer or fish and crab from the shore year-round. There are picnic tables and outdoor grills. Hours at Fort Macon are November–February 8:00 A.M. to 6:00 P.M.; March and October 8:00 A.M. to 7:00 P.M.; April, May, September 8:00 A.M. to 8:00 P.M.; June, July, August 8:00

A.M. to 9:00 P.M.; swimming area 10:00 A.M. to 6:00 P.M. and fort 9:00 A.M. to 5:30 P.M.

Directions: From I-95 take Route 70 east through Goldsboro, Kinston and New Bern. In Morehead City cross the bridge to Atlantic Beach and turn left on Route 58 east for Fort Macon State Park.

North Carolina Aquarium— Pine Knoll Shores

N.C.'s Age of Aquariums

North Carolina has a unique network of aquariums to foster understanding and appreciation of coastal aquatic habitats. The three facilities—Pine Knoll Shores, Fort Fisher, and Roanoke Island—are the state's most visited facilities and they are open at no charge.

The **Pine Knoll Shores Aquarium** is situated within the 290-acre Theodore Roosevelt Natural Area near Atlantic Beach. One of Pine Knoll Shores' major exhibits focuses on the endangered sea turtle. The story of the loggerhead turtle is explained from nesting through life at sea. Live turtles are on display, and a model nest reveals how deeply the eggs are laid and how difficult the climb is for the newly hatched turtles. Children can take a sea turtle quiz after viewing the exhibit. To give the turtles a better chance for survival the aquarium releases sea turtles they've nursed in aquarium hospital tents.

Aquarium volunteers man the Close Encounter tank. this hands-on exhibit gives young and old the chance to pick up and investigate sea stars, spider crabs, whelks, window pane flounders, horseshoe crabs, sea urchins and other aquatic specimens. Interpretative panels identify the animals found in the touch tank.

In addition to exhibits, the calender of events includes live demonstrations, field trips, boat excursions, snorkeling classes, films, lectures, craft workshops and children's classes. There are also special events like the Bogue Banks Photography Exhibit, Saltwater Arts Week and Hurricane Awareness Week. Just outside the aquarium, within the Theodore Roosevelt Natural Area, is the Hoffman Nature Trail which takes you through a maritime forest. There is a great diversity of plants and animals within this protected area.

The aquarium is open 9:00 A.M. to 5:00 P.M. Monday through Saturday and 1:00 to 5:00 P.M. on Sundays. Closed on Thanksgiving, Christmas and New Year's Day.

Directions: From I-95 take Route 70 east through Goldsboro,

Kinston and New Bern. At Morehead City take the bridge to Atlantic Beach. Go west five miles on Route 58.

North Carolina Maritime Museum

Nautical But Nice

The **North Carolina Maritime Museum** in Beaufort offers a series of diverse activities as well as exhibits. Innovative both in scope and design, the weathered wooden museum, built in 1985, blends well with the town's historic district as it is modeled on an early U.S. lifesaving service station.

The exhibit area resembles the hold of a large wooden ship and displays several historical boats. The life-size North Carolina spritsail skiff and the lapstrake sailing dinghy both seem to be in full sail as their rigging reaches toward the vaulted ceiling. Other vessels are represented by scale models, which include 18th and 19th-century square-riggers, shrimp trawlers, sharpies, shad boats, schooners and other local work boats. One model is the historic *Snapdragon*, captained by War of 1812 privateer, Otway Burns.

The museum's theme "Down to the Sea" includes both maritime artifacts and natural history. Exhibits of coastal birds, fish and mammals acquaint visitors with North Carolina's rich natural resources. A small aquarium area has live specimens from the state's estuaries and offshore waters.

The museum has a small craft program that preserves the records of North Carolina boat building as well as fostering the art of wooden boat building. Ambitious new plans call for expansion to a waterfront building across from the main museum. This new location will house the Harvey W. Smith Watercraft Center.

Boat building is just one of the hands-on activities at this museum. The educational staff conducts excursions focusing on birding, fossil hunting, canoeing, wildflower and mushroom walks plus trips to Shackleford Banks, Cape Lookout National Seashore, Croatan National Forest and other nearby destinations. The museum also hosts lectures, video programs, art exhibits and numerous special events. The first weekend of May is the annual Spring Gathering of Small Wooden Boats. Upwards of 75 boats participate in the races, demonstrations and clinics. Another popular event, the Strange Seafood Exhibition, takes place yearly on the third Thursday in August. This is no place for the timid as culinary offerings include bluefish mousse, shark creole, whelk chowder, sea lettuce soup, periwinkles in butter, stingray casserole, eel salad, sea urchin roe and marinated octopus. These far from everyday items can be tasted, and if you enjoy them a

Exhibits at the North Carolina Maritime Museum in Beaufort acquaint visitors with coastal marine life and boat building techniques from the past and present.

recipe collection is available for home preparation, presuming you can find the ingredients.

The North Carolina Maritime Museum, 315 Front Street, is

open at no charge Monday–Friday 9:00 A.M. to 5:00 P.M., Saturday 10:00 A.M. to 5:00 P.M. and Sunday 2:00 to 5:00 P.M. To obtain a detailed four-month calendar of events call (919)728-7317.

Directions: From I-95 take Route 70 east through Goldsboro, Kinston and New Bern. Just past Morehead City you'll cross a high bridge and a drawbridge. Make a right turn at the first traffic light after the drawbridge. You will be on Turner Street. Go three blocks and you are on Front Street. Turn right and the North Carolina Maritime Museum is immediately on your right.

WILMINGTON AND VICINITY

Bald Head Island

Isolated Splendor

Some spots are better served by being less publicized, treasures discovered by an intrepid few. If any spot deserves such protection it's **Bald Head Island**, a veritable ocean Eden.

Bald Head Island is a 12,000-acre natural wonderland including a great salt marsh and tidal creek that extend across 6,000 acres at the mouth of the Cape Fear River, a few nautical miles off the coast at Southport (a 45-minute drive from Wilmington). If you cross the island's maritime forest and scale the spinal dunes you'll find miles of secluded ocean beaches. Even on summer holiday weekends, yours may be the only footprints in the sand.

Although people are scarce here, wildlife is abundant. More than 180 species of birds pass through or reside on this island. You're apt to spot white ibis, great blue herons, snowy egrets, black-bellied plovers and a wide variety of other waterfowl. In the dense foliage of loblolly pines, live oaks, palmetto, sabal palms, bay and holly trees you may see raccoons, opossum and an occasional fox. Alligator walks are sponsored by the Bald Head Conservancy, but these elusive reptiles have to be sought out. You may see one or more of the island's 40 loggerhead sea turtles. In summer they come ashore to lay their eggs, and in early autumn the hatchlings head out to sea.

Though man has inhabited Bald Head sporadically since 300 A.D. when Indian campsites were established here, the disruption of the natural harmony of the island has been slight. The residents on the island (about 40) get around in electric golf carts, traveling no more than 12–15 mph. Most vacationers choose to rent accommodations on the island, but day-trippers are welcome to take the short 3½-mile ferry ride from Southport.

Golfers have discovered the appeal of Bald Head's 18-hole course designed by Master's consultant George Cobb. The 7,040-yard course winds through maritime forests and alongside massive dunes. Fortunately the alligators rarely find their way to the picturesque fresh water lagoons that curve through 15 fairways. Golfers and other visitors need to remember that ferry reservations are a must; call (919)457-5003. Tee times should be reserved on holidays and weekends; call (919)457-5000, ext. 211.

Fishermen have long known that Bald Head's Frying Pan Shoals are one of the best sportfishing locations north of the Caribbean. Anyone who longs for an unpopulated beach will delight in the vast stretches on Bald Head. Shell-seekers find the pickings abundant, and surfers need have no fear of careening into bathers.

Those anxious to explore the island can rent golf carts, bicycles or canoes. The principal landmark on the island is Old Baldy, the oldest standing lighthouse in North Carolina. This 90-foot tower, erected in 1817, was the island's second lighthouse. The first, built in 1796, was precariously perched near the edge of the Cape Fear River. Its hazardous location prompted its demolition in 1813. During the Civil War, Old Baldy was part of Fort Holmes, an earthenworks fort built by the Confederates to protect Wilmington, one of the South's few open links to Europe. The fort was evacuated in 1865, but Old Baldy continued in operation until 1903. Other points of interest are the island chapel, the quaint beach cottages that served as quarters for the lighthouse staff in the early 1900s and the old Coast Guard boat house which has been converted to a private home.

If you plan a one-day visit, get an early start. Bald Head is an environment you'll want to savor. For overnight visits call the island rental agents. In North Carolina call (800)722-6450, ext. 275; outside North Carolina call (800)443-6305, ext. 275.

Directions: From I-95 take Route 70 east to the Goldsboro area. Pick up Route 117 south to Route 17 at Wilmington. Continue south on Route 17 to the intersection with Route 87. Take Route 87 for slightly less than 20 miles. At the intersection of Route 87 and Route 133 (there is a flashing light), bear right on Route 133 and follow it to Southport. In Southport turn left on Hwy 221, Howe Street (there will be a traffic light at this intersection). Continue about 1.5 miles to the next traffic light and turn left on Moore Street. The Bald Head Island ferry terminal is approximately one mile on the right.

Brunswick Town and Southport

The Layered Look

Along the wooded banks of the Cape Fear River are reminders of two pivotal periods of American history. The excavated ruins of **Brunswick Town**, a colonial port community, date back to 1726. Lying diagonally across this razed town are the massive sand mounds that once formed the Civil War embankments of Fort Anderson. There are approximately 50 fenced foundations and excavations to view on this walk through history.

Brunswick Town was founded by Maurice Moore, whose father was governor of South Carolina. The town rapidly became a major naval port between the colonies and Europe and the seat of government for New Hanover County. Just outside the town's environs was Russellborough, the country estate of two North Carolina governors—Arthur Dobbs and William Tryon.

Governor Dobbs moved to the Brunswick Town area from New Bern in 1758 when he purchased Russellborough, a plantation house built by Captain John Russell. Dobbs, with notions of what was fitting, changed the estate's name to Castle Dobbs. At age 73 he married 15-year-old Justine Davis at Brunswick Town's St. Philips Church, the best preserved ruin from this 18th-century town. He is supposedly buried within its walls.

After Dobb's death in March 1765, William Tryon purchased the estate. He renamed it Castle Tryon and lived there until 1770 when Tryon Palace in New Bern was sufficiently completed to be habitable (see Tryon Palace selection).

When relations with the mother country worsened, Brunswick Town was severely affected. The Stamp Act created an economic hardship for merchants by making them affix expensive stamps to all their documents and goods. This injustice so enraged residents that one of the first incidents of armed resistance to England occurred here when angry taxpayers surrounded Castle Tryon holding the Royal Governor under house arrest. They unloaded and distributed unstamped goods from two docked ships and prevented another vessel from delivering stamps. After this show of strength ships entered and cleared this port without stamps.

The town's location on the Cape Fear River made it vulnerable to naval attack. In 1748 when the British were at war with Spain, the town was held by Spanish privateers for three tumultuous days. It was the proceeds of the Spanish ship seized and commandeered by Brunswick townsfolk that paid for the construction of St. Philips Church.

Even before the British burned Brunswick Town in 1776 it had been superseded by the rival port of Wilmington. The last residents left at the beginning of the American Revolution. In 1842 the entire town site was sold to the owner of Orton Plantation (see selection) for $4.25.

The Confederates discovered new worth for this once prosperous site in the early days of the Civil War. The land proved an excellent vantage point for a fort to protect Wilmington. Two five-gun batteries and smaller gun emplacements were set along protective sand mounds that straddled the old town site. Wood and bricks from the colonial ruins were salvaged to build the barracks. Fort Anderson was manned until February 19, 1865, a month after nearby Fort Fisher fell to Union troops. At that time the Confederate position became untenable, and the fort was abandoned.

The story of colonial America, the Revolutionary War and the Civil War is recounted at the visitors center. Brunswick Town is open without charge April through October, Monday–Saturday 9:00 A.M. to 5:00 P.M. and Sunday 1:00 to 5:00 P.M. From November through March hours are Tuesday–Saturday 10:00 A.M. to 4:00 P.M. and Sunday 1:00 to 4:00 P.M.

If Brunswick Town is a reminder of the past, just up the road is **Southport**, a seacoast village that suggests the past without losing its links with the present. In fact the town got a real dose of notoriety when *Crimes of the Heart* was filmed at a local residence. The now famous Northrup House, at 229 Caswell Street, is available for weekly rentals, call (919)457-5258. It's a charming example of Victorian architecture and Hollywood allure. The Old Brunswick Court House was also featured in the film. The best way to get a sense of Southport—breathe the sea air and hear the local legends—is to take a horse-drawn carriage tour. Call Southport Carriage (919)457-9475 or 457-9125, for details. Southport is also a good spot to stop for lunch at one of the several waterside restaurants.

Directions: From I-95 take Route 70 east to Goldsboro. Go south on Route 117. From Wilmington take NC 133 south and follow the roadside directional signs to Brunswick Town. If you want to see Southport first then take Route 17 south from Wilmington. At the intersection with Route 87 bear left and follow Route 87 into Southport. From Southport you would take NC 133 north to reach Brunswick Town.

Fort Fisher and North Carolina Aquarium

Mounds Bar

During the Civil War **Fort Fisher** grew from a small defensive bulwark into the largest earthenwork fort in the Confederacy.

271

Named in honor of the commander of the Sixth North Carolina Regiment who lost his life at First Manassas, the fort was of vital importance to the Southern cause because it protected supply lines providing munitions, provisions and clothing for soldiers and civilians alike.

In 1861 when troops under Captain Bolles first took command of Confederate Point (now Federal Point) they constructed two sand batteries. By the summer of 1862 the bulwark had been expanded to include a battery of land defense, four batteries of sea defense and a quadrilateral field work.

On July 4, 1862, a forward-looking commander, Colonel William Lamb, surveyed the fort and declared that "one of the Federal frigates could have cleared it out with a few broadsides." To remedy this he started to build a fort "of such magnitude it could withstand the heaviest fire of any guns in the American Navy."

At times as many as a thousand men—upwards of 500 slaves and free blacks plus soldiers—worked to build this extensive fortification. It was called the Malakoff of the South because it was modeled on the Malakoff Tower, the Russian redoubt that protected Sebastopol from land and sea attack by Great Britain and France during the Crimean War. When completed, Fort Fisher provided one mile of sea defense with 22 guns and a third of a mile of land defense with 25 guns. It was constructed of earth to absorb heavy bombardment. Even after the war Fort Fisher was considered a model of fort construction and used as an example in West Point classrooms.

For awhile it looked like all this effort would pay off. Despite its strategic significance Union troops did not attack the lower Cape Fear River area because they lacked sufficient land and navy power. But by December 1864 they had amassed a fleet of 56 warships and 6,500 men under Major General Butler. Against this were the 1,430 men at Fort Fisher and General Hoke's 6,000-man force just five miles up river. The fort was bombarded on Christmas Eve and Christmas Day but proved impervious to assault. Federal troops withdrew, only to return on January 12, 1865.

The odds shifted; now the Union force numbered 8,000 with five ironclads and 58 warships mounting 627 guns. This massive strike force began bombarding the fort. On January 15 after six hours of hand-to-hand combat the fort was captured. The naval bombardment during this and the December assault was the heaviest naval attack of land fortifications up to that time in history. Little more than a month after Fort Fisher fell, Wilmington, the capital of Confederate blockade-running, was evacuated. The Confederate cause was lost soon after that.

Today the visitor center at this state historic site provides de-

tailed information on the construction and the way of life at Fort
Fisher. Diaries of blockade runners and an account of the two
battles fought here help tell the story. An audio-visual presentation completes the background, and throughout the day site
personnel offer guided walks. A gravel path runs from the center
up along the remaining mounds and past the restored palisade
fence. Much of the fort is now under water as the beach line has
changed considerably since 1865. The fort is open at no charge
April–October, Monday–Saturday 9:00 A.M. to 5:00 P.M. and Sunday 1:00 to 5:00 P.M. November–March hours are Tuesday–Saturday 10:00 A.M. to 4:00 P.M. and Sunday 1:00 to 4:00 P.M.; closed
on Mondays.

After visiting the fort, stop down the road at the **Fort Fisher
North Carolina Aquarium** (see Pine Knoll Shores selection).
Here you'll see a large mounted exhibit on the fish of this region
plus an extensive shark exhibit. Just outside the aquarium is a
Marsh Trail through a maritime shrub thicket. Salt spray from
the ocean gives the trees a close-cut, hedge-like appearance. The
trail also winds through marsh meadow, salt marsh, tidal basin,
dune and beach.   Hours at the aquarium are Monday– Saturday
9:00 A.M. to 5:00 P.M. and 1:00 to 5:00 P.M. on Sundays. Closed
on Thanksgiving, Christmas and New Year's Day.

One last option is to catch the ferry from the Fort Fisher terminal to Southport (see selection). It's a 30-minute crossing with
frequent summer departures. From mid-September to mid-May
a ferry leaves in just a little under every two hours.

Directions: From I-95 take Route 421 to Wilmington. Continue
past Wilmington approximately 20 miles. Fort Fisher is directly
off Route 421.

Moores Creek National Battlefield

War and Peace

Now trees are reflected in the quiet water of the narrow stream,
the landscape is serene, but over 200 years ago the scene at
Moores Creek Bridge was quite different. At daybreak on February 27, 1776, a violent clash occurred here that prompted North
Carolina to become the first colony to vote for independence.

More than a month earlier on January 10, Royal Governor Josiah Martin called upon his loyal subjects to put down "a most
daring, horrid and unnatural Rebellion." Martin's rallying call
did not muster as many Loyalists as he hoped, but a force of
1,600 was organized. The battle lines were drawn when the Patriots also mobilized. The fledgling armies met at Moores Creek.

The Patriots, though outnumbered, were well positioned, occupying hastily constructed breastworks along the banks of

273

Moores Creek. In addition to securing their position, the Patriots also removed the planks from the bridge over the creek and greased the girders.

The Loyalists' advance force of 75 Highland broadswordsmen was cut down after they made their way across Moores Creek. Only one Patriot died while 30 Loyalists were killed and 40 more wounded. The Loyalists' retreat turned into a rout, and by week's end almost all the Loyalists who took part in this battle were captured and disarmed. The leaders were banished and the soldiers paroled to their homes.

This early Patriot victory had far-reaching consequences. It ended royal authority in North Carolina and discouraged Loyalist sentiment. Combined with the repulsing of the British sea force off Charleston, South Carolina, it forestalled a full-scale invasion of the South. Historian Edward Channing stated that "Had the South been conquered in the first half of 1776, it is entirely conceivable that rebellion would never have turned into revolution."

An audio-visual program at the park's visitors center helps put this brief but important encounter in perspective. The museum exhibits include a Highland pistol and broadsword plus a diorama of the battle. Visitors can spend up to two hours exploring the battlefield. There is a .7-mile History Trail that covers the high spots of the Revolutionary War battle. To see more of the 86-acre park take the three-mile Tarheel Trail, which begins at the end of the History Trail. This trail traces the production of naval stores, the principal industry of this region in the 18th century. While hiking these trails keep an eye out for snakes. The park is home to several species of poisonous snakes, but they rarely venture onto the open trails.

The Moores Creek National Battlefield is open at no charge 8:00 A.M. to 5:00 P.M. daily. During daylight saving time the park stays open until 6:00 P.M. It is closed Christmas and New Year's Day.

Directions: From I-95 take either Route 701 to Route 421 or continue south on I-95 to Route 421 exit. Follow Route 421 south to the intersection with Route 210, turn right on Route 210 and continue for 5 miles. Moores Creek National Battlefield will be on your left.

Orton Plantation

Down the Garden Path

Winifred, the heroine Carol Burnett played in *Once Upon a Mattress*, would certainly be happy at **Orton Plantation**. Winifred's sobriquet was "Girl of the Swamps," and at Orton the Carolina

274

Surviving both the Revolution and Civil War as a rice plantation, Orton Plantation is particularly lovely in spring when azaleas, dogwood and over 10,000 pansies bloom in the gardens.

waters lap along the edges of the gardens at this once prosperous rice plantation.

The 20-acre estate is on a peninsula jutting out into rice fields at the edge of the Cape Fear River. Dr. James Sprunt, grandfather of one of the current plantation owners, had a profound interest in the Orient and established a missionary school in China. It is not surprising therefore to see lattice-like chinoiserie bridges gracefully curve over narrow portions of the lakes that protrude finger-like amid the gardens. A sign on one bridge reads, "The Ancient Chinese believed that evil spirits followed them but could not turn. The crooked bridges forced the evil spirits to fall overboard and drown."

One of the plantation's formal areas is the **Scroll Garden**. Its curves and arabesques were suggested by the patterns of a paisley shawl. The bedding plants within the garden change with the seasons. The best time to visit Orton is in the spring when azaleas, flowering fruit trees, dogwoods and 10,000 pansies add color to the grounds.

Don't expect a lot of blooms at other times of the year as this is more a natural area than a garden. You'll see avenues of oak lining the self-guided walking path. Plan to spend between 45 minutes to an hour along the trail. You'll discover that the lagoons are a popular nesting spot for a wide variety of waterfowl.

At the far end of the gardens you'll see a colonial burying ground with the imposing tomb of early Orton's owner "King" Roger Moore. His brother Colonel Maurice Moore first owned the land on which Orton was built. But it was Roger who made his home here and developed the land into one of the most famous of the lower Cape Fear plantations. The Indians destroyed Roger Moore's first house, but in 1735 he built a 1½-story house. Additions by later owners have made it an outstanding example of Greek Revival architecture. The plantation house, still privately owned and not open for tours, can be seen from the garden path. The fact that the house survived both the American Revolution and the Civil War is amazing. Nearby plantations were burned by the British in 1776. Others suffered from invading Northern troops, but Orton was saved because it served as a hospital for Union wounded.

Admission is charged. Orton Plantation Gardens are open March through August 8:00 A.M. to 6:00 P.M. and September through November 8:00 A.M. to 5:00 P.M.

Directions: From I-95 southbound take US 421 east at Dunn. When you get near Wilmington pick up NC 133 south to Orton. If you are heading north on I-95 take US 74 east near Lumberton. Just outside of Wilmington take NC 133 south of the city to Orton.

Poplar Grove Plantation, Airlie Gardens and Greenfield Gardens

Peanuts and Posies

At **Poplar Grove Plantation** near Wilmington you can enjoy history, the arts, nature, recreation and dining. The history of this antebellum peanut plantation dates to 1795 when it was purchased by James Foy, Jr., the first of five generations of Foys to make their home at Poplar Grove. The plantation has maintained only 16 of the original 628 acres, but there are reminders that this was once a self-supporting agricultural community. Barnyard animals still fill the pens, and a blacksmith works in his shop. Outbuildings include a tenant house, smoke house, herb cellar, out-kitchen and a turpentine and salt works display.

Costumed guides detail the Foys' struggle during the Civil War as they escort you through the third floor exhibit rooms. A family account of 1862 notes that Union soldiers confiscated four horses, 50 bushels of ground corn, 300 pounds of bacon and 300 bee hives—the total value of the loss was estimated at $1,370.

The parlor, which ordinarily would have been on the first floor, is filled with Foy family pieces. One unusual item is the two-seat engagement chair, rather like a modern loveseat. There is also an 1850 ladies' bedroom and a children's room from the 1800s.

The museum rooms are on the upstairs level to accommodate dining rooms on the first and second floor. Lunch, which does not require reservations, is available Monday–Saturday 11:30 A.M. to 2:30 P.M. and on Sunday 12:00 to 2:30 P.M. A plantation-style dinner is served on the second floor Tuesday–Saturday, starting at 6:00 P.M. Reservations should be made by 4:00 P.M. the evening you wish to enjoy the Main House's hospitality.

Another part of the Poplar Grove experience is the **Cultural Arts Center** located in a barn on the rolling grounds below the house. Skills practiced in the 1800s are demonstrated in the basket shop and the weaving room. Poplar Grove also hosts various special events including square dancing in the old barn and hayrides beneath the Spanish moss-draped oaks. The spring is particularly appealing as the grounds are planted with camellias and azaleas.

Be sure to save time to browse through Poplar Grove's Scotts Hill Country Store. You can sample penny candy and check out the hand-crafted items. There are even rocking chairs and a swing on the front porch to provide a little southern-style relaxation. Poplar Grove Plantation is open February–December 9:00 A.M. to 5:00 P.M. Monday–Saturday and 12:00 to 5:00 P.M. Sunday. There is a fee for the house tour.

If you are in the Wilmington area during the spring there is another estate you won't want to miss—**Airlie Gardens**. This five-acre garden only opens when the azaleas bloom and is a great spot for taking photographs. A rose-covered bridge spans a tranquil azalea-banked lake. The pastel blossoms are reflected in the quiet water, and swans add their serene grace to the scene.

Another focal lake-side spot is the jasmine-covered stone pergola that dates back to the Civil War.

This is primarily a natural garden but close to the Airlie Mansion, which is not open to the public. Within sight of the mansion, near the chapel, is the spring garden, the only formal garden on the estate. There is a nominal charge to tour the gardens. Call for exact times for tours, (919)763-9991.

Another garden that is particularly appealing in the spring is **Greenfield Gardens**. This five-acre city park is open without charge. In a cypress-studded lake you'll see the reflection of thousands of azalea blossoms. Canoe and paddle boats can be rented if you want to become part of the postcard-pretty scene.

Directions: From I-95 take Route 74 to Wilmington, then head north on Route 17 for 9 miles for Poplar Grove Plantation. For Airlie Gardens take the Wrightsville Beach Highway accessible from downtown Wilmington off 17th Street. Greenfield Gardens is on S. Third Street, Route 421 south. All are well marked.

USS *North Carolina* Battleship Memorial

The Showboat

On six occasions during WW II the Japanese claimed they'd sunk the North Carolina, but like Molly Brown the battleship proved unsinkable. The North Carolina, the first of ten fast battleships, was nicknamed The Showboat after the river steamer in a Broadway musical.

Now, on summer evenings at 9:00 P.M. the North Carolina presents its own story The Immortal Showboat, a sound-and-light spectacle. The story of the North Carolina's participation in all twelve major naval offensives in World War II's Pacific Theater is dramatically re-created. The crew races to man their battle stations as Japanese torpedoes and Kamikaze attack. The voices of world leaders, sound effects, music and 400 lights combine to bring the past to life. The show's memorable climax simulates the firing of a torpedo. If you overnight in the Wilmington area don't miss this nightly performance.

During the day portions of nine decks of the North Carolina are open to the public. A less dramatic but no less comprehensive recital of the ship's history is given in a ten-minute orientation film that precedes the self-guided walking tour. There are two routes, one marked blue and one marked red; the red route avoids difficult climbs and excessive stairs.

To establish a time period, tunes popular during the North Carolina's six years of active duty, 1941–47, are piped through the ship. At designated hours you'll also hear reveille, mail call, liberty and chow call.

During summer evenings a sound-and-light spectacle relives the combat history of the USS North Carolina. The battleship, berthed at Wilmington, serves as a memorial to the nearly 10,000 North Carolinians who gave their lives in World War II.

You'll discover that a battleship of this size—it had a crew of 2,339 (144 officers and 2,195 enlisted men)—has just about everything a small city has. The galley which served 7,200 meals a day was the equivalent of a gigantic restaurant. Other facilities included a barber shop, laundry, post office, a hospital (sick bay), a series of 13 machine shops plus the quarters, which, though not as elegant as a hotel, did provide ample, if not comfortable, sleeping berths. At times, part of the mess hall (dining area) was used as a movie theater, a chapel and even a gymnasium.

During the summer you can stop for a soft drink at the Soda Fountain, though you'll notice the prices have gone up. Old ads offer Pepsi and Hershey bars for five cents. Another bit of hands-on fun is the opportunity to turn the throttle that once drove this 44,800-ton ship. Old navy hands may also appreciate the chance to sit in the captain's chair on the bridge. When you reach the Combat Information Center notice the radar. When the *North Carolina* was constructed radar was in its infancy. The development of radar was the single most valuable technical advance for combatant ships. The *North Carolina* had an early model search radar, the CXAM, or bedsprings as it was called because of the appearance of the antenna. This was replaced during the war by a large dish antenna, a replica of which is now installed in the foremast.

It's when you start checking out the roughly 125 guns on deck that you realize you are walking the equivalent of 52 battlefields. Guadacanal, the Gilbert and Marshall Islands, the Marianas, Leyte, Luzon, Iwo Jima, Okinawa and the Japanese mainland were all part of the *North Carolina*'s combat history. Like her sailors she wears her battle decorations on the bridge for all to see. Plan to spend between an hour-and-a-half and two hours on this tour.

Despite the *North Carolina*'s participation in the major confrontations in the Pacific, she lost only ten men with 67 wounded. Today the battleship is not only a window on the past. It is also a memorial to the 10,000 North Carolinians who perished in World War II. The Roll of Honor lists the war dead by county.

The USS *North Carolina* Battleship Memorial is open daily 8:00 A.M. to 8:00 P.M. during the summer months and until sunset the rest of the year. Admission is charged with a nominal addition for the nightly evening show, starting the first Friday in June through Labor Day. The grandstand across from the ship's port bow holds 1,000 spectators, so seating is rarely a problem.

Directions: From I-95 take US 74/76 or US 421 east to Wilmington. As you approach the city on either route, signs will direct you to the proper exit. The *North Carolina* is three miles from Wilmington.

Wilmington's Historic Homes

Take an Old-Fashioned Walk

In 1524 Verrazzano explored the Cape Fear region for France. But it was almost 200 years later before the first permanent settlement was established in this region at Brunswick. Fourteen more years passed before Wilmington was incorporated in 1739.

These early North Carolina settlements were port rivals, but Wilmington prospered because of its location at the juncture of two branches of the Cape Fear River. If the river accounted for Wilmington's early growth, the railroad later led to its second spurt. In 1840 the Wilmington & Wildon RR opened western

North Carolina to trade with Wilmington. By 1850, Wilmington was the largest city in the state.

These two eras of prosperity and growth are still apparent when you stroll through the historic district, which encompasses 200 city blocks. This large urban district is listed on the National Register of Historic Places.

The best way to appreciate the rich history of this district is by joining a 90-minute guided walking tour. These old-fashioned walks are given Tuesday through Saturday on the hour from 10:00 A.M. to 3:00 P.M. Tickets can be purchased at the Center Box Office, 118 Princess Street, or you can join the group at the corner of Third and Prince Streets and purchase your ticket directly from the guide.

The tours include a visit to two house museums—the Burgwin-Wright and Latimer houses—which can also be explored on your own. The **Burgwin-Wright House** dates from 1770 and the Latimer House from 1852. In design and decor they offer an instructive comparison of 18th and 19th-century styles.

Edgar Allan Poe would have loved the house John Burgwin built over the massive stone foundations of the colonial town jail. It's interesting to speculate on the use he envisioned for the dungeons, as he did include a trapdoor leading to these subterranean hideaways. These lower depths also contained the remains of a tunnel to the Cape Fear River.

This elegant home was the second residence of John Burgwin, the treasurer of the colony under Royal Governor Dobbs. The influence of the British West Indies can be seen in the double balustraded porches on the front and back of the house.

For a time during the American Revolution, Burgwin's business partner lived here, and at his death his step-son, Joshua Grainger Wright, purchased the house. The Wrights were displaced briefly towards the end of the war. In 1781 after the Battle of Guilford Court, Lord Cornwallis commandeered this, "the most considerable house in town," for an 18-day stay. The British general even found a use for the dungeons, using them to incarcerate his prisoners of war.

The Burgwin-Wright House's rich history and architectural style prompted the National Society of Colonial Dames of America to purchase it for the North Carolina state headquarters. Since acquiring the house in 1934 the Society has painstakingly restored and decorated it, returning both the interior and exterior to its 18th-century appearance. They have also restored the parterre garden and out-kitchen. Tours of the Burgwin-Wright House, 224 Market Street, are given Tuesday–Saturday 10:00 A.M. to 4:00 A.M. A nominal admission is charged.

The second historic house that opens its doors to the public (during the same hours) is the **Zebulon Latimer House** at 126

South Third Street. Feelings did not run as high in 1852 as they did in the late 1800s to the notion of northerners establishing themselves in southern communities. So Zebulon Latimer of Glastonbury, Connecticut had no trouble when he set up his business in Wilmington. In fact, he won one of the local belles, Elizabeth Savage. This forward-looking couple built a Victorian style "Italianate" four-story mansion. Three generations of Latimers enjoyed this spacious residence before it was purchased in 1963 as the headquarters for the Lower Cape Fear Historical Society.

The Society was able to acquire 65 percent of the original Empire and Victorian furniture. You'll feel as if the family has just stepped out; the house is so steeped in Latimer family history. The front parlor abounds with decorative touches popular during the Victorian era—peacock feathers, a mixture of designs in the rug and fabrics, and lace coverings on the tables. The formal dining room on the first floor was decorated after the house was electrified (it was the first in the city to add this new invention). You'll see the original dining room on the ground floor along with the in-house kitchen. The Latimer House garden is particularly splendid in the spring. The Victorian garden is enhanced by the ornate cast iron porch frieze.

If time permits there are several additional points of interest in Wilmington's historic district. Just a block down Orange Street (#114) from the Latimer House is **St. John's Museum of Art**. Three historic buildings house the permanent collection and rotating exhibits of this active museum. The 1804 brick Masonic Lodge was the meeting hall for the first Masonic Lodge in North Carolina. Another building was once a tavern. The museum encompasses both North Carolina and other American painters and sculptors. It is open at no charge Tuesday–Saturday 10:00 A.M. to 5:00 P.M. and Sunday 2:00 to 5:00 P.M..

Up Market Street is North Carolina's oldest local history museum, the **New Hanover County Museum of the Lower Cape Fear**. Ambitious plans are underway to completely remodel and expand this museum. Completion is planned for 1991. The museum's scale model of Wilmington between 1840–1900 captures the city when it was the largest in the state. The museum also focuses on the effects of the Civil War on this region. They have a 30-foot model of the Battle of Fort Fisher. Another popular museum exhibit is the simulated trolley ride, a real favorite with the kids. The museum is open at no charge Tuesday–Saturday 9:00 A.M. to 5:00 P.M. and Sunday 2:00 to 5:00 P.M..

Down along the Cape Fear River at the corner of Red Cross and Water Streets you'll find the **Wilmington Railroad Museum**, recalling another bit of local history when the railroad was the city's leading industry. Old railroad car and locomotive memorabilia date back to 1840. There is no charge for this museum, open Tuesday–Saturday 10:00 A.M. to 5:00 P.M. and Sunday 1:00 to 5:00 P.M..

If you want to browse through Wilmington's unique boutiques, head down Water Street to Ann Street for the Chandler's Wharf shops and waterside restaurants. Another excellent shopping area is the Cotton Exchange in the 300 block of North Front Street. This turn-of-the-century building houses fashionable boutiques and diverse shops. You'll find restaurants here as well.

Directions: From I-95 take Route 74 east to Wilmington. After you cross the Cape Fear River turn left on Third Street for the visitor center on your right just past Market Street. The Burgwin-Wright House is at Market and Third Street, and the Zebulon Latimer House is at Third and Orange Streets. You can also take Route 421 off I-95 for an alternative route to Wilmington. Plans call for I-40 to link I-95 and Wilmington by 1990.

Outdoor Historical Dramas

First for Freedom
The story of the adoption of the Halifax Resolves, one of the most important documents of the American Revolutionary period and the first formal declaration of independence from Great Britain by an American colony.
Presented: late June through early August, Wednesday–Saturday 8:30 P.M.
First for Freedom
P.O. Box 1776
Halifax, NC 27839
(919)583-1776, (919)586-7191.

From This Day Forward
This drama tells the story of the persecution of the Waldensians in Italy and their immigration to and triumph in America.
Presented: mid-July through mid-August, Thursday–Saturday 8:30 P.M.
Old Colony Players, Inc.
P.O. Box 12
Valdese, NC 28690
(704)874-0176

Horn in the West
An account of the pioneers who settled the Appalachian Mountain Region on the threshold of the American Revolution.
Presented: late June through mid-August at 8:30 P.M.; dark Mondays.
Horn in the West
P.O. Box 295
Boone, NC 28607
(704)264-2120

The Liberty Cart (this may not be running, call ahead)
The story of the development of eastern North Carolina from 1755–1865.
Presented: Thursday through Saturday, mid-July to mid-August at 8:15 P.M.
Liberty Cart
P.O. Box 470
Kenanville, NC 28349
(919)296-0721

Listen and Remember

The story of early pioneers of the Old Waxhaws Settlement, including the parents and family of the young Andrew Jackson, and the impact of the Revolutionary War upon these settlers.
Presented: June, Friday and Saturday at 8:30 P.M.
Listen and Remember
Box 1776
Waxhaw, NC 28173
(704)843-2300

The Lost Colony

Sir Walter Raleigh's attempts to establish the first English settlement in the New World on Roanoke Island are the subject of the nation's oldest outdoor drama.
Presented: early June–late August, daily, dark Sundays 8:30 P.M.

The Lost Colony
P.O. Drawer 40
Manteo, NC 27954
(919)473-3414

Micajah

The story of Micajah Autry, a North Carolina teacher and lawyer, who died at the Alamo.
Presented: late June through early July at 8:30 P.M.
Micajah
Box 52
Autryville, NC 28318
(919)525-4930

Strike at the Wind

A musical depiction of the adventures of Berry Lowrie and the Lumbee Indians of Robeson County.
Presented: July through August, Thursday–Saturday at 8:30 P.M.
Strike at the Wind
P.O. Box 1059
Pembroke, NC 28372
(919)521-3112

The Sword of Peace

A recounting of the Quakers' peaceful resistance during the American Revolution.
Presented: late June through mid-August, Thursday–Saturday
8:30 P.M.
Sword of Peace
P.O. Box 535
Snow Camp, NC 27349
(919)376-6948

Unto These Hills

The story of the Eastern Band of Cherokee Indians from the time of DeSoto's exploration of Cherokee territory through the Trail of Tears.
Presented: mid-June through August nightly (dark Sunday)
Unto These Hills
P.O. Box 398
Cherokee, NC 28719
(704)497-2111

Worthy is the Lamb

A musical drama about the life of Christ.
Presented: mid-June through early September, Tuesday–Saturday 8:30 P.M.
Worthy is the Lamb
P.O. Box 1004
Swansboro, NC 28584
(800)662-5960 or (919)393-8373

Calendar of Events

JANUARY

Early:

Hatteras Island, *Old Christmas*, (919)995-4240.
Beech Mountain Ski Resort, *Winterfest*, (704)387-2011.
Appalachian Ski Mountain & Ski Hawksnest, *Southeast Region Winter Special Olympics*, (704)295-9311.

Mid:

Fort Fisher SHS, *Commemoration of the Fall of Ft. Fisher*, (919)458-5538.

FEBRUARY

Early:

Sugar Mountain Resort, *Sugar Mountain Pro-Am Ski Race*, (704)898-4521.
Charlotte, *Camellia Show*, (704)366-0207.
Grove Park Inn, *Jazz Festival*, (800)438-5800.

Mid:

Southern Pines, *Sandhills Cayman Classic Championship-Golf*, (919)692-2114 ext. 249, (800)323-2114.

Late:

Latta Place, *Hornet's Nest Reenactment Weekend*, (704)875-2312.
Moores Creek National Battlefield, *Anniversary of Battle of Moores Creek*, (919)283-5591.
Sugar Mountain Resort, *Sugarbear's Birthday Celebration*, (704)898-4521.

MARCH

Early:

Asheville Community Theater, *Asheville Storytelling Festival*, (704)251-2819.
Biscoe, *Star Fiddlers Convention*, (919)428-2759.

Mid:

Tannenbaum Park, *Battle of Guilford Courthouse Commemoration*, (919)288-8259.
Guilford Courthouse National Military Park, *Anniversary of the Battle of Guilford Courthouse*, (919)288-1776.
Latta Place, *Hornet's Nest Reenactment Weekend*, (704)875-2312.
NC Executive Mansion, Spring Tours (through May), (919)733-3456.

Historic Pinehurst Harness Horse Training Track, *Open House*, (919)295-2599.

Bentonville Battleground SHS, *Anniversary of the Battle of Bentonville*, (919)594-0789.

Historic Tryon Palace Complex, *Tryon Palace Symposium on the Decorative Arts*, (919)638-1560.

Chimney Rock Park, *Photo Contest* (through mid-December), (704)625-9611.

Hezekiah Alexander Homesite, *Rites of Spring*, (704)568-1774.

Late:

Poplar Grove Historic Planation, *Peanut Festival*, (919)686-7820, (919)686-9989.

Duke Homestead SHS, *Tobacco History Day*, (919)477-5498.

Fayetteville, *Dogwood Festival* (or April depending on blooms), (919)433-1543, (919)483-5311.

Fremont, *Daffodil Festival*, (919)242-6037.

Mooresville, *Old Time Fiddlers & Bluegrass Convention*, (704)663-7527.

Chimney Rock Park, *Easter Sunrise Service* (changes with the holiday), (704)625-9611.

APRIL

Early:

Pope Air Force Base/Ft. Bragg, *Open House*, (919)394-4183.

Charles B. Aycock Birthplace SHS, *Living History Days*, (919)242-5581.

NC Zoological Park, *Zoo Fling*, (919)876-5606.

Beaufort County, *Tulip Festival*, (919)946-2504.

Wilmington, *NC Azalea Festival* (dates change with blooming cycle), (919)763-0905.

New Bern, *Spring Historic Homes & Garden Tour*, (919)633-6448.

Latta Place, *Springtime on the Plantation*, (704)875-2312.

Hamilton, *Ft. Branch's Living History Program*, (919)792-2044.

Tryon Palace Gardens, *Historic Tryon Palace & Tulips by Twilight* and *Tryon Palace Gardener's Sunday*, (919)638-1560.

Reed Gold Mine SHS, *Gold Rush Run*, (704)786-8337.

Southern Pines, *Pleasure Horse Driving Show*, (919)295-2599.

Stoneybrook Farm, *Stoneybrook Steeplechase*, (919)692-8000.

Mid:

Southern Pines, *House & Gardens Tour*, (919)692-2106.

Historic Halifax State Historic Site, *Halifax Day*, (919)583-7191.

Biltmore Estate, *Festival of Flowers* (through mid-May), (704)255-1700, (800)543-2961.

Pinehurst Village, *Easter Egg Hunt* (changes with the season), (919)295-6842.

Topsail Island, *Easter Sunrise Service on the Beach*, (919)328-0666.
Spirit Square, *Charlotte Festival*, (704)375-4796.
Jamesville, *Herring Festival*, (919)792-5006.
Statesville, *Carolina Dogwood Festival*, (704)873-2892.
Grifton, *Shad Festival*, (919)524-5168.

Late:

Louisburg, *National Whistlers Convention*, (919)496-2521.
Smithfield, *Ham & Yam Festival*, (919)934-0887.
Topsail Island, *Spring Jubilee*, (919)328-0666.
Old Salem, *Spring Festival*, (919)721-7300.
Yadkinville, *Bluegrass Contest & Fiddlers Convention*, (919)463-5624.
Zebulon B. Vance Birthplace SHS, *Spring Pioneer Living Day*,
    (704)645-6706.
Reed Gold Mine SHS, *Heritage Day*, (704)786-8337.
Bennett Place SHS, *Commemoration of Confederate Surrender*,
    (919)383-4345.
Beaufort, *Music Festival*, (919)728-5442.
Alamance Battleground SHS, *18th-Century Live-In & Militia Muster*,
    (919)227-4785.
Chadbourn, *Strawberry Festival,*, (919)654-5106.
New Bern, *Spring Arts Festival*, (919)638-2577.
Southern Pines, *Springfest*, (919)692-3211.
Greensboro, *Walking Tour*, (919)272-6617.
Chimney Rock Park, *Coors/Pirelli/Chimney Rock Hillclimb*, (704)625-
    9611.
Pinehurst, *Spring Horse Carriage Drive*, (919)295-2599.
State Capitol, *Last Signal Message Reenactment*, (919)733-4994.

MAY

Early:

Wright Brothers National Memorial, *Wright Brothers Fly-In*, (919)473-
    2138.
Beaufort, *Traditional Wooden Boat Show*, (919)728-7317.
Duke Homestead SHS, *Farm Day & Spring Open House*, (919)477-
    5498.
Statesville, *Weekend in the Village Street Festival*, (704)872-7416.
Ocracoke, *Crab Festival*, (919)928-6711.
Fayetteville, *Sunday-on-the-Square*, (919)323-1776.
Raleigh Capitol Square, *Confederate Memorial Weekend*, (919)266-
    1861.
Burlington, *Alamance Balloon Fest*, (800)637-3804.
Jockey's Ridge State Park, *Hang Gliding Spectacular*, (919)441-4124.
Pine Knoll NC Aquarium, *Sea Turtle Release*, (919)247-4003.
Kannapolis Village Park, *Spring Fever Fest*, (704)932-4164.
Blandwood Mansion, *National Historic Preservation Week*, (919)272-
    5003.

Zebulon B. Vance Birthplace SHS, *Zebulon B. Vance Day*, (704)645-6706.

Mid:

Alamance Battleground SHS, *Anniversary of the Battle of Alamance*, (919)227-4785.

Carolina Beach, *Pleasure Island Spring Festival*, (919)458-7116.

White Lake, *Water Festival*, (919)862-4368.

Carthage, *Buggy Festival*, (919)947-2504.

Emerald Isle, *Beach Music Festival*, (919)354-2250.

Thomas Wolfe Memorial SHS, *A Day in May*, (704)253-8304.

Late:

Castle McCulloch, *NC Medieval Faire* (through mid-June), (919)887-4383.

Greensboro Historical Museum, *Dolley Madison's Birthday*, (919)373-2043.

Lake Lure, *Stagecoach Day Clogging Festival*, (704)625-9611.

Mooresville, *Lake Norman Festival*, (704)664-3898.

Wilkesboro, *Arts Festival*, (919)667-2841.

Latta Place, *Living History Tour*, (704)875-2312.

Burlington, *Bluegrass Festival*, (919)228-7344.

Grandfather Mountain, *Nature Photograph Weekend*, (704)733-2013.

Union Grove, *Old Time Fiddler's & Bluegrass Festival*, (704)539-4417.

Tryon Palace Complex, *Colonial Living Day*, (919)638-1560.

Bethabara Park, *Revolutionary War Encampment*, (919)924-8191.

USS NC Battleship Memorial, *Memorial Day Observance*, (919)762-1829.

Duke Homestead SHS, *To Work the Land*, (919)477-5498.

JUNE

Early:

Alamance Co. Historical Museum, *Fiddlers' Picnic*, (919)226-8254.

Mt. Airy, *Bluegrass & Old Time Fiddlers Convention*, (919)786-6830.

USS NC Battleship Memorial, *The Immortal Showboat Sound & Light Spectacular* (through early September), (919)762-1829.

Manteo, *Dare Day Festival*, (919)473-1101, ext. 319.

Bald Head Island, *Turtle Nesting & Turtle Walks*, (800)722-6450 NC only, (800)443-6305.

Raleigh State Fairgrounds, *Carolina Barbecue Championship Cook-off*, (919)846-9758.

Jockey's Ridge State Park, *Triathalon of Windsports*, (919)441-4124.

Kill Devil Hills, *Wright Brothers Fly-In*, (919)473-2138.

Flat Rock Playhouse, summer season (through early September), (704)693-0134.

Elizabeth II SHS, Sailors, Sea Chanties & Salt Pork (living history through late August), (919)473-1144.
Bath, *Spring Open House*, (919)923-3971.
Jockey's Ridge State Park, *Rogallo Kite Festival*, (919)441-4124.
Hezekiah Alexander Homesite, *Summer Sampler Living History*, (704)568-1774.

Mid:

Beech Mountain, *Storytelling Festival*, (704)387-9283.
Brevard, *Spring Art Show*, (704)885-8268.
Norwood, *Reenactment of the Battle at Colson's Mills*, (704)982-6492.
Spivey's Corner, *National Hollerin' Contest*, (919)567-2156.
Poplar Grove Historic Plantation, *Summer Arts & Crafts Fair*, (919)686-4868, (919)686-9989.
Bakersville, *NC Rhododendron Festival*, (704)688-2344, (919)688-3113.
Tweetsie Railroad, *Railroader's Day*, (704)264-9061.

Late:

Banner Elk, *Blue Ridge Hearthside Craft Fair*, (704)963-5252.
Tobacco Farm Life Museum, *Anniversary Celebration*, (919)284-3431.
Charles B. Aycock Birthplace SHS, *Farmer's Day*, (919)242-5581.
Grandfather Mountain, *Singing on the Mountain*, (704)733-2013.
Beaufort, *Old Homes Tour*, (919)728-5225.

JULY

Early:

Beech Mountain, *Roasting of the Hog*, (704)387-9283.
Bethabara Park, *Independence Day Celebration*, (919)924-8191.
Old Salem, *4th of July Weekend*, (919)721-7300.
Tweetsie Railroad, *Independence Day Celebration*, (704)264-9061.
Hickory Ridge Homestead, *Old-Fashioned 4th*, (704)264-2120.
High Point Museum, *4th of July Celebration*, (919)885-6859.
Ocracoke, *Sandsculpture Contest*, (919)928-4531.
Sword of Peace Drama Site, *Snow Camp July 4th*, (919)376-6948.
USS NC Battleship Memorial, *4th of July Fireworks*, (919)762-1829.
West Jefferson, *Christmas in July Festival*, (919)246-9550.
Asheville, *Shindig-on-the-Green Summer Series* (through August), (800)257-1300.
Maggie Valley, *Freedom Festival Arts & Crafts Fair*, (704)456-8170.
Wright Brothers National Memorial, *Wright Kite Festival*, (919)441-6235.
Thomas Wolfe Memorial SHS, *In the Good Old Summertime*, (704)253-8304.
Grandfather Mountain, *Highland Games & Gathering of Scottish Clans*, (704)733-2013.

Mid:

Spencer Shops SHS, *Railfan Day*, (704)636-2889.
Chinqua-Penn, *Children's Workshops*, (919)349-4576.
Maggie Valley, *Folkmoot, USA*, (704)452-2997.
Fort Bragg, *CAPEX* (Capabilities Exercise), (919)396-6893, (919)396-2906.

Late:

Duke Homestead SHS, *Curing Barn Party*, (919)477-5498.

AUGUST

Early:

Tweetsie Railroad, *Tweetsie Cloggin Jamboree*, (704)264-9061.
Scotland Neck, *Crepe Myrtle Festival*, (919)826-3373.
Asheville, *Mountain Dance & Folk Festival*, (800)257-1300.
Asheville, *Gee Haw Whimmy Diddle World Competition*, (704)298-7928.
High Point, *Shakespeare Festival*, (800)672-6273 NC only, (919)841-6273.
Murfreesboro, *Watermelon Festival*, (919)398-5922.
Jefferson, *Ashe Co. Old Time Fiddlers' Convention*, (919)246-9945.
House in the Horseshoe SHS, *Anniversary Battle Reenactment*, (919)947-2051.
Pine Knoll NC Aquarium, *Hurricane Awareness Week*, (919)247-4003.
Brevard, *Summer Art Show*, (704)885-8268.

Mid:

NC Maritime Museum, *Strange Seafood Exhibition*, (919)728-7317.
Kitty Hawk Connection, *Wacky Watermelon Weekend & Windsurfing Regatta*, (919)441-4124.
Grandfather Mountain, *Press Photographers Camera Clinic*, (704)733-2013.
Fort Raleigh National Historic Site, *Gossyp Feaste*, (919)473-2111.
Wright Brothers National Memorial, *Orville Wright's Birthday & National Aviation Day*, (919)473-2138.

Late:

Duke Homestead SHS, *Herb Day*, (919)477-5498.
Hendersonville, *NC Apple Festival*, (704)692-3135, (704)693-6336.

SEPTEMBER

Early:

Spencer Shops SHS, *Golden Days of Railroading*, (704)636-2889.
Morgantown, *Historic Morgantown Festival*, (704)437-8888, (704)437-8863.
NC Zoological Park, *Grandparent's Day*, (919)879-7200.

Mid:

Zebulon B. Vance SHS, *Fall Pioneer Living Days & Militia Encampment*, (704)645-6706.

Executive Mansion, *Fall Tours*, (919)733-3456.

Chimney Rock Park, *Coca-Cola Chimney Rock Hillfall*, (704)625-9611.

Maggie Valley, *Singing in the Valley*, (704)456-8448.

Late:

Benson, *Mule Days*, (919)894-3825.

Castle McCulloch, *Oktoberfest*, (919)878-4383.

Jamestown, Guilford Native American Assn. *Pow Wow*, (919)273-8686.

Tanglewood Park, *NC State Chili Championship*, (800)443-4093, NC only (919)723-4386.

Grandfather Mountain, *Cycling Hill Climb*, (704)295-3700.

Country Doctor Museum, *Museum Day*, (919)235-4165.

Charles B. Aycock Birthplace SHS, *Harvest Day*, (919)242-5581.

Malcolm Blue Farm, *Historic Crafts & Skills Festival*, (919)944-3840.

Bennett Place SHS, *Living History Encampment*, (919)383-4345.

Chinqua-Penn Plantation, *Children's Summer Memories Adventure*, (919)349-4576.

OCTOBER

Early:

Wilmington, *Riverfest*, (919)343-1639.

North Wilkesboro, *Brushy Mountain Apple Festival*, (919)667-3322.

Thomas Wolfe Memorial SHS, *Birthday Celebration*, (704)253-8304.

John C. Campbell Folk School, *Fall Festival*, (704)837-2775.

Tweetsie Railroad, *Autumn Leaves Crank-Up*, (704)264-9061.

Latta Place, *Folklife Festival*, (704)875-2312.

Duke Homestead SHS, *Mock Tobacco Auction*, (919)477-5498.

Alamance Battleground SHS, *Colonial Living Week*, (919)227-4785.

Brevard, *Fall Art Show*, (704)885-8268.

Hendersonville, *National Chrysanthemum Society Show*, (704)693-0589.

Mid:

Fort Bragg, *Oktoberfest Internationale*, (919)396-6893, (919)396-2906.

Maggie Valley, *Autumn Leaves Arts & Crafts Festival*, (704)456-8170.

Spencer Shops SHS, *Antique Auto Show*, (704)636-2889.

Laurinburg, *John Blue House Cotton Festival*, (919)277-2585.

Late:

Tryon Palace Complex, *Chrysanthemum Festival*, (919)638-5781.

Jockey's Ridge State Park, *Outer Banks Stunt Kite Competition*, (919)441-4124.

Valle Crucis, *Country Fair*, (704)963-4609.
Brunswick Town SHS, *Heritage Days*, (919)371-6613.
Hickory Ridge Homestead, *Apple Festival*, (704)264-2120.
Valle Crucis, *Civil War Living History Enactment*, (704)262-4089.
Cannon Village, *Scarecrow Festival*, (704)938-3200.
Reed Gold Mine SHS, *The Deadly Saga of the Mad Miner-Halloween Celebration*, (704)786-8337.
Maggie Valley, *America's Clogging Hall of Fame Competition*, (704)891-3435.
Snow Camp, *Colonial Living & Molasses Festival*, (919)376-6948.
Poplar Grove Historic Plantation, *Halloween Festival & Monster Bash*, (919)686-4868, (919)686-9989.

NOVEMBER

Early:

Charles B. Aycock Birthplace SHS, *Birthday Celebration*, (919)242-5581.
Castle McCulloch, *Highland Games*, (919)887-4383.
Hamilton, *Historic Hamilton Day*, (919)798-7461.
James K. Polk Memorial SHS, *Living History*, (704)889-7145.
Duke Homestead SHS, *Christmas Day by Candlelight*, (919)477-5498.
New Bern, *Candlelight Tour of Historic Homes*, (919)638-8558.
Pinehurst, *Fall Horse Carriage Drive*, (919)295-2599, (919)692-2449.
Pine Knoll NC Aquarium, *Sea Harvest Sampler*, (919)247-4003.

Mid:

Blowing Rock, *Victorian Christmas* (through December), (704)295-7851.
Charles B. Aycock Birthplace SHS, *Education Week*, (919)242-5581.

Late:

Asheville, *Light Up Your Holidays Festival* (through December), (704)259-5807, (800)257-1300 NC only, (800)548-1300.
Biltmore Estate, *Christmas at Biltmore* (through December), (704)255-1700.
Nags Head, *Thanksgiving Windsurfing Regatta*, (919)441-4124.
Wrightsville Beach, *Holiday Flotilla*, (919)256-4303, (919)256-3771.
Latta Place, *Latta Family Christmas & Musicale*, (704)875-2312.
Blandwood Mansion, *Christmas at Blandwood* (through mid-December), (919)272-5003.
Bethabara Park, *Annual Christmas Tours* (through mid-December), (919)924-8191.
Old Salem, *Home Moravian Church Candle Tea* (through early December), (919)768-6968.
Cannon Village, *Christmas in the Village* (through December 24), (704)938-3200.

Banner Elk, Avery Co., *Christmas Festival*, (through mid-December), (704)898-5605.

Peterson Doll Museum, *Lilliputian Christmas* (through January), (919)884-1594, (919)884-2222, ext. 36.

DECEMBER

Early:

State Capitol Raleigh, *Capitol Christmas*, (919)733-4994.

Executive Mansion, *Christmas Open House*, (919)733-3456.

Southport, *Christmas By the Sea Festival*, (919)457-6964.

Wilmington, *Old Wilmington By Candlelight*, (919)762-0492.

Brunswick Town SHS, *Christmas Open House*, (919)371-6613.

Grove Park Inn, *Christmas Celebration* (through December), (704)252-2711, (800)438-5800.

Hezekiah Alexander Homesite, *A Colonial Christmas*, (704)568-1774.

Tobacco Museum of NC, *Christmas at the Tobacco Museum*, (919)284-3431.

McAdenville, *Christmastown, USA*, (704)824-3551, ext. 260.

Chinqua-Penn, *Christmas for Children*, (919)349-4576.

Chinqua-Penn, *Christmas Candlelight Tours* (through late December), (919)349-4576.

Poplar Grove Plantation, *Christmas Through the Ages*, (919)686-4868, (919)686-9989.

Alamance Co. Historical Museum, *Christmas Tour of Homes & Candlelight Tea*, (919)226-8254.

Alamance Battleground SHS, *Christmas Open House*, (919)227-4785.

Stagville Center, *Christmas Open House*, (919)477-9835.

Greensboro Historical Museum, *Holiday Open House*, (919)373-2043.

Historic Halifax SHS, *Country Christmas*, (919)583-7191.

High Point Museum, *Christmas Open House*, (919)885-6859.

Reed Gold Mine SHS, *A Colonial German Christmas*, (704)786-8337.

Maggie Valley, *Christmas in the Valley* (through December), (704)926-1388.

Fayetteville, *Horse & Carriage Rides & Christmas Caroling on the Commons*, (919)483-2073.

Joel Lane House, *Christmas Open House*, (919)786-0796.

Southern Pines, *Christmas Open House/Historic Homes in Moore Co.*, (919)295-3613.

Thomas Wolfe Memorial SHS, *Victorian Christmas*, (704)253-8304.

House in the Horseshoe SHS, *Christmas Open House & Candlelight Tour*, (919)947-2051.

Bennett Place SHS, *Christmas Open House*, (919)383-4345.

Duke Homestead SHS, *Christmas By Candlelight & Craft Sale*, (919)477-5498.

Cupola House-Edenton, *Wassail Bowl*, (919)482-2637, (919)482-3663.

James Iredell House SHS, *Groaning Board*, (919)482-2637, (919)482-3663.

Elizabeth II SHS, *Christmas Open House*, (919)473-1144.

James K. Polk Memorial SHS, *Christmas at the Polk Place*, (704)889-7645.

Tryon Palace Complex, *Christmas Celebration Tours* (through late December), (919)638-1560.

Murfreesboro, *Candlelight Christmas*, (919)398-5922.

Mid:

NC Museum of Life and Science, *Santa Train*, (919)477-0431, (919)477-0432.

Edenton, *Christmas Candlelight Tour of Private Homes*, (919)482-2637, (919)482-3663.

Hickory Ridge Homestead, *Christmas at the Homestead*, (704)264-2120.

Southern Pines, *Christmas Horse Carriage Drive*, (919)692-6386.

Old Salem, *Salem Christmas*, (919)721-7300.

West Point on the Eno, *Christmas Open House*, (919)560-4355.

Oakwood, *Candlelight Tour of Homes in Historic Oakwood*, (919)834-0887.

Wright Brothers National Memorial, *Man Will Never Fly Memorial Society & First Flight Commemoration*, (919)473-2138.

Late:

Raleigh, NC Symphony Orchestra's *New Year's Eve Concert*, (800)868-6666 NC only, (800)552-8666.

INDEX

Acknowledgments

I would like to express my heartfelt thanks to Rebecca Moore and David Little with North Carolina Travel and Tourism Division of the Department of Commerce. Their helpful assistance made my travels through North Carolina highly productive and immensely enjoyable.

My visits to the state's many attractions were aided by the friendly assistance of the staff at each site. I regret that space does not permit me to list each individual. I would be remiss, however, if I did not thank those who spent days with me helping me to cover their region thoroughly. Without their help *The North Carolina One-Day Trip Book* would not be in your hands. My thanks to: Crystal Craft formerly of the Charlotte Convention and Visitors Bureau (CVB), Dave Everett with Maggie Valley Area Chamber of Commerce, Dot Fuss with Craven County Tourism Development Authority, Jane Peterson of Cape Fear CVB, Tracy Hurst of Pinehurst CVB, Florence Brown of Fayetteville CVB, Becky Vohoska of Raleigh CVB, Carol Vilas of Durham CVB Board, Snooky Bond of Historic Albemarle, Dorrie O'Neil Harty of Dare County Tourist Board, Holly Jeffus of Burlington/Alamance County CVB, Nancy Sebastian of High Point CVB, Shelly Green of Winston-Salem CVB, Sherri Moretz of NC High Country Host, and both Bill and Bruce Hensley of Hensley Communications. For providing memorable experiences, I would also like to thank Kelly Davis, of Mattamuskeet Wildlife Refuge, Jack Vail of Spencer Shops and Becky Reid of Bald Head Island.

TO HELP YOU PLAN AND ENJOY YOUR TRAVEL IN THE MID-ATLANTIC AREA

THE WALKER WASHINGTON GUIDE $7.95

The seventh edition of the "Guide's guide to Washington," completely revised by Katherine Walker, builds on a 25-year reputation as the top general guide to the capital. Its 320 pages are packed with museums, galleries, hotels, restaurants, theaters, shops, churches, as well as sites. Beautiful maps and photos. Indispensable.

**ADVENTURE VACATIONS IN
FIVE MID-ATLANTIC STATES** $9.95

This all-season guide to making the most of free time in PA, MD, VA, WV and NC features hiking, biking, cross-country skiing, trail riding, sailing and canoeing; also archeological digs, mystery weekends, crafts and specialty workshops, and lending a hand and elder-hosteling. Tips on planning, costs, equipment and special attractions included.

MARYLAND ONE-DAY TRIP BOOK $10.95

From boiling rapids and rugged trails high in the western mountains to frontier forts, horse country, Baltimore's urban treasures, the Chesapeake Bay and the plantations and preserves of the Eastern Shore, Maryland is more than you can imagine!

PHILADELPHIA ONE-DAY TRIP BOOK $8.95

And you thought Independence Hall and the Liberty Bell were all Philadelphia had to offer? Norman Rockwell Museum, Pottsgrove Mansion, Daniel Boone Homestead, Covered Bridges and Amish Farms are among 101 exciting one-day trips featured.

ONE-DAY TRIPS THROUGH HISTORY $9.95

Describes 200 historic sites within 150 miles of the nation's capital where our forebears lived, dramatic events occurred and America's roots took hold. Sites are arranged chronologically starting with pre-history.

THE VIRGINIA ONE-DAY TRIP BOOK $8.95

Jane Ockershausen Smith, one of the most experienced travel writers in the Mid-Atlantic area, admits to being surprised by the wealth of things to see and do in the Old Dominion. With 101 sites divided into seven geographic regions, this is the perfect guide for anyone who is anywhere in Virginia.

Also:

Florida One-Day Trips (from Orlando). What to do after you've done Disney. **$7.95**

Call it Delmarvalous. How to talk, cook and "feel to hum" on the Delaware, Maryland, and Virginia Peninsula. **$7.95**

A Shunpiker's Guide to the Northeast. Wide open routes that shun turnpikes and interstates between Washington and Boston. Maps and directions included. **$9.95**

Footnote Washington. Tracking the engaging, humorous and surprising bypaths of capital history by one of the city's most popular broadcasters. **$8.95**

Mr. Lincoln's City. An illustrated guide to the Civil War sites of Washington, as readable as it is informative. **$17.95**

General Lee's City. Relive the turbulent life of Confederate Richmond through 150 photographs, 17 maps and five auto tours with site-by-site descriptions. Companion to *Mr. Lincoln's City.* **$16.95**

Walking Tours of Old Washington and Alexandria. Paul Hogarth's exquisite watercolors of grand old buildings, lovingly reproduced and arranged in seven guided walking tours. **$24.95**

Order Blank for all EPM books described here. Mail with check to:

EPM Publications, Inc.
Box 490, McLean, VA 22101

Title	Quantity	Price	Amount	Shipping
The North Carolina One-Day Trip Book		$11.95		$2.00 each book

Subtotal _____

Virginia residents, add 4½% tax _____

Name _____ Shipping _____

Street _____

City _____ State _____ Zip _____

Total _____

Remember to enclose names, addresses and enclosure cards for gift purchases.
Please note that prices are subject to change. Thank you.

Photo credit: Lise Metzger

About the Author

Traveler-writer Jane Ockershausen has written six previous books on the Mid-Atlantic region for one-day trippers. She currently writes feature articles for *AAA World* and a weekly column on the region for *The Washington Times*. Her work has also appeared in *The Washingtonian*, *Historic Preservation*, the *Journal* Newspapers, *The Baltimore Sun*, *Mid-Atlantic Country*, *The Chicago News* and *The Oregonian*. She is a member of the Society of American Travel Writers and the American Society of Journalists and Authors.